The 163 best
Paleo
Slow Cooker
recipes

The 163 best Paleo Slow Cooker recipes

100% Gluten-Free

Judith Finlayson

Robert
ROSE

Some of the recipes in this book appeared in the following books, often in a slightly different form: *Delicious & Dependable Slow Cooker Recipes* (2002), *175 Essential Slow Cooker Classics* (2006), *Healthy Slow Cooker* (2006), *Slow Cooker Comfort Food* (2009), *Vegetarian Slow Cooker* (2010) and *The 150 Best Slow Cooker Recipes* (2011).

For complete cataloguing information, see page 246.

Design and Production: Joseph Gisini/PageWave Graphics Inc.
Editor: Carol Sherman
Copy Editor: Karen Campbell-Sheviak
Cover Photography: Colin Erricson
Interior Photography: Colin Erricson and Mark T. Shapiro
Associate Photography: Matt Johannsson
Food Styling: Kathryn Robertson and Kate Bush
Prop Styling: Charlene Erricson

Cover Image: Classic Beef Stew (page 136) with Cauliflower Mash (page 242)
Image on Page 16: New World Bouillabaisse (page 106)

We acknowledge the financial support of the Government of Canada through the Book Publishing Industry Development Program (BPIDP) for our publishing activities.

Published by Robert Rose Inc.
120 Eglinton Avenue East, Suite 800, Toronto, Ontario, Canada M4P 1E2
Tel: (416) 322-6552 Fax: (416) 322-6936
www.robertrose.ca

Printed and bound in Canada

1 2 3 4 5 6 7 8 9 TC 21 20 19 18 17 16 15 14 13

Contents

Acknowledgments

It is hard to believe that this is my 15th cookbook! I've been very fortunate in that, with a few tweaks, the same team has been in place since day one. These are the people who work together to take masses of words and numbers and transform them into beautiful books. So, once again, thanks to you all:

The team at PageWave Graphics, Kevin Cockburn, Joseph Gisini and Daniella Zanchetta for their excellent work in designing my books and overseeing the photo shoots;

Photographer Colin Erricson and his associate Matt Johannsson for taking the pictures that make my recipes look so beautiful;

Food stylist Kathryn Robertson and prop stylist Charlene Erricson for creating the raw material from which the photographers work;

And last, but not least, my editor Carol Sherman, who has been a consistent support and helpmate for all these years.

I also need to thank the back-of-the-house folks who work so hard to ensure that once they are produced, my books find a warm welcome in the marketplace:

Marian Jarkovich, for her marketing expertise;

Nina McCreath, for her multilingual capacity, which helps to ensure that my books are translated into other languages; and,

Martine Quibell, for her outstanding skills as a publicist;

Of course, none of this would be possible without the constant love and support of my number-one fan, work mate and friend, my darling husband, Bob Dees.

Introduction

I am someone who loves to cook — and to eat — delicious food and I've been fortunate enough to turn my passion into a successful career as a cookbook author. I have always emphasized using fresh whole foods in both my work and my personal life, but as my awareness of the role that diet plays in health grew and developed, I have become increasingly focused on the benefits of healthy eating. Over the years, research has shown that food can provide much more than daily sustenance. What we eat (or don't eat) has the power to prevent and even cure many illnesses, from type-2 diabetes to cardiovascular disease. I strongly believe — and am a walking testament to this belief — that over the long term we can dramatically influence our health status by eating smarter to get the most out of food.

These days, for more and more people, eating smarter means eating "Paleo." The basic premise behind this dietary framework is that we should follow the model of our hunter-gatherer ancestors, eating food that is as close to its natural state as possible because it fits with us genetically. There are many excellent books on the subject (see Resources, page 245) and I urge you to explore them. The full extent of the benefits of Paleo eating and the range of conditions it can address are far beyond the scope of this book.

Although it had been simmering in the background for some time, the Paleo diet was launched as a concept in 1985 when *The New England Journal of Medicine* published an article called "Paleolithic Nutrition" by a doctor named Boyd Eaton. In 2002, Loren Corbain moved the subject to the front burner with the publication of his book *The Paleo Diet*. His work was the catalyst that popularized the idea, and in recent years, many others have taken up the Paleo cause.

My own journey to Paleo eating began with a gradual awareness that I had a problem digesting gluten. This prompted me to experiment with eliminating gluten from my diet, beginning in the fall of 2011. Coincidentally, late in 2009, I had been diagnosed with idiopathic paroxysmal atrial fibrillation — quite a mouthful for what boils down to a particular kind of irregular heart beat with no known origin. AFib, as it is commonly described, comes and goes, on (to those afflicted with the paroxysmal type) something resembling a whim. The most serious problem with the illness is that because your heart is pumping in an irregular fashion, blood may not be properly pumped out, which can lead to a stroke.

I won't bore you with the details, but my doctors prescribed drug therapy 101 (aspirin and a beta blocker), which I failed. Although it fixed my AFib,

I had an alarming allergic reaction to both of the drugs, not to mention suffering extremely debilitating side effects from the beta-blocker. (I have never done well with drugs and up to that point had been fortunate enough to be able to mostly avoid them.) The specialist's solution was to promote me to a regimen of stronger drugs. After a quick Google search, I discovered that these new drugs were far more likely to promote an allergic reaction than the ones I had been on. At that point, I visited my family physician, fired the specialist and became what is described as a self manager of my illness.

I spent the next two years researching AFib and gradually identified a link between my stomach and my heart problems via the vagus nerve. I can't take a tremendous amount of credit for what turned out to be the mother lode discovery in treating my AFib: deciding to eliminate gluten from my diet. I realized I was often feeling lethargic and bloated and that my stomach was easily upset and decided to go gluten-free for a while to see if it helped.

Four months after eliminating gluten from my diet, I made an interesting connection: I realized I was no longer having AFib attacks or any irregular heart beats at all. Since at that point I had not come across anything in the medical literature that suggested a connection between stomach and heart, I was inclined to dismiss my empirical discovery. Over the holiday season I indulged in foods containing gluten and sure enough, early in the new year, I had my final AFib attack. As a result, I no longer eat gluten and at the time of this writing, I'm heading into my second year of being AFib-free.

I now know that some medical researchers have identified a possible link between cardiac symptoms and gastrointestinal problems, but sadly, this information does not seem to have filtered down to on-the-ground practitioners. In my own case, I believe my irregular heartbeat was an autoimmune response to food sensitivities, which although focused on gluten, might be activated to a lesser degree by legumes, certain grains and some starches. In other words, I now pay very close attention to what is happening in my stomach because I view it as the canary in the coal mine warning of impending disaster.

That said, I am a foodie, a cook and a cookbook author. And although I adhere to the principles of a Paleo diet, it is against my principles to eat anything that doesn't taste good. Fortunately, the two are not mutually exclusive. There are many recipes (163 to be precise) in this book, all of which I enjoy and which I hope you will find equally delicious.

— Judith Finlayson

Eating and Cooking Paleo

The basic premise behind the Paleo approach is that we should follow a diet very similar to that of our hunter-gatherer ancestors, eating food that is as close to its natural state as possible. Proponents cite anthropological evidence, noting that while our genes haven't changed in the past 10,000 years, our eating habits did with the advent of agriculture. At that point, our health apparently took a turn for the worse: the origins of problems such as dental cavities and bone malformations, and indications of protein and mineral deficiencies, among other symptoms. In the modern era, when refining and processing food is the order of the day, the link between the foods we eat today and the so-called diseases of civilization that afflict our society, such as diabetes, heart disease and obesity, became increasingly obvious. In the Paleolithic era, people ate only whole nutrient-dense foods. Nothing was processed and there were no potentially harmful additives, all of which proponents point to as the reason for the excellent health our hunter-gatherer ancestors enjoyed.

There are many excellent books on the virtues of the Paleo diet (see Resources, page 245) but it is beyond the scope of this book to provide a complete overview. However, key points include:

- increasing your consumption of protein in the form of naturally raised (pasture-fed) meat, and wild (sustainably caught) fish and seafood. Among other benefits, when naturally sourced (not feed-lot raised or grown on fish farms), all of these foods are higher in healthy omega-3 fatty acids (which our modern diet is lacking) than their "conventional" counterparts.
- limiting your carbohydrate sources to include fresh fruits and vegetables that are low in starch, as well as certain nuts and seeds. Choose organically grown plant foods whenever possible.
- forgetting most of what you have been taught about fat. So long as it is "natural," fat is fine. Unfortunately, the refined oils most people consume (such as canola, corn, peanut, safflower and sunflower) are very bad for our health (see Fats, page 12).

Eating Paleo is defined as much by what is off-limits as it is by what you are allowed to consume: no grains (even whole grains) or legumes, both of which are very irritating to the digestive system; and no refined sugars and oils or other processed foods. For various reasons, all these foods promote inflammation, which sets the stage for the development of chronic disease.

People who choose to eat Paleo do so for a number of reasons. These include:

- losing weight, which is based on the premise that (contrary to conventional wisdom) all calories are not created equal. (The most thorough documentation of this premise I've come across is contained in *Good Calories, Bad Calories* by Gary Taubes.) By emphasizing the consumption of protein, the Paleo diet boosts metabolism and promotes weight loss.

- regulating blood sugar levels, which helps to manage illnesses such as hypoglycemia and type-2 diabetes. Virtually all acceptable Paleo foods are low on the glycemic index.
- improving digestive health, which may control illnesses such as irritable bowel syndrome. Carbohydrates such as grains and legumes are extremely hard to digest. Poorly digested carbohydrates may lead to more serious problems, such as nutrient malabsorption and various intestinal disorders.
- healing intestinal permeability, also known as leaky gut syndrome, which has been linked to a wide variety of conditions from Crohn's disease to rheumatoid arthritis. When carbohydrates are not properly digested, they can bypass the later stages of digestion, entering the bloodstream only partially digested. Your body sees these food particles as invaders and attacks them in what is effectively an autoimmune response.

Proponents of the Paleo diet range from those who are zealous about adhering to a "caveman diet" to others who take a much more relaxed approach, allowing, for instance, the inclusion of some starchy vegetables, or probiotic-containing dairy products such as kefir, which, by improving gut flora, help to heal a leaky gut. Since no one knows with absolute certainly what hunter-gatherer societies actually ate (its extremely likely that they did eat some naturally fermented food, for instance) in selecting the recipes for this book, I have chosen to treat Paleo as a guideline rather than a catechism.

While I have paid close attention to the orthodoxy of Paleo eating, I have also taken a few liberties by using products such as canned tomatoes (see page 13) because this is a slow cooker book, and people use their slow cookers for convenience. Also, as noted, people choose to eat Paleo for a variety of reasons, and foods that work for one strategy may be mutually exclusive to another. For instance, some people with joint-related issues may have problems with deadly nightshade vegetables such as tomatoes and eggplant, while those with problems such as bloating or IBS often find help in following the FODMAP (fermentable oligo-, di, and monosaccharides and polyols) strategy. For instance, FODMAP advises avoiding vegetables belonging to the Brassica family, such as cabbage and broccoli. For these reasons, all the recipes in this book are not likely to appeal to everyone. However, I have assumed that people dealing with specific conditions will know what to avoid and will choose recipes that suit their individual needs. In other words, I take the position that when eating Paleo, one size doesn't fit all.

In the following pages I have included a rationale for including some ingredients that may not be considered appropriate on a Paleo diet.

Salt

By eating lots of fresh foods our Paleo ancestors consumed an abundance of potassium. They also consumed very little salt, and this combination (a high ratio of potassium to salt) is a prescription for healthy blood pressure, among other benefits. However, in my opinion, salt *per se* has been unjustly demonized within the Paleo community.

There are two basic problems with salt in the modern diet: we eat too much of it, most of which (roughly 85%) comes from processed foods, and the kind of salt we are likely to consume is not real salt. Refined table salt is pure sodium chloride, stripped of any beneficial minerals and chemically treated to improve the color. Worse still, it contains additives to prevent caking, some of which may be harmful to our health.

Our bodies need a certain amount of salt to function. It helps to maintain fluid in our blood cells and carries information to our nerves and muscles. In some respects, salt is like certain essential fatty acids, our bodies can't manufacture it. Although rare, hyponatremia, a condition where the body doesn't get enough sodium (most commonly seen in endurance sports) may have serious consequences. Several years ago a friend's grandmother ended up in hospital after taking her doctor's recommendation to reduce her salt intake so seriously that she virtually eliminated salt from her diet. We need to obtain it from our diet.

Salt also dramatically enhances the flavor of food. Consequently, I have used a moderate amount of salt in my recipes. I always use *sel gris*, also known as Celtic sea salt, as my everyday cooking salt, or *fleur de sel* and Maldon salt as basic finishing salts. All these "real" salts contain beneficial trace minerals and, if consumed in appropriate quantities, should not have negative effects on your health.

Fats

The sad truth is that most of the cooking oils we commonly consume and which are readily available in supermarkets are bad for us. This includes refined vegetable oils such as corn and safflower oil as well as hydrogenated oils, which have been identified as harmful for some time. These oils have been refined, bleached and chemically treated. They have been processed using solvents and other undesirable chemicals so they will have a higher smoke point and a longer shelf life. They are also likely to contain an unhealthy ratio of omega-6 to omega-3 fatty acids. They are outlawed on the Paleo diet because, among other concerns, they have been linked with chronic inflammation, which is a precursor to many diseases of civilization.

The default fat in this book is extra virgin olive oil. I use it most often because it is a stable oil with a mild flavor and acceptable smoke point. The Olive Oil Council claims that extra virgin olive oil has a smoke point of 410°F (210°C), which means that is the temperature at which it burns, creating harmful toxins. I take a more cautious approach. I treat extra virgin olive oil as if it has a smoke point of 350°F (180°C) and use it for medium-heat cooking, such as softening vegetables. In recipes where they fit the flavor profile I have, from time to time, suggested alternatives such as clarified butter, ghee, coconut oil, or even beef tallow or pure lard, all of which are usually Paleo-approved. All these fats are safe for cooking at higher heats. (Clarified butter has a smoke point of 480°F/249°C; beef tallow is 400°F/200°C and lard is 375°F/190°C.)

Although it goes against conventional wisdom (please consult the Resources section for further reading, page 245) old-fashioned animal fats are actually healthy alternatives to refined cooking oils. If you have access to them and they fit the flavor profile of your dish, feel free to use pure lard, beef tallow, chicken fat (schmaltz) or duck or goose fat. Do not use packaged lard. It is made from the fat of poorly raised animals and as a result is too high in omega-6 fatty acids. It is also likely to be hydrogenated, which means it contains deadly trans fats. I buy lard from my butcher, who renders it from the fat of pasture-raised pigs. It keeps for a long time in the freezer.

Potatoes

Potatoes are a controversial vegetable in the Paleo world because they are starchy and have a high glycemic index, which can cause blood sugar to spike. I take the position that when eating Paleo, choosing to consume potatoes is an individual decision. They are not right for people who have difficulty processing carbohydrates or for those with autoimmune problems that may be affected by some of the compounds they contain. I have used them in a number of recipes because they improve the result. Potatoes are a great thickener (in my opinion, a preferable alternative to refined ingredients such as cornstarch) and they can be used to add flavor and creamy texture to dishes in place of cream.

In addition to adding flavor, potatoes also provide a wide range of nutrients. As for that pesky glycemic index, when combined with vegetables that are high in fiber or healthy fat, their glycemic response is mitigated. With a nod to the Paleo orthodox, it's hard to believe that hunter-gatherers weren't eating wild potatoes since evidence shows that potatoes have been cultivated in South America since about 8,000 BC.

Cauliflower rice is usually used as a substitute for starchy potatoes. But people with digestive problems, such as IBS, who are following a FODMAP approach may want to avoid cauliflower, which belongs to the Brassica family. They may find potatoes a preferable substitute.

Tomatoes

There are many excellent "canned" tomato products on the market, and because most people use a slow cooker for convenience, I have used them in some recipes in this book. To make the best tomato choices, look for those that are organically grown, with no salt added, and come in glass jars or BPA (bisphenol-A) free cans. When using canned tomatoes (or any canned product) check to make sure they are gluten-free. A surprising number do contain gluten. Moreover, manufacturers are constantly changing their formulae and gluten may suddenly appear in a previously gluten-free product.

If you don't want to use canned products you can easily substitute the following:

One 28 oz (796 mL) can of tomatoes =
4 cups (1 L) peeled chopped fresh tomatoes

One 14 oz (398 mL) can diced tomatoes =
2 cups (500 mL) peeled diced tomatoes

1 tbsp (15 mL) tomato paste =
2 tbsp (30 mL) minced reconstituted sun-dried tomatoes

When I call for tomato paste, it is because I want an intense hit of tomato flavor. I, personally, have no problem with using a brand that I purchase at my local natural foods store. It contains only organic tomatoes and salt. Commercial brands are not likely to be as unadulterated and should be avoided.

Prepared tomato sauce: some prepared tomato sauces are very pure and, in my opinion, are acceptable when eating Paleo. I buy a version at my local natural foods store that is made from organically grown ingredients, contains a minimal amount of salt and comes in a glass jar. If you are unhappy about your prepared options you can always make your own tomato sauce (see page 220).

Dairy Products

Traditional Paleo wisdom is that dairy products are forbidden. Many people, particularly those on Paleo diets, cannot tolerate the lactose in dairy products. However, I have broken with tradition and included a few fermented milk products for two reasons: first, they dramatically improve the result and second, because, in my opinion, the healthy bacteria they contain outweigh any potential negative effects, particularly for those suffering from digestive disorders and/or leaky gut.

When dairy products have been fermented properly, virtually all of the lactose disappears (it is devoured by the fermenting bacteria), which is why it is important to make your own or use only those made by trusted artisanal providers. Not only are the lactic acid bacteria in properly fermented milk products such as yogurt and sour cream linked with a variety of health benefits, including improved digestion, recent studies suggest that the acids in fermented milk products may also reduce the impact of certain foods on blood glucose response.

Butter is basically milk fat and it contains virtually no lactose or milk proteins. Even people with a dairy allergy usually don't have problems consuming butter. Clarified butter, which is pure milk fat, is good for cooking on high heat because it has a high smoke point. Ghee is basically clarified butter, but avoid commercially made ghee because it often contains additives.

Sour cream

Make your own sour cream or purchase it from a trusted provider (not a mass market brand) to ensure that virtually all the lactose has been eliminated in the process of fermentation and that it does not contain any additives.

Making sour cream or crème fraîche is not difficult. But proper fermentation takes about 12 hours and requires a starter, such as buttermilk. The less-processed your base cream is, the better your results in terms of digestibility. If you are using a commercial starter, follow the instructions. If using buttermilk or yogurt (with active cultures) you will need about 1 tbsp (15 mL) per cup (250 mL) of heavy cream. Stir well, cover lightly, and set aside at room temperature for at least 12 hours. When the mixture has thickened, cover tightly and refrigerate for up to 2 weeks.

Green Peas

Some people following a Paleo diet mistakenly eliminate sweet green peas. While fresh green peas are classified as legumes in the botanical sense, they do not qualify as dietary legumes. The fundamental difference is that sweet green peas are not dried; they are a vegetable that can be eaten raw or just lightly cooked. Dietary legumes, on the other hand, are grown specifically for their seed and are categorized as pulses. They often need to be pre-soaked for an extensive period and invariably require a long cooking time.

Sweet Corn

In the Paleo world, sweet corn is seriously misunderstood. It is a vegetable, not a grain, and is acceptable on a Paleo diet, so long as it is organically grown. Starchier field corn, which is allowed to dry on the stalk, is the grain. Field corn is doubly problematic because most is grown from genetically modified seed, unlike sweet corn.

Vinegar

I am very comfortable using fermented vinegars in recipes. I have little doubt that our Paleolithic ancestors accidentally stumbled upon the juice of fermented fruit and found a use for it. In addition, vinegar can be a healthy addition to contemporary diets. For instance, recent studies show that consuming vinegar may reduce the glycemic response in both healthy individuals and those with diabetes.

Soy Sauce

I do not mind eating small amounts of fermented soy, so my gluten-free product of choice to replace regular soy sauce is a gluten-free tamari sauce. It tastes good, is readily available and inexpensive. If you are avoiding soy, use liquid aminos or coconut aminos. People have strong feelings about both these products, so research, taste and make your own decision.

Maple Syrup

Recent research is showing that pure maple syrup, which Native North American hunter-gatherers taught the early settlers to make, may actually be a superfood. It is loaded with beneficial compounds, which may be anti-inflammatory and of benefit to people managing type-2 diabetes. As a result, I have used it occasionally as a sweetener in recipes.

Slow Cooker Basics

A Low-Tech Appliance

Slow cookers are amazingly low-tech. The appliance usually consists of a metal casing and a stoneware insert with a tight-fitting lid. For convenience, you should be able to remove the insert from the metal casing. This makes it easier to clean and increases its versatility, not only as a vessel for refrigerating dishes that have been prepared to the Make Ahead stage, but also as a serving dish. The casing contains the heat source, electrical coils that usually surround the stoneware insert. These coils do their work using the energy it takes to power a 100-watt light bulb. Because the slow cooker operates on such a small amount of energy, you can safely leave it turned on while you are away from home.

Shapes, Sizes and Configurations

Slow cookers are generally round or oval in shape and range in size from 1 to 8 quarts. The small round ones are ideal for dips and fondues, as well as some soups, main courses and desserts. The smaller oval ones (approximately $1\frac{1}{2}$ to 4 quarts) are extremely versatile, as they are small enough to work well with smaller quantities but have enough volume to accommodate some full-batch recipes. The larger sizes, usually oval in shape, are necessary to cook big-batch dishes and those that need to be cooked in a dish or pan that can fit into the stoneware.

I have recommended slow cooker sizes for all my recipes. However, please be aware that so many new models are coming onto the market that I have not been able to test all the configurations myself. Use your common sense. The stoneware should be about one-third to three-quarters full. Pieces of meat that can feed a large number of people (such as pork butt cooked in a minimal amount of liquid) may fit quite nicely into some of the smaller oval shapes, but dishes that contain an abundance of vegetables and liquid will likely need a model that can accommodate greater volume. The smaller oval cookers are extremely versatile because the larger bottom surface can accommodate chunks of fish or larger pieces of meat such as half a brisket. Because I use my slow cookers a lot for entertaining, I feel there is a benefit to having at least two: a smaller ($1\frac{1}{2}$ to 4 quart), which is ideal for preparing dips, roasting nuts or making recipes with smaller yields, and a larger (6 to 8 quart) oval one, which I use most of the time to cook recipes with larger yields as well as those calling for a baking dish or pan set inside the stoneware. Once you begin using your slow cooker, you will get a sense of what suits your needs.

Some manufacturers sell a "slow cooker" that is actually a multi-cooker. These have a heating element at the bottom, and in my experience they cook faster than traditional slow cookers. Also, since the heat source is at the bottom, the food is likely to scorch unless it is stirred.

Your slow cooker should come with a booklet that explains how to use the appliance. I recommend that you read this carefully and/or visit the manufacturer's website for specific information on the model you purchased.

There are now so many models, shapes and sizes of slow cookers on the market that it is impossible to give one-size-fits-all instructions for using them.

Cooking Times

Over the years I've cooked in a wide variety of slow cookers and have found that cooking times can vary substantially from one to another. This is true even among different models sold under the same brand. The quality control on some of the lower-priced models may not be as rigorous as it should be, which accounts for some of the difference. That said, I've also found that some of the newer slow cookers tend to cook much more quickly than those that are a few years old. Please bear these discrepancies in mind if you follow my recipes and find that your food is overcooked. Although it may not seem particularly helpful if you're just starting out, the only firm advice I can give is *Know your slow cooker.* After trying a few of these recipes, you will get a sense of whether your slow cooker is faster or slower than the ones I use, and you will be able to adjust the cooking times accordingly. Other variables that can affect cooking time are extreme humidity, power fluctuations and high altitude. Be extra vigilant if any of these circumstances affect you.

Cooking Great-Tasting Food

The slow cooker's less-is-better approach is, in many ways, the secret of its success. The appliance does its work by cooking foods very slowly — from about 200°F (95°C) on the Low setting to 300°F (150°C) on High. This slow, moist cooking environment enables the appliance to produce mouthwatering pot roasts, briskets and many kinds of soups and stews. It also helps to ensure success with delicate puddings and custards, among other dishes. In fact, I'm so pleased with the slow cooker's strengths that there are many dishes I wouldn't cook any other way — for instance, pot roast, beef brisket or short ribs, beef, veal and lamb shanks and many kinds of stew.

Some benefits of long, slow cooking:

- it breaks down the tough connective tissue of less tender cuts of meat;
- it allows the seasoning in complex sauces to intermingle without scorching;
- it makes succulent stews that don't dry out or stick to the bottom of the pot; and
- it ensures success with delicate dishes such as puddings and custards.

Entertaining Worthy

I often use my slow cookers to help prepare the meal when I entertain, and as you use this book you'll notice recipes that have been identified as "Entertaining Worthy." Some of these, such as Osso Buco with Lemon Gremolata, Braised Swordfish and Chocolate Flan with Toasted Almonds, are clearly "special occasion" dishes, but many, including Mexican-Style

Chicken Soup, Savory Braised Pork and Poached Quince, may strike you as pretty down-home, particularly if you're trying to impress guests. All of which is to say, my selections are entirely subjective and very much reflect my own approach to entertaining. While every now and again I like to pull out the stops and do a bang-up elegant dinner party, most of the time I prefer to have one or two couples over for a casual Friday night meal. And on those evenings the kinds of dishes everyone prefers tend to be classic low-key comfort foods, which in my opinion are truly "entertaining worthy."

Understanding Your Slow Cooker

Like all appliances, the slow cooker has its unique way of doing things, so you need to understand how it works and adapt your cooking style accordingly. Years ago, when friends learned I was writing my first slow cooker cookbook, many had the same response: "Oh, you mean that appliance that allows you to throw the ingredients in and return home to a cooked meal!"

"Well, sort of," was my response. Over the years I've learned to think of my slow cooker as an indispensable helpmate, and I can hardly imagine living without its assistance. But I also know that it can't work miracles. Off the top of my head, I can't think of any great dish that results when ingredients are merely "thrown together." Success in the slow cooker, like success in the oven or on top of the stove, depends upon using proper cooking techniques. The slow cooker saves you time because it allows you to forget about the food once it is in the stoneware. But you still must pay attention to the advance preparation. Here are a few tips that will help to ensure slow cooker success.

Brown Meat and Soften Vegetables

Although it requires an extra pan, I am committed to browning most meats and softening vegetables before adding them to the slow cooker. In my experience this is not the most time-consuming part of preparing a slow cooker dish — it usually takes longer to peel and chop the vegetables, which you have to do anyway. But it dramatically improves the quality of the dish for two reasons. Not only does browning add color, it begins the process of caramelization, which breaks down the natural sugars in foods and releases their flavor. It also extracts the fat-soluble components of foods, which further enriches the taste. Moreover, tossing spices in with the softened vegetables helps to produce a sauce in which the flavors are better integrated than they would be if this step were skipped.

Reduce the Quantity of Liquid

As you use your slow cooker, one of the first things you will notice is that it generates liquid. Because slow cookers cook at a low heat, tightly covered, liquid doesn't evaporate as it does in the oven or on top of the stove. As a result, food made from traditional recipes will be watery. So the second rule of successful slow cooking is to reduce the amount of liquid. Because I don't want to reduce the flavor, I prefer to cook with stock rather than water.

Cut Root Vegetables into Thin Slices or Small Pieces

Perhaps surprisingly, root vegetables — carrots, parsnips and particularly potatoes, if you are using them — cook even more slowly than meat in the slow cooker. Root vegetables should be thinly sliced or cut into small pieces: no larger than 1-inch (2.5 cm) cubes.

Pay Attention to Cooking Temperature

To achieve maximum results, less tender cuts of meat should be cooked as slowly as possible. Expect to cook whole cuts of meat such as brisket and roasts for 8 to 10 hours on Low to become truly succulent. If you're short of time and at home during the day, cook whole cuts of meat on High for 1 to 2 hours before switching the temperature to Low. As noted in Food Safety in the Slow Cooker (see page 22), if adding cold ingredients, particularly large cuts of meat, to the slow cooker, set it on High for an hour before lowering the temperature.

Some delicate desserts need to be cooked on High. In these recipes, a Low setting is not suggested as an option. For recipes that aren't dependent upon cooking at a particular temperature, the rule of thumb is that 1 hour of cooking on High equals 2 to $2\frac{1}{2}$ hours on Low.

Don't Overcook

Although slow cooking reduces your chances of overcooking food, it is still not a "one size fits all" solution to meal preparation. If you want your slow cooker to cook while you are away, you should plan your day carefully if you have more delicate meats such as chicken in the pot. It is very easy to overcook poultry, which shouldn't require more than 6 hours on Low. If cooking white meat, which dries out easily, reduce the cooking time to 5 hours. Because legs and thighs stand up well in the slow cooker, I remove the skin before cooking to reduce the fat content in the sauce.

Use Ingredients Appropriately

Some ingredients do not respond well to long, slow cooking and should be added during the last 30 minutes, after the temperature has been increased to High. These include peas, leafy greens and seafood. I love to cook with peppers, but I've learned that most become bitter if cooked for too long. The solution to this problem is to add peppers to recipes during the last 30 minutes of cooking. All the recipes in this book address these concerns in the instructions.

Whole-Leaf Herbs and Spices

For best results use whole rather than ground spices in the slow cooker. Whole spices such as cinnamon sticks, vanilla beans, dried thyme and oregano leaves release their flavors slowly throughout the long cooking period, unlike ground spices, which tend to lose flavor during slow cooking. If you're using fresh herbs, add them finely chopped, during the last hour of cooking, unless you include the whole stem (this works best with thyme and rosemary).

I recommend the use of cracked black peppercorns rather than ground pepper in many of my recipes because they release flavor slowly during the long cooking process. "Cracked pepper" can be purchased in the spice sections of supermarkets, but I like to make my own with a mortar and pestle. A rolling pin or even a heavy can on its side will also break up the peppercorns for use in slow-cooked dishes. If you prefer to use ground black pepper, use one-quarter to one-half the amount of cracked black peppercorns called for in the recipe.

Using Dishes and Pans in the Slow Cooker

Some dishes, notably puddings and custards, need to be cooked in an extra dish that is placed in the slow cooker stoneware. Not only will you need a large oval slow cooker for this purpose, finding a dish or pan that fits into the stoneware can be a challenge. I've found that standard 7-inch (18 cm) square, 4-cup (1 L) and 6-cup (1.5 L) ovenproof baking dishes or soufflé dishes are the best all-round pans for this purpose, and I've used them to cook most of the custard-like recipes in this book.

Before you decide to make a recipe requiring a baking dish, ensure that you have a container that will fit into your stoneware. I've noted the size and dimensions of the containers used in all relevant recipes. Be aware that varying the size and shape of the dish is likely to affect cooking times.

Making Smaller Quantities

Over the years many people have asked me for slow cooker recipes that make smaller quantities, suitable for one or two people. Since most recipes reheat well or can be frozen for future use, making a big-batch recipe can be an efficient strategy for having a delicious, nutritious meal on hand for those nights when there is no time to cook. However, since more and more households comprise single people or couples who want to enjoy the benefits of using a slow cooker, I have noted those recipes that are suitable for being halved. Since slow cookers depend on volume to operate efficiently, it is important to use a small slow cooker (approximately $1\frac{1}{2}$ to $3\frac{1}{2}$ quarts) when cutting a recipe in half.

Making Ahead

Most of the recipes in this book can be partially prepared ahead of time and held for up to two days in the refrigerator, which is a great time saver for busy days. (Look for the Make Ahead instructions accompanying appropriate recipes.) If a recipe contains meat, for food safety reasons you cannot brown it ahead of time, nor can uncooked meat be combined with vegetables and held. For small pieces of meat, such as diced bacon, ground meat or sausage meat, that are fully cooked with vegetables before being placed in the stoneware, it is important to ensure that the mixture cools quickly to a safe temperature. Therefore I recommend placing these mixtures in a shallow container, then refrigerating them. This ensures that they are out of the danger zone within the preferred 30 minutes.

As a rule of thumb, I recommend refrigerating mixtures in a separate container, then transferring them to the stoneware. However, some vegetarian dishes can be preassembled in the stoneware and refrigerated, in which case be sure not to turn the slow cooker on before dropping the stoneware into the casing — the dramatic temperature change could crack it.

Maximize Slow Cooker Convenience

To get the most out of your slow cooker, consider the following:

- Prepare ingredients to the cooking stage the night before you intend to cook to keep work to a minimum in the morning.
- Cook a recipe overnight and refrigerate until ready to serve.
- Make a big-batch recipe and freeze a portion for a second or even a third meal.

Food Safety in the Slow Cooker

Because it cooks at a very low temperature for long periods of time, cooking with a slow cooker requires a bit more vigilance about food safety than does cooking at higher temperatures. The slow cooker needs to strike a delicate balance between cooking slowly enough that it doesn't require your attention and fast enough to ensure that food reaches temperatures that are appropriate to inhibit bacterial growth. Bacteria grow rapidly at temperatures higher than 40°F (4°C) and lower than 140°F (60°C). Once the temperature reaches 165°F (74°C), bacteria are killed. That's why it is so important to leave the lid on when you're slow cooking, particularly during the early stages. This helps to ensure that bacteria-killing temperatures are reached in the appropriate amount of time.

Slow cooker manufacturers have designed the appliance to ensure that bacterial growth is not a concern. So long as the lid is left on and the food is cooked for the appropriate length of time, that crucial temperature will be reached quickly enough to ensure food safety. Unless you have made part of the recipe ahead and refrigerated it, most of the ingredients in my recipes are warm when added to the slow cooker (the meat has been browned and the sauce has been thickened on the stove top), which adds a cushion of comfort to any potential concerns about food safety.

The following tips will help to ensure that utmost food safety standards are met:

- Keep food refrigerated until you are ready to cook. Bacteria multiply quickly at room temperature. Do not allow ingredients to rise to room temperature before cooking.
- Do not partially cook meat or poultry and refrigerate for subsequent cooking. If you're browning meat before adding it to the slow cooker, do so just before placing it in the slow cooker. When cooking meat, try to get it to a high temperature as quickly as possible.

- If cooking a large cut of meat, such as a pot roast, which has been added to the stoneware without being browned, set the temperature at High for at least an hour to accelerate the cooking process.
- Pay attention to the make-ahead instructions for recipes that can be partially prepared in advance of cooking, as they have been developed to address food safety issues.
- If you're making part of a recipe ahead and it contains cooked meat such as sausage or ground beef mixed with vegetables, cool the mixture to a safe temperature (less than 40°F/4°C) as quickly as possible. To ensure it doesn't stay in the danger zone any longer than 30 minutes, spread the mixture in a shallow container (use more than one, if necessary), cover and refrigerate immediately. Or (this works in some recipes) refrigerate precooked meat such as ground beef or sausage and vegetables in separate containers and assemble when ready to cook. Do not brown meat until you're ready to cook. Browning meat, then refrigerating it encourages the growth of harmful bacteria.
- Do not put frozen meat, fish or poultry into a slow cooker. Unless otherwise instructed, thaw frozen food before adding to the slow cooker. Frozen fruits and vegetables should usually be thawed under cold running water to separate them before being added to recipes.
- Limit the number of times you lift the lid while food is cooking. Each time the lid is removed it takes approximately 20 minutes to recover the lost heat. This increases the time it takes for the food to reach the "safe zone."
- If the power goes out while you are away, discard the food if it has not finished cooking. If the food has cooked completely, it should be safe for up to 2 hours.
- Refrigerate leftovers as quickly as possible.
- Do not reheat food in the slow cooker.

Testing for Safety
If you are concerned that your slow cooker isn't cooking quickly enough to ensure food safety, try this simple test. Fill the stoneware insert with 8 cups (2 L) of cold water. Set temperature to Low for 8 hours. Using an accurate thermometer and checking quickly (because the temperature drops when the lid is removed), check to ensure that the temperature is 185°F (85°C). If the slow cooker has not reached that temperature, it's not heating food fast enough to avoid food safety problems. If the temperature is significantly higher than that, the appliance is not cooking slowly enough to be used as a slow cooker.

Leftovers
Many slow cookers have a Warm setting, which holds the food at 165°F (74°C). Programmable models will automatically switch to Warm when the time is up. Cooked food can be kept warm in the slow cooker for up to 2 hours. At that point it should be transferred to small containers so it cools as rapidly as possible and then be refrigerated or frozen. Because the appliance heats up so slowly, food should never be reheated in a slow cooker.

Starters and Snacks

Spicy Tamari Almonds
and Maple Orange Pecans

Spicy Tamari Almonds

◆ Entertaining Worthy
◆ Can Be Halved
(see Tips, below)

Tips

If you are halving this recipe, be sure to use a small (1½ to 2 quart) slow cooker.

Gluten-free tamari sauce tastes good, is readily available and inexpensive. If you are avoiding soy, use liquid aminos or coconut aminos.

I love eating these tasty tidbits as pre-dinner nibbles with a glass of cold white wine. Tamari is usually a wheat-free soy sauce (check the label), but if you prefer, you can substitute coconut aminos.

• **Small (2 to 3½ quart) slow cooker**

2 cups	unblanched whole raw almonds	500 mL
¼ tsp	cayenne pepper	1 mL
2 tbsp	gluten-free tamari sauce or coconut aminos (see Tips, left and page 15)	30 mL
1 tbsp	extra virgin olive oil	15 mL
	Fine sea salt	

1. In slow cooker stoneware, combine almonds and cayenne. Place a clean tea towel, folded in half (so you will have 2 layers), over top of stoneware to absorb moisture. Cover and cook on High for 45 minutes.

2. In a small bowl, combine tamari and olive oil. Add to hot almonds and stir thoroughly to combine. Replace tea towel. Cover and cook on High for 1½ hours, until nuts are hot and fragrant, stirring every 30 minutes and replacing towel each time. Sprinkle with salt to taste. Store in an airtight container.

Maple Orange Pecans

◆ Entertaining Worthy
◆ Can Be Halved
(see Tips, below)

Tips

If you are halving this recipe, be sure to use a small (1½ to 2 quart) slow cooker.

Research is showing that pure maple syrup may actually be a superfood. It is loaded with beneficial compounds, which may be anti-inflammatory and of benefit to people managing type-2 diabetes.

I love snacking on these sweet, flavorful nuts, and they also make a great addition to salads or a garnish for desserts.

• **Small (2 to 3½ quart) slow cooker**
• **Baking sheet, lined with waxed paper**

¼ cup	pure maple syrup (see Tips, left)	60 mL
1 tbsp	grated orange zest	15 mL
½ tsp	ground cinnamon	2 mL
Pinch	cayenne pepper, optional	Pinch
2 cups	raw pecan halves	500 mL
	Sweet paprika	

1. In slow cooker stoneware, combine maple syrup, orange zest, cinnamon and cayenne, if using.

2. Cover and cook on High for 30 minutes to meld flavors. Add pecans and stir well. Place a clean tea towel, folded in half (so you will have 2 layers), over top of stoneware to absorb moisture. Cover and cook on High for 1 hour, until nuts release their aroma and are nicely toasted. Spread out on prepared baking sheet. Sprinkle with paprika to taste and let cool (coating will harden). Store in an airtight container.

Spicy Cashews

Tip

Check your chili powder blend to make sure it doesn't contain gluten. Some manufacturers add ingredients that contain gluten.

These zesty nuts are somewhat addictive. For a holiday gift, make up a batch or two and package in pretty jars. If well sealed, the nuts (this works as well for the almonds, left and below) will keep for up to 10 days.

- **Small (maximum 3$\frac{1}{2}$ quart) slow cooker**

2 cups	whole raw cashews	500 mL
1 tsp	chili powder (see Tip, left)	5 mL
$\frac{1}{2}$ tsp	cayenne pepper	2 mL
$\frac{1}{4}$ tsp	ground cinnamon	1 mL
1 tsp	fine sea salt	5 mL
1 tbsp	extra virgin olive oil	15 mL

1. In slow cooker stoneware, combine cashews, chili powder, cayenne and cinnamon. Stir to combine thoroughly. Cover and cook on High for 1$\frac{1}{2}$ hours, stirring every 30 minutes, until nuts are nicely toasted.

2. In a small bowl, combine sea salt and olive oil. Add to nuts in slow cooker and stir to thoroughly combine. Transfer mixture to a serving bowl and serve hot or let cool.

Almonds with Thyme

Tip

So long as you are getting enough potassium in your diet, consuming an appropriate amount of pure sea salt, which contains a smattering of beneficial minerals, should not be problematic.

I completely agree with Elizabeth David, the late food writer, who wrote: "Nothing yet invented so sets the gastric juices to work as the sight of a plateful of freshly roasted and salted almonds."

- **Small (maximum 3$\frac{1}{2}$ quart) slow cooker**

2 cups	unblanched whole raw almonds	500 mL
$\frac{1}{2}$ tsp	freshly ground white pepper	2 mL
1 tbsp	fine sea salt, or to taste	15 mL
2 tbsp	extra virgin olive oil	30 mL
2 tbsp	fresh thyme leaves	30 mL

1. In slow cooker stoneware, combine almonds and white pepper. Cover and cook on High for 1$\frac{1}{2}$ hours, stirring every 30 minutes, until nuts are nicely toasted.

2. In a bowl, combine salt, olive oil and thyme. Add to hot almonds in stoneware and stir thoroughly to combine. Spoon mixture into a small serving bowl and serve hot or let cool.

Caper-Studded Caponata

◆ **Entertaining Worthy**

Tips

I like to "sweat" eggplant and drain it of excess moisture because I find it doesn't soak up as much oil when browning. *To sweat eggplant:* Place the cubed eggplant in a colander and sprinkle liberally with salt. Leave for 30 minutes to 1 hour until the moisture comes to the surface. (If time is short, blanch the pieces for a minute or two in heavily salted water.) In either case, rinse thoroughly in fresh cold water and, using your hands, squeeze out the excess moisture. Pat dry with paper towels and it's ready to cook.

You can also use salt-cured capers in this recipe, but they will need to soak in cold water for about 30 minutes, then thoroughly rinsed under cold running water before adding to the recipe.

Make Ahead

Complete Step 2. Cover and refrigerate for up to 2 days. When you're ready to cook, complete the recipe.

This recipe differs from most caponata because it contains a sweet pepper and capers. I find it particularly delicious. Serve it on celery sticks, hearts of romaine lettuce or Napa cabbage, Oven-Baked Kale Chips (page 241) or thinly sliced cucumber. It also makes a great finish for a simple piece of grilled fish or a topping for Zucchini Noodles (page 153).

- Small (approx. 2 quart) slow cooker
- Large sheet of parchment paper

1	medium eggplant (about 1 lb/500 g), peeled, cut into 1/2-inch (1 cm) cubes and drained of excess moisture (see Tips, left)	1
3 tbsp	red wine vinegar (see page 15)	45 mL
1 tbsp	liquid honey	15 mL
2 to 3 tbsp	extra virgin olive oil	30 to 45 mL
4	cloves garlic, minced	4
1 tsp	cracked black peppercorns	5 mL
1/2 tsp	sea salt	2 mL
1/4 cup	finely chopped reconstituted sun-dried tomatoes (see Tips, page 29)	60 mL
1/2	red bell pepper, seeded and diced	1/2
2 tbsp	drained capers	30 mL
1/4 cup	finely chopped parsley leaves	60 mL

1. In a small bowl, combine vinegar and honey. Stir until combined. Set aside.

2. In a skillet, heat 2 tbsp (30 mL) of the oil over medium-high heat. Add sweated eggplant, in batches, if necessary, and cook, stirring and tossing, until it begins to brown, about 3 minutes per batch, adding more oil, if necessary. Transfer to slow cooker stoneware. Add garlic, peppercorns and salt to pan and cook, stirring, for 1 minute. Add sun-dried tomatoes and vinegar mixture and stir to combine. Stir into stoneware.

3. Place a large piece of parchment over the eggplant mixture, pressing it down to brush the food and extending up the sides of the stoneware so it overlaps the rim. Cover and cook on Low for 6 hours or High for 3 hours, until mixture is hot and bubbly. Lift out parchment and discard, being careful not to spill the accumulated liquid into the mixture. Stir in bell pepper and capers. Cover and cook on High for 15 minutes, until bell pepper is soft and flavors blend. Transfer to a serving bowl and garnish with parsley. Serve warm or at room temperature.

Eggplant Caviar

◆ Entertaining Worthy
◆ Can Be Halved
(see Tips, below)

Tips

If you are halving this recipe, be sure to use a small (1½ to 2 quart) slow cooker.

Use sun-dried tomatoes packed in extra virgin olive oil, or dry-packed sun-dried tomatoes, which should be soaked in 1 cup (250 mL) boiling water for 15 minutes before being used. In case you have any concerns about sun-dried tomatoes being "Paleo," according to James Trager (in his book *The Food Chronology*) humans were drying and smoking food as early as 12,000 BC.

Make Ahead

You can make Eggplant Caviar up to 2 days ahead. Cover and refrigerate until you're ready to serve.

Although its origins are Mediterranean, this flavorful spread has become a favorite around the world. What's more, it's loaded with nutrition. Serve it well chilled with sliced veggies. Spears of Belgian endive or hearts of romaine make for a particularly elegant presentation. It is also tasty spread on Oven-Baked Kale Chips (page 241).

- **Small (2 to 3½ quart) slow cooker**
- **Food processor**

1	medium eggplant (about 1 lb/500 g), peeled, cut into 2-inch (5 cm) cubes and drained of excess moisture (see Tips, page 28)	1
1 tbsp	cumin seeds	15 mL
2 tbsp	extra virgin olive oil, divided (approx.)	30 mL
½ tsp	cracked black peppercorns	2 mL
4	cloves garlic, minced	4
½ cup	diced peeled tomatoes	125 mL
4	green onions, white part only with just a hint of green, chopped	4
1	roasted red bell pepper, seeded and chopped	1
2	reconstituted sun-dried tomatoes, drained and chopped (see Tips, left)	2
½ cup	coarsely chopped parsley leaves	125 mL
2 tbsp	red wine vinegar (see page 15)	30 mL
	Fine sea salt and freshly ground black pepper	

1. In a large dry skillet over medium heat, toast cumin seeds, stirring, until fragrant, about 3 minutes. Transfer to a mortar and pestle or a spice grinder and pound or grind as finely as you can. Set aside.

2. In same skillet, heat 1 tbsp (15 mL) of the oil over medium heat. Add sweated eggplant, in batches, if necessary and cook, stirring and tossing, until it begins to brown, about 3 minutes per batch, adding more oil, if necessary. Transfer to slow cooker stoneware. Add reserved cumin, peppercorns, garlic and tomatoes. Cover and cook on Low for 4 hours or High for 2 hours.

3. Transfer to a food processor and process until smooth. Add green onions, roasted pepper, sun-dried tomatoes, parsley and vinegar and pulse until blended. Season with salt and pepper to taste. Chill thoroughly.

Chilly Dilly Eggplant

◆ Entertaining Worthy

Tip

I am very comfortable using fermented vinegars in recipes. I have little doubt that our Paleolithic ancestors accidently stumbled upon the juice of fermented fruit and found a use for it. In addition, there is evidence that vinegar is a healthy addition to contemporary diets. Recent studies show that consuming vinegar reduces the glycemic response in both healthy individuals and those with diabetes.

Make Ahead

You'll achieve maximum results if you make this a day ahead and chill thoroughly before serving, or cook overnight, purée in the morning and chill.

This is a versatile recipe, delicious as a dip with raw vegetables or a tasty vegetable chip such as Oven-Baked Kale Chips (page 241). It makes a wonderful addition to a mezes or tapas-style meal. Although it is tasty warm, the flavor dramatically improves if it is thoroughly chilled before serving.

- **Small (maximum 3½ quart) slow cooker**
- **Blender or food processor**

2	large eggplants (each about 1½ lbs/750 g), peeled, cut into 1-inch (2.5 cm) cubes and drained of excess moisture (see Tips, page 28)	2
2 to 3 tbsp	extra virgin olive oil	30 to 45 mL
2	medium onions, chopped	2
4	cloves garlic, chopped	4
1 tsp	dried oregano	5 mL
1 tsp	sea salt	5 mL
½ tsp	freshly ground black pepper	2 mL
1 tbsp	balsamic or red wine vinegar (see Tip, left)	15 mL
½ cup	chopped fresh dill fronds	125 mL
	Dill sprigs, optional	
	Finely chopped black olives, optional	

1. In a skillet, heat 2 tbsp (30 mL) of the oil over medium heat. Add sweated eggplant, in batches, if necessary and cook, stirring and tossing, until it begins to brown, about 3 minutes per batch, adding more oil, if necessary. Transfer to slow cooker stoneware.

2. In same pan, using more oil, if necessary. Add onions and cook, stirring, until softened, about 3 minutes. Add garlic, oregano, salt and pepper and cook for 1 minute. Transfer to slow cooker and stir to combine thoroughly. Cover and cook on Low for 7 to 8 hours or on High for 4 hours, until vegetables are tender.

3. Transfer contents of slow cooker, in batches, if necessary, to a blender or food processor. Add vinegar and dill fronds and process until smooth, scraping down sides of bowl at halfway point. Taste for seasoning and adjust. Spoon into a small serving bowl and refrigerate thoroughly. Garnish with sprigs of dill and chopped black olives, if using.

Braised Tomato Topping

◆ **Entertaining Worthy**

Tip

Look for canned tomatoes that are organically grown, with no salt added, and come in glass jars or BPA (bisphenol-A) free cans. When using canned tomatoes (or any canned product) check to make sure they are gluten-free.

Make Ahead

Complete the recipe. Cover and refrigerate for up to 3 days. Bring to room temperature before serving.

This luscious tomato topping, which is reminiscent of a fresh tomato salad, is simply delicious and a wonderful treat in the midst of winter, when succulent local field tomatoes are only a faint memory. It is delicious served over grilled portobello mushroom tops or spread on spears of Belgian endive or Oven-Baked Kale Chips (page 241). It also makes a great accompaniment to grilled meat or fish, or a topping for Zucchini Noodles (page 153) or Kelp Noodles (page 220).

- **Small to medium (1½ to 3½ quart) slow cooker**
- **Large sheet of parchment paper**

¼ cup	extra virgin olive oil, divided	60 mL
1	can (28 oz/796 mL) diced tomatoes, drained (see Tip, left)	1
2	cloves garlic, minced	2
2 tsp	dried oregano	10 mL
½ tsp	sea salt	2 mL
2 tbsp	finely chopped parsley leaves	30 mL
	Freshly ground black pepper	

1. In slow cooker stoneware, place 2 tbsp (30 mL) of the olive oil and swirl to coat bottom. Add tomatoes and sprinkle with garlic, oregano and salt. Drizzle with remaining olive oil. Place a large piece of parchment over the tomatoes, pressing it down to brush the food and extending up the sides of the stoneware so it overlaps the rim.

2. Cover and cook on Low for 6 hours or High for 3 hours, until mixture is hot and bubbly. Lift out parchment and discard, being careful not to spill the accumulated liquid into the tomato mixture. Stir in parsley and season with pepper to taste. Transfer to a serving dish and let cool to room temperature.

Oh-So-Retro Swedish Meatballs

Makes about 30 meatballs

♦ Entertaining Worthy

Tips

Many people on Paleo diets cannot tolerate the lactose in dairy products. However, butter contains only a minimal amount of lactose. If you are concerned about the fact that cows were not domesticated until the Neolithic era, you can substitute properly fermented goat's milk products for dairy. Hunter-gatherers have been drinking goat's milk since about 10,000 BC.

Sandor Katz (in his book *The Art of Fermentation*) sees fermentation as a "coevolutionary force" and he notes that humans have been consuming fermented food since prehistoric times. When dairy products have been fermented properly, virtually all of the lactose disappears. The lactic acid bacteria in properly fermented milk products such as yogurt and sour cream are linked with a variety of health benefits, including improved digestion. Recent studies suggest that the acids in fermented milk products may also reduce the impact of certain foods on blood glucose response.

These were a cocktail party standard when I was growing up, and they are firmly lodged in my food memory bank. I like to serve them in a shallow serving dish or a deep platter, speared with cocktail toothpicks. If my experience is any measure, they will disappear in a flash. Make sure your guests have napkins or a plate to catch any drips.

- Small to medium (2 to 3½ quart) slow cooker

1 lb	lean ground beef, preferably sirloin	500 g
½ cup	almond flour	125 mL
1	onion, grated	1
1	egg, beaten	1
2 tsp	finely grated lemon zest	10 mL
2 tbsp	freshly squeezed lemon juice	30 mL
½ tsp	sea salt	2 mL
½ tsp	allspice	2 mL
	Freshly ground black pepper	
2 tbsp	extra virgin olive oil or clarified butter (see page 12)	30 mL
1 tbsp	coconut flour	15 mL
½ tsp	cracked black peppercorns	2 mL
2 cups	beef stock, heated to the boiling point	500 mL
½ cup	sour cream or crème fraîche (see Tips, left and page 14)	125 mL
½ cup	finely chopped dill fronds	125 mL

1. In a bowl, combine ground beef, almond flour, onion, egg, lemon zest and juice, salt, allspice and pepper to taste. Mix well. Using your hands, shape into balls about ½ inch (1 cm) in diameter.

2. In a large skillet, heat oil over medium-high heat. Add meatballs, in batches, and cook, stirring, until nicely browned, about 4 minutes per batch. Transfer to slow cooker stoneware as completed. Add coconut flour to pan and cook, stirring, until frothy but not browning, about 2 minutes. Stir in peppercorns. Add beef stock and cook, stirring, until mixture comes to a boil and thickens, about 2 minutes. Pour over meatballs.

3. Cover and cook on Low for 6 hours or on High for 3 hours, until meatballs are cooked through. Using a slotted spoon, transfer meatballs to a serving dish. Add sour cream and dill to stoneware and stir well. Pour over meatballs and serve.

Country Terrine

Tips

This terrine can be made in almost any kind of baking dish that will fit into your slow cooker. I have a variety of baking pans that work well: a small loaf pan, approximately 8 by 5 inches (20 by 12.5 cm), makes a traditionally shaped terrine; a round 4-cup (1 L) soufflé dish or a square 7-inch (18 cm) baking dish produces slices of different shapes.

Although brandy is not a Paleo ingredient, it adds great flavor to this terrine. Feel free to omit it if you prefer.

To purée garlic, use a fine-tooth grater such as Microplane.

Placing a weight on a terrine while it cools compacts the meat and ensures it has a uniform texture. I keep a brick wrapped in plastic wrap for this purpose. It fits nicely into my loaf pan.

This is a simple terrine, mildly flavored and nicely moist. Served with a spirited condiment such as Dijon mustard or some cornichons, it's a real treat. Enjoy this on thinly sliced cucumber slices or wedges of sweet red pepper, or plated and eaten with a fork. I can't think of a better companion for a leisurely glass of wine.

- Loaf pan, earthenware terrine or soufflé dish, lightly greased (see Tips, left)
- Large (minimum 5 quart) oval slow cooker
- Instant-read thermometer

1½ lbs	boneless pork shoulder, including fat, coarsely chopped	750 g
8 oz	stewing veal, coarsely chopped	250 g
4 oz	smoked bacon, trimmed of rind, cubed	125 g
2 tsp	cracked black peppercorns	10 mL
1 tsp	sea salt	5 mL
3 tbsp	brandy or cognac, optional (see Tips, left)	45 mL
1	onion, grated	1
2	cloves garlic, puréed (see Tips, left)	2
2 tbsp	fresh thyme leaves	30 mL

1. In a meat grinder (or food processor in batches), grind pork, veal and bacon, transferring to a bowl as completed. Mix well. Add peppercorns, salt, brandy, if using, onion, garlic and thyme and mix well. Cover and refrigerate overnight.

2. When you're ready to cook, transfer mixture to prepared pan. Cover tightly with foil and secure with a string. Place in stoneware and add hot water to come about halfway up the sides of the pan.

3. Cover and cook on High about 4 hours, until juices run clear or an instant-read thermometer inserted into the center of the terrine registers 160°F (71°C). Chill overnight, weighted down (see Tips, left) before serving.

Hot Anchovy-Garlic Dunk

◆ **Entertaining Worthy**

Tip

For a smoother blend, put the garlic and anchovies through a garlic press before adding to the stoneware.

Traditionally, this is served with celery or carrot sticks, or broccoli or cauliflower florets, but almost anything tastes good in the ambrosial brew. I even serve it with beautiful little Brussels sprouts cooked to the point where they are just slightly underdone. My guests spear them on fondue forks and dunk them in the hot bath. Even one who is usually no fan of Brussels sprouts loves them. Crisp leaves of baby bok choy and Belgian endive also work well.

- **Small (maximum 3½ quart) slow cooker**
- **Fondue forks**

2	cloves garlic, minced	2
¾ cup	extra virgin olive oil	175 mL
2 tbsp	butter	30 mL
8	anchovy fillets, finely chopped (see Tip, left)	8
	Freshly ground black pepper	
	Crudités (see Introduction, above)	

1. In slow cooker stoneware, combine garlic, olive oil, butter, anchovies and pepper to taste. Cover and cook on High for about 30 minutes, until mixture is hot and anchovies have begun to dissolve. Stir well to incorporate anchovies into sauce. Turn heat to Low.

2. Arrange crudités on a serving plate or platter. Give each guest a plate and fondue fork and allow them to help themselves.

Slow-Roasted Garlic

Tips

Double or triple this recipe to suit your needs.

Roasted garlic is an easy enhancement for simple soups, gravy or vinaigrette. Just whisk in the desired quantity. It also makes a great topping for grilled vegetables and can be stirred into mayonnaise to make a Roasted Garlic Aïoli (see Variations, page 238).

If you like to have roasted garlic on hand to use as a condiment, here is a very easy way to make it. The garlic cooks away in the slow cooker, and you can forget about it while you do other things. Store for up to 2 days tightly covered in the refrigerator or frozen in small portions for up to 3 months.

- **Small (approx. 2 quart) slow cooker**
- **Food processor**
- **Large sheet of parchment paper**

30	cloves peeled garlic (about 2 heads)	30
2 tbsp	extra virgin olive oil	30 mL

1. Lay parchment on a flat work surface and mound garlic in the middle. Spoon olive oil over garlic. Lift 2 opposite sides of parchment to meet in the middle, then fold them over to form a seal. Continue folding until flush with garlic. Fold remaining sides over to form a package. Place in stoneware, seam side down. Cover and cook on High for 4 hours, until garlic is nicely caramelized.

New World Leek
and Pepper Soup

Soups

New World Leek and Pepper Soup

Serves 8

◆ **Can Be Halved**
(see Tips, below)

Tips

If you are halving this recipe, be sure to use a small (approx. 2 quart) slow cooker.

To clean leeks: Fill a sink full of lukewarm water. Split the leeks in half lengthwise and submerge them in the water, swishing them around to remove all traces of dirt. Transfer to a colander and rinse thoroughly under cold water.

For the best flavor, toast cumin seeds and grind them yourself. *To toast cumin seeds:* Place in a dry skillet over medium heat and cook, stirring, until fragrant, about 3 minutes. Immediately transfer to a spice grinder or mortar and grind finely.

This soup is tastiest when made with sweet potatoes, but if you prefer substitute an equal quantity of acorn squash.

If you prefer, use one red and one green bell pepper.

Make Ahead

Complete Step 1. Cover and refrigerate for up to 2 days. When you're ready to cook, complete the recipe.

I call this soup "new world" because it's a variation on the classic French leek and potato soup, using sweet potatoes and peppers, two ingredients that Christopher Columbus introduced to Europe during his explorations of the Americas. Serve small quantities as a prelude to a celebratory meal, or add a tossed green salad for a light supper.

- **Medium to large (3½ to 5 quart) slow cooker**
- **Blender or food processor**

2 tbsp	extra virgin olive oil or butter	30 mL
4	large leeks, white part with just a bit of green, cleaned and thinly sliced (see Tips, left)	4
4	cloves garlic, minced	4
1 tbsp	ground cumin (see Tips, left)	15 mL
½ tsp	sea salt	2 mL
½ tsp	cracked black peppercorns	2 mL
6 cups	chicken or vegetable stock, divided	1.5 L
3	medium sweet potatoes (about 2 lbs/1 kg), peeled and cut into 1-inch (2.5 cm) cubes (see Tips, left)	3
2	green bell peppers, diced (see Tips, left)	2
1	long red chile pepper, minced, optional	1
	Sea salt, optional	
	Roasted red pepper strips, optional	
	Finely snipped chives	

1. In a large skillet, heat oil over medium heat. Add leeks and cook, stirring, until softened, about 5 minutes. Add garlic, cumin, salt and peppercorns and cook, stirring, for 1 minute. Add 2 cups (500 mL) of the stock and stir well. Transfer to slow cooker stoneware.

2. Add remaining 4 cups (1 L) of stock and sweet potatoes. Cover and cook on Low for 6 hours or on High for 3 hours, until potatoes are tender. Add green peppers and chile pepper, if using. Cover and cook on High for 20 minutes, until peppers are tender. Season to taste with salt, if using.

3. Purée using an immersion blender. (If you don't have an immersion blender, do this in a blender or food processor, in batches.) To serve, ladle soup into bowls and garnish with roasted red pepper strips, if using, and chives.

French-Style Pumpkin Soup with Leeks

◆ **Entertaining Worthy**
◆ **Can Be Halved**
(see Tips, below)

Tips

If you are halving this recipe, be sure to use a small (2 to 3½ quart) slow cooker.

If you are using the outer stalks of celery, peel them before chopping; the top layer is very fibrous. The inner stalks (hearts) can be used without peeling.

Substitute an equal quantity of winter squash, such as butternut or acorn, for the pumpkin.

Make Ahead

Complete Step 1. Cover and refrigerate for up to 2 days. When you're ready to cook, complete the recipe.

In France there are many variations of this deliciously light and beautifully flavored soup. Here I have suggested a basic version that is simply perfect as is. If you're inclined to gild the lily, try adding the mussels (see Variation, below), my husband's favorite.

- **Medium to large (3½ to 5 quart) slow cooker**
- **Blender or food processor**

2 tbsp	butter or extra virgin olive oil	30 mL
2	leeks, white part only with just a hint of green, cleaned and thinly sliced (see Tips, page 38)	2
2	stalks celery, diced (see Tips, left)	2
2	carrots, peeled and diced	2
½ tsp	sea salt	2 mL
½ tsp	cracked black peppercorns	2 mL
4 cups	chicken or vegetable stock, divided	1 L
4 cups	cubed (1 inch/2.5 cm) peeled pumpkin (see Tips, left)	1 L
	Finely snipped chives	

1. In a skillet over medium heat, melt butter. Add leeks, celery and carrots and cook, stirring, until softened, about 7 minutes. Add salt and peppercorns and cook, stirring, for 1 minute. Add 2 cups (500 mL) of the stock and bring to a boil.

2. Transfer to slow cooker stoneware. Stir in pumpkin and remaining 2 cups (500 mL) of stock. Cover and cook on Low for 6 to 8 hours or on High for 3 to 4 hours, until pumpkin is tender. Purée using an immersion blender. (If you don't have an immersion blender, do this in a blender or food processor, in batches.) Ladle into bowls, and garnish liberally with chives.

Variation

Pumpkin and Mussel Soup: In a large saucepan, bring ½ cup (125 mL) dry white wine and 1 tsp (5 mL) fennel seeds to a boil. Add 2 lbs (1 kg) cleaned mussels. Cover and cook until all the mussels have opened, about 5 minutes. Discard any that have not opened. Drain, reserving cooking liquid. Remove mussels from their shells. Strain cooking liquid through a fine sieve or paper coffee filter, discarding any sediment. About 20 minutes before the soup has finished cooking, add mussels and cooking liquid to stoneware and cook on High until heated through and flavors meld, about 10 minutes. If cooking ahead of time, combine shelled mussels with strained cooking liquid and refrigerate until ready to use.

Coconut-Spiked Pumpkin Soup with Cumin and Ginger

Serves 6 to 8

- ◆ **Entertaining Worthy**
- ◆ **Can Be Halved**
  (see Tips, below)

Tips

If you are halving this recipe, be sure to use a small (approx. 2 quart) slow cooker.

For the best flavor, toast cumin seeds and grind them yourself. *To toast cumin seeds:* Place in a dry skillet over medium heat, and cook, stirring, until fragrant, about 3 minutes. Immediately transfer to a spice grinder or mortar and grind finely.

You may need to adjust the quantity of salt depending upon the saltiness of the stock you're using.

If you like heat, increase the quantity of cayenne to ½ tsp (2 mL).

Coconut milk should be gluten-free. However, some brands contain guar gum, which, although it does not contain gluten, is not recommended for people with celiac disease. Check the label.

Make Ahead

Complete Step 1. Cover and refrigerate for up to 2 days. When you're ready to cook, complete the recipe.

Here's a hearty soup with Asian flavors that makes a nice centerpiece for lunch or a light supper or an elegant starter to a more substantial dinner.

- **Medium to large (3½ to 5 quart) slow cooker**
- **Blender or food processor**

2 tbsp	extra virgin coconut oil	30 mL
2	onions, finely chopped	2
2	carrots, peeled and diced	2
2	stalks celery, diced (see Tips, page 39)	2
4	cloves garlic, minced	4
2 tbsp	minced gingerroot	30 mL
1 tbsp	ground cumin (see Tips, left)	15 mL
½ tsp	sea salt (see Tips, left)	2 mL
½ tsp	cracked black peppercorns	2 mL
5 cups	chicken or vegetable stock, divided	1.25 L
6 cups	cubed (½ inch/1 cm) peeled pumpkin or orange squash, such as butternut	1.5 L
¼ tsp	cayenne pepper (see Tips, left)	1 mL
2 tbsp	freshly squeezed lime juice	30 mL
1 cup	coconut milk (see Tips, left)	250 mL

1. In a skillet, heat oil over medium heat. Add onions, carrots and celery and cook, stirring, until softened, about 7 minutes. Add garlic, ginger, cumin, salt and peppercorns and cook, stirring for 1 minute. Add 1 cup (250 mL) of the stock and bring to a boil. Transfer to slow cooker stoneware.

2. Add remaining 4 cups (1 L) of stock and pumpkin. Cover and cook on Low for 6 hours, until pumpkin is tender. Purée using an immersion blender. (If you don't have an immersion blender, do this in a blender or food processor, in batches, and return to stoneware.)

3. In a small bowl, combine cayenne and lime juice, stirring until cayenne dissolves. Add to slow cooker along with coconut milk. Stir well. Cover and cook on High for 15 minutes to meld flavors.

Curried Parsnip Soup

Serves 8

◆ Entertaining Worthy
◆ Can Be Halved
(see Tips, below)

Tips

If you are halving this recipe, be sure to use a small (approx. 2 quart) slow cooker.

If you are using large parsnips in this recipe, cut away the woody core and discard.

Curry powder should be simply a blend of spices, which are gluten-free, but some manufacturers add wheat starch so be sure to check the label.

While fresh green peas are classified as legumes in the botanical sense, they do not qualify as dietary legumes. The fundamental difference is that they are not dried; they are a vegetable that can be eaten raw or just lightly cooked. Dietary legumes, on the other hand, are grown specifically for their seed and are categorized as pulses. They often need to be pre-soaked for an extensive period and invariably require a long cooking time.

Make Ahead

Complete Step 1. Cover and refrigerate for up to 2 days. When you're ready to cook, complete the recipe.

Flavorful and elegant, this soup makes a great introduction to a more substantial meal. Served with salad, it is also a satisfying supper.

- **Medium to large (3½ to 5 quart) slow cooker**
- **Blender or food processor**

1 tbsp	extra virgin coconut oil	15 mL
2	onions, finely chopped	2
4	cloves garlic, minced	4
2 tsp	ground cumin (see Tips, page 73)	10 mL
1 tsp	ground coriander	5 mL
½ tsp	sea salt	2 mL
½ tsp	cracked black peppercorns	2 mL
1	piece (1 inch/2.5 cm) cinnamon stick	1
1	bay leaf	1
6 cups	chicken or vegetable stock	1.5 L
4 cups	sliced peeled parsnips (about 1 lb/500 g) (see Tips, left)	1 L
2 tsp	curry powder (see Tips, left), dissolved in 4 tsp (20 mL) freshly squeezed lemon juice	10 mL
2 cups	sweet green peas, thawed if frozen (see Tips, left)	500 mL
½ cup	coconut milk, plus additional for drizzling	125 mL

1. In a skillet, heat oil over medium heat. Add onions and cook, stirring, until softened, about 3 minutes. Add garlic, cumin, coriander, salt, peppercorns, cinnamon stick and bay leaf and cook, stirring, for 1 minute. Transfer to slow cooker stoneware. Add stock.

2. Add parsnips and stir well. Cover and cook on Low for 6 hours or on High for 3 hours, until parsnips are tender. Discard cinnamon stick and bay leaf. Purée using an immersion blender. (If you don't have an immersion blender, do this in a blender or food processor, in batches, and return to stoneware.)

3. Add curry powder solution, green peas and coconut milk. Cover and cook on High for 20 minutes, until peas are tender and coconut milk is heated through. Ladle into bowls and drizzle with additional coconut milk.

Cabbage Borscht

Serves 8

◆ **Can Be Halved**
(see Tips, below)

Tips

If you are halving this recipe, be sure to use a small (approx. 2 quart) slow cooker.

If you prefer a smoother soup, do not purée the vegetables in Step 2. Instead, wait until they have finished cooking, and purée the soup in the stoneware using an immersion blender before adding the vinegar and cabbage. Allow the soup time to reheat (cook on High for 10 or 15 minutes) before adding the cabbage to ensure that it cooks.

I am very comfortable using fermented vinegar in recipes (see page 15). Recent studies show that consuming vinegar reduces the glycemic response in both healthy individuals and those with diabetes.

Make Ahead

Complete Steps 1 and 2. Cover and refrigerate for up to 2 days. When you're ready to cook, complete the recipe.

This hearty soup makes a soul-satisfying meal, particularly in the dark days of winter.

- **Medium to large (3½ to 5 quart) slow cooker**
- **Blender or food processor**

1 tbsp	extra virgin olive oil	15 mL
2	onions, finely chopped	2
4	stalks celery, diced	4
2	carrots, peeled and diced	2
4	cloves garlic, minced	4
1 tsp	caraway seeds	5 mL
½ tsp	sea salt	2 mL
½ tsp	cracked black peppercorns	2 mL
1	can (28 oz/796 mL) tomatoes with juice, coarsely chopped, divided (see page 13)	1
1 tbsp	coconut sugar	15 mL
3	medium beets, peeled and diced	3
1	potato, peeled and diced, optional (see page 13)	1
4 cups	beef stock or vegetable stock	1 L
1 tbsp	red wine vinegar (see Tips, left)	15 mL
4 cups	finely shredded cabbage	1 L
	Sour cream, optional (see page 14)	
	Finely chopped dill	

1. In a skillet, heat oil over medium heat. Add onions, celery and carrots and cook, stirring, until softened, about 7 minutes. Add garlic, caraway seeds, salt and peppercorns and cook, stirring, for 1 minute.

2. Transfer to a blender or food processor fitted with a metal blade (see Tips, left). Add half the tomatoes with juice and process until smooth. Transfer to slow cooker stoneware.

3. Add remaining tomatoes, coconut sugar, beets, and potato, if using, to stoneware. Add stock.

4. Cover and cook on Low for 6 hours or on High for 3 hours, until vegetables are tender. Add vinegar and cabbage, in batches, stirring until each is submerged. Cover and cook on High for 20 to 30 minutes, until cabbage is tender. To serve, ladle into bowls, add a dollop of sour cream, if using, and garnish with dill.

Cranberry Borscht

Serves 6 to 8

- ◆ **Entertaining Worthy**
- ◆ **Can Be Halved**
  (see Tips, below)

Tips

If you are halving this recipe, be sure to use a small (2 to 3½ quart) slow cooker.

Make your own sour cream (see page 14) or purchase it from a trusted provider to ensure the lactose has been eliminated in the process of fermentation and that it does not contain any additives.

Make Ahead

Cook overnight in the slow cooker, finish the next morning and chill during the day.

Served cold in chilled bowls, this fresh, fruity soup is one of my favorite preludes to an outdoor dinner on a warm night. Many years ago, I learned about adding cranberries to borscht from a recipe created by New York restaurateur George Lang. Their fruity tang provides just enough tartness to round out the soup. This soup is also good served hot.

- **Medium to large (3½ to 5 quart) slow cooker**
- **Blender or food processor**

6	beets (about 2½ lbs/1.25 kg), peeled and chopped	6
	Leaves from beets, washed, coarsely chopped and set aside in refrigerator	
4	cloves garlic, chopped	4
5 cups	beef or vegetable stock	1.25 L
½ tsp	sea salt	2 mL
	Freshly ground black pepper	
1 cup	cranberries	250 mL
2 tbsp	coconut sugar	30 mL
	Zest and juice of 1 orange	
	Sour cream (see Tips, left)	
	Chopped fresh dill fronds, optional	

1. In slow cooker stoneware, combine beets, garlic, stock, salt, and pepper to taste. Cover and cook on Low for 6 hours or on High for 3 hours, until beets are tender.

2. Add cranberries, coconut sugar, orange zest and juice and beet leaves. Cover and cook on High for 30 minutes or until cranberries are popping from their skins.

3. Purée using an immersion blender. (You can also do this in batches in a food processor or blender.) If serving cold, transfer to a large bowl and chill thoroughly, preferably overnight.

4. When ready to serve, spoon into individual bowls, top with sour cream and garnish with dill, if using.

Beet Soup with Lemongrass and Lime

Serves 6

◆ **Can Be Halved**
(see Tips, below)

Tips

If you are halving this recipe, be sure to use a small (approx. 2 quart) slow cooker.

Coconut cream is a thicker, richer version of coconut milk. You can purchase it in stores with a well-stocked Asian foods section. If you can't find it, spoon off the thick layer that rises to the top of a can of coconut milk.

Make Ahead

Ideally, make this soup the day before you intend to serve it so it can chill overnight in the refrigerator.

This Thai-inspired soup, which is served cold, is elegant and refreshing. Its jewel-like appearance and intriguing flavors make it a perfect prelude to any meal. I especially like to serve it at summer dinners in the garden.

- **Medium to large (3½ to 5 quart) slow cooker**
- **Blender or food processor**

2 tbsp	extra virgin coconut oil	30 mL
1	onion, chopped	1
4	cloves garlic, minced	4
2	stalks lemongrass, trimmed, smashed and cut in half crosswise	2
2 tbsp	minced gingerroot	30 mL
2 tsp	cracked black peppercorns	10 mL
½ tsp	sea salt	2 mL
6 cups	chicken or vegetable stock, divided	1.5 L
6	beets (about 2½ lbs/1.25 kg), peeled and chopped	6
1	red bell pepper, diced	1
1	long red chile pepper, seeded and diced, optional	1
	Grated zest and juice of 1 lime	
	Sea salt, optional	
	Coconut cream, optional (see Tips, left)	
	Finely chopped cilantro leaves	

1. In a skillet, heat oil over medium heat. Add onion and cook, stirring, until softened, about 3 minutes. Add garlic, lemongrass, ginger, peppercorns and salt and cook, stirring, for 1 minute. Add 2 cups (500 mL) of the stock and stir well. Transfer to slow cooker stoneware.

2. Add remaining 4 cups (1 L) of stock and beets. Cover and cook on Low for 6 hours or on High for 3 hours, until beets are tender. Add red pepper and chile pepper, if using. Cover and cook on High for 30 minutes, until peppers are tender. Discard lemongrass.

3. Purée using an immersion blender. (You can also do this in batches in a food processor or blender.) Transfer to a large bowl. Stir in lime zest and juice. Season to taste with salt, if using. Cover and refrigerate until thoroughly chilled, preferably overnight.

4. Ladle into bowls, drizzle with coconut cream, if using, and garnish with cilantro.

Wild Mushroom Soup

Serves 8

♦ **Can Be Halved**
(see Tips, below)

Tips

If you are halving this recipe, be sure to use a small (approx. 2 quart) slow cooker.

If you prefer, use half chicken, beef or vegetable and half mushroom stock.

Although brown rice miso is made from fermented beans and rice, it is gluten-free. Because it is fermented, it is good for the digestion. It also adds great flavor to this soup but if you are averse to using any product made from legumes or grains, feel free to omit it.

Make Ahead

Complete Steps 1 and 2. Cover and refrigerate for up to 2 days. When you're ready to cook, complete the recipe.

Not only is this hearty soup the perfect antidote to a bone-chilling day but mushrooms, particularly shiitake, are also great immune system boosters. A steaming mug will help you beat off lurking winter viruses, and I can't imagine anything more satisfying after coming in from the cold.

• **Medium to large (3½ to 5 quart) slow cooker**

1	package (½ oz/14 g) dried porcini mushrooms	1
1 cup	hot water	250 mL
1 tbsp	extra virgin olive oil	15 mL
2	leeks, white part with just a bit of green, cleaned and thinly sliced (see Tips, page 51)	2
2	carrots, peeled and diced	2
2	stalks celery, diced (see Tips, page 39)	2
2	cloves garlic, minced	2
½ tsp	sea salt	2 mL
½ tsp	cracked black peppercorns	2 mL
1	bay leaf	1
8 oz	fresh shiitake mushrooms, stems discarded and caps thinly sliced	250 g
8 oz	cremini mushrooms, trimmed and quartered	250 g
6 cups	chicken, beef, vegetable or mushroom stock (see Tips, left)	1.5 L
1 cup	water	250 mL
¼ cup	brown rice miso, optional (see Tips, left) Finely snipped chives	60 mL

1. In a bowl, combine porcini mushrooms and hot water. Let stand for 30 minutes. Drain through a fine sieve, reserving liquid. Pat mushrooms dry with paper towel and chop finely. Set aside.

2. In a skillet, heat oil over medium heat. Add leeks, carrots and celery and cook, stirring, until softened, about 7 minutes. Add garlic, salt, peppercorns, bay leaf and reserved reconstituted porcini mushrooms and cook, stirring, for 1 minute. Stir in reserved mushroom soaking liquid. Transfer to slow cooker stoneware.

3. Add shiitake and cremini mushrooms. Stir in stock and water. Cover and cook on Low for 6 hours or on High for 3 hours. Stir in miso. Cover and cook on High for 15 minutes to meld flavors. Discard bay leaf. Ladle soup into bowls and garnish with chives.

Fennel-Laced Celery Soup

◆ Entertaining Worthy
◆ Can Be Halved
  (see Tips, below)

Tips

If you are halving this recipe, be sure to use a small (approx. 2 quart) slow cooker.

The potato in this recipe has been used to add flavor and, more importantly, to replace cream, which is traditionally used as a thickener and emulsifier. If you are concerned about eating this starchy vegetable, the relatively high fiber content of both the celery and fennel and the presence of fat mitigate the glycemic response. However, if you cannot consume potatoes for other dietary reasons, omit it. The soup will be tasty anyway.

Make Ahead

Complete Step 1. Cover and refrigerate for up to 2 days. When you're ready to cook, complete the recipe.

The hint of fennel adds a delightfully different accent to this almost-classic cream of celery soup. The potato disappears after the ingredients are puréed, providing creaminess, which would otherwise be achieved with the addition of cream (see Tips, left). Serve this as a prelude to an elegant meal or as the centerpiece to a light soup and salad dinner.

- **Medium to large (3½ to 5 quart) slow cooker**
- **Blender or food processor**

2 tbsp	butter or extra virgin olive oil	30 mL
4 cups	diced celery (about 12 stalks) (see Tips, page 39)	1 L
2	onions, finely chopped	2
1	bulb fennel, trimmed, cored and chopped	1
4	cloves garlic, minced	4
1 tsp	dried thyme	5 mL
½ tsp	sea salt	2 mL
½ tsp	cracked black peppercorns	2 mL
6 cups	chicken or vegetable stock, divided	1.5 L
1	potato, peeled and shredded (see Tips, left)	1
	Finely chopped chives	

1. In a skillet, melt butter over medium heat. Add celery, onions and fennel and cook, stirring, until softened, about 5 minutes. Add garlic, thyme, salt and peppercorns and cook, stirring, for 1 minute. Add 2 cups (500 mL) of the stock. Transfer to slow cooker stoneware.

2. Add remaining 4 cups (1 L) of the stock and potato. Cover and cook on Low for 6 hours or on High for 3 hours, until vegetables are tender. Purée using an immersion blender. (If you don't have an immersion blender, do this in a food processor or blender, in batches, and return to slow cooker.) To serve, ladle into bowls and garnish with chives.

Santa Fe–Style Vegetable Soup

Serves 6 to 8

◆ **Can Be Halved**
(see Tips, below)

Tips

If you are halving this recipe, be sure to use a small (approx. 2 quart) slow cooker.

Sweet corn is a vegetable, not a grain, and is acceptable on a Paleo diet so long as it is organically grown. It is starchier field corn that is allowed to dry on the stalk that is actually a grain. Field corn is also problematic because most is grown from genetically modified seed.

To roast peppers: Preheat oven to 400°F (200°C). Place pepper(s) on a baking sheet and roast, turning two or three times, until skin on all sides is blackened, about 25 minutes. Transfer pepper(s) to a heatproof bowl. Cover with a plate and let stand until cool. Remove and, using a sharp knife, life skins off. Discard skins and slice according to recipe instructions.

Make Ahead

This soup can be partially prepared before it is cooked. Complete Step 1. Cover and refrigerate for up to 2 days. When you're ready to cook, continue with the recipe.

Here's a flavorful, rib-sticking soup with lots of pizzazz and universal appeal. New Mexico chiles add an enticing, slightly smoky flavor, but ancho or guajillo chiles also work well. The lime, roasted red pepper and cilantro finish provides a nice balance to the sweet potatoes. If you are a heat seeker, add the jalapeño pepper.

- **Medium to large (3½ to 5 quart) slow cooker**
- **Blender or food processor**

2 tbsp	extra virgin olive oil	30 mL
2	onions, finely chopped	2
4	cloves garlic, minced	4
1 tsp	dried oregano	5 mL
½ tsp	sea salt	2 mL
6 cups	chicken or vegetable stock	1.5 L
4 cups	cubed (about ½ inch/1 cm) peeled sweet potatoes or butternut squash	1 L
2	dried New Mexico, ancho or guajillo chile peppers	2
2 cups	boiling water	500 mL
1	jalapeño pepper, finely chopped, optional	1
2 cups	sweet corn kernels, thawed if frozen (see Tips, left)	500 mL
1 tsp	finely grated lime zest	5 mL
2 tbsp	freshly squeezed lime juice	30 mL
2	roasted red peppers, cut into thin strips	2
	Finely chopped cilantro leaves	

1. In a skillet, heat oil over medium heat. Add onions and cook, stirring, until softened, about 3 minutes. Add garlic, oregano and salt and cook, stirring, for 1 minute. Transfer to slow cooker stoneware. Add stock and stir to combine.

2. Add sweet potatoes and stir to combine. Cover and cook on Low for 6 hours or on High for 3 hours, until sweet potatoes are tender.

3. Thirty minutes before the soup has finished cooking, in a heatproof bowl, soak dried chile peppers in boiling water for 30 minutes, weighing down with a cup to ensure they remain submerged. Drain, discarding soaking liquid and stems and chop coarsely. Add to stoneware.

4. Purée using an immersion blender. (If you don't have an immersion blender, do this in a blender or food processor, in batches, and return to stoneware.) Add corn, lime zest and juice. Cover and cook on High for 30 minutes, until corn is tender. When ready to serve, ladle soup into warmed bowls and garnish with red pepper strips and cilantro.

"Vichyssoise" with Celery Root and Watercress

Serves 6 to 8

- ◆ **Entertaining Worthy**
- ◆ **Can Be Halved**
  (see Tips, below)

Tips

If you are halving this recipe, be sure to use a small (approx. 2 quart) slow cooker.

Since celery root oxidizes quickly on contact with air, be sure to use it as soon as you have peeled and chopped it, or toss it with 1 tbsp (15 mL) lemon juice to prevent discoloration.

The potato in this recipe has been used to add flavor and, more importantly, to replace cream, which is traditionally used as a thickener and emulsifier. If you are concerned about eating this starchy vegetable, the relatively high fiber content of the celery root and the presence of fat mitigate the glycemic response. However, if you cannot consume potatoes for other dietary reasons, omit it. The soup will be tasty anyway.

Make Ahead

Complete Step 1. Cover and refrigerate for up to 2 days. When you're ready to cook, complete the recipe.

This refreshing soup is delicious and easy to make, and can be a prelude to the most sophisticated meal. More nutritious than traditional vichyssoise, it has a pleasing nutty flavor that may be enhanced with a garnish of chopped toasted walnuts. In the summer, I aim to have leftovers in the refrigerator and treat myself to a small bowl for a yummy afternoon snack.

- **Medium to large (3½ to 5 quart) slow cooker**
- **Blender or food processor**

2 tbsp	butter or extra virgin olive oil	30 mL
3	leeks, white and light green parts only or white part with just a bit of green, cleaned and coarsely chopped (see Tips, page 51)	3
2	cloves garlic, minced	2
½ tsp	sea salt	2 mL
½ tsp	cracked black peppercorns	2 mL
6 cups	chicken or vegetable stock	1.5 L
1	large celery root (celeriac), peeled and sliced	1
1	potato, peeled and shredded, optional (see Tips, left)	1
2	bunches (each about 4 oz/125 g) watercress, tough parts of the stems removed	2
	Sea salt, optional	
	Toasted chopped walnuts	
	Watercress sprigs, optional	

1. In a skillet, melt butter over medium heat. Add leeks and cook, stirring, until softened, about 5 minutes. Add garlic, salt and peppercorns and cook, stirring, for 1 minute. Transfer to slow cooker stoneware. Stir in stock.

2. Add celery root and potato, if using, and stir well. Cover and cook on Low for 6 hours or on High for 3 hours, until celery root and potato are tender. Add watercress, in batches, stirring after each to submerge the leaves in the liquid.

3. Purée using an immersion blender. (You can also do this in batches in a food processor or blender.) Transfer to a large bowl. Season to taste with salt, if using. Cover and refrigerate until thoroughly chilled, about 4 hours.

4. Ladle into bowls and garnish with walnuts and/or watercress, if using.

Leafy Greens Soup

Serves 8

◆ **Can Be Halved**
(see Tips, below)

Tips

If you are halving this recipe, be sure to use a small (approx. 2 quart) slow cooker.

To clean leeks: Fill a sink full of lukewarm water. Split the leeks in half lengthwise and submerge them in the water, swishing them around to remove all traces of dirt. Transfer to a colander and rinse thoroughly under cold water.

The potato in this recipe has been used to add flavor and to thicken and emulsify the soup. If you have concerns about eating potatoes, omit the ingredient. You will have a thinner but still delicious soup.

Make Ahead

Complete Step 1. Cover and refrigerate for up to 2 days. When you're ready to cook, complete the recipe.

This delicious country-style soup is French in origin. Sorrel, which has an intriguing but bitter taste, adds delightful depth to the flavor. Sorrel is available from specialty greengrocers or at farmers' markets during the summer, but if you're unsuccessful in locating it, arugula or parsley also work well in this recipe.

- **Medium to large (3½ to 5 quart) slow cooker**
- **Blender or food processor**

2 tbsp	butter or extra virgin olive oil	30 mL
6	small leeks, white and light green parts only or white part with a bit of green, cleaned and thinly sliced (see Tips, left)	6
4	cloves garlic, minced	4
1 tsp	dried tarragon	5 mL
½ tsp	sea salt	2 mL
½ tsp	cracked black peppercorns	2 mL
6 cups	chicken or vegetable stock, divided	1.5 L
2	medium potatoes, peeled and cut into ½-inch (1 cm) cubes (see Tips, left)	2
4 cups	packed torn Swiss chard leaves (about 1 bunch)	1 L
1 cup	packed torn sorrel, arugula or parsley leaves	250 mL

1. In a large skillet, melt butter over medium heat. Add leeks and cook, stirring, until softened, about 5 minutes. Add garlic, tarragon, salt and peppercorns and cook, stirring, for 1 minute. Add 2 cups (500 mL) of the stock and bring to a boil. Transfer to slow cooker stoneware.

2. Stir in remaining 4 cups (1 L) of stock and potatoes. Cover and cook on Low for 8 hours or on High for 4 hours, until potatoes are tender. Add Swiss chard and sorrel, in batches, stirring after each to submerge the leaves in the liquid. Cover and cook on High for 20 minutes, until greens are tender.

3. Purée using an immersion blender. (You can also do this in batches in a food processor or blender.) Spoon into individual serving bowls and serve immediately.

Down-Home Chicken Gumbo

Serves 6

◆ **Can Be Halved**
(see Tips, page 56)

Tips

Always buy sausage from a butcher you trust. It should be made from pasture-fed meat, with no added gluten.

Check the label of your Cajun seasoning to make sure it doesn't contain gluten. The quantity and whether you add cayenne depend upon how hot your chorizo is. If you're in doubt, err on the side of caution. You can always pass hot pepper sauce at the table.

Tomato paste is, basically, a highly concentrated tomato purée. I buy mine at a natural foods store. It contains only organic tomatoes and salt. However, commercially prepared versions may contain a panoply of dreadful ingredients, from high fructose corn syrup to hidden gluten and even MSG. Check the label. If you can't buy a suitable product or have concerns about using any prepared foods, substitute sun-dried tomatoes.

Make Ahead

Complete Step 1. Cover and refrigerate for up to 2 days. When you're ready to cook, complete the recipe.

This is a much more delicious version of the chicken gumbo soup I enjoyed as a child, which, I'm sorry to say, came out of a can. Despite the difference in quality, it evokes an abundance of pleasant food memories — I could still enjoy it almost every day of the week.

• **Medium to large (3½ to 5 quart) slow cooker**

1 tbsp	extra virgin olive oil	15 mL
8 oz	fresh chorizo sausage, removed from casings (see Tips, left)	250 g
2	onions, finely chopped	2
4	stalks celery, diced (see Tips, page 39)	4
4	cloves garlic, minced	4
1 to 2 tsp	Cajun seasoning (see Tips, left)	5 to 10 mL
1 tsp	cracked black peppercorns	5 mL
½ tsp	sea salt	2 mL
1	bay leaf	1
2 tbsp	tomato paste (see page 13) or ¼ cup (60 mL) minced reconstituted sun-dried tomatoes	30 mL
1	can (14 oz/398 mL) diced tomatoes with juice	1
4 cups	chicken stock	1 L
1 lb	skinless boneless chicken thighs, cut into bite-size pieces	500 g
2 cups	sliced okra (¼ inch/0.5 cm) (see Tips, page 110)	500 mL
1	red bell pepper, seeded and diced	1
¼ tsp	cayenne pepper, optional (see Tips, left) Finely chopped green onions	1 mL

1. In a skillet, heat oil over medium heat. Add sausage, onions and celery and cook, stirring, until sausage is cooked through, about 7 minutes. Add garlic, Cajun seasoning to taste, peppercorns, salt and bay leaf and cook, stirring, for 1 minute. Stir in tomato paste. Add tomatoes with juice and bring to a boil.

2. Transfer to slow cooker stoneware. Stir in stock and chicken. Cover and cook on Low for 5 hours or on High for 2½ hours, until hot and bubbly. Stir in okra, bell pepper and cayenne. Cover and cook on High for 20 minutes, until okra is tender. Discard bay leaf. Garnish with green onions.

Variation

Andouille, a spicy smoked pork sausage used in Cajun cooking, is traditionally used in gumbo. If you can find uncooked butcher-made andouille, by all means use it here. However, most andouille is precooked and heavily smoked, which wouldn't work in this recipe.

Mulligatawny Soup

Serves 8

◆ **Can Be Halved**
(see Tips, page 56)

Tips

Most people (except those with a serious dairy allergy) should benefit from consuming properly made yogurt (see page 14). It introduces probiotic bacteria into the gut, which have been linked with a variety of health benefits.

If you don't have leftover chicken, you can cook the chicken in the soup. Add half a whole chicken breast or two chicken thighs (skin-on, bone-in) to the stoneware along with the potatoes. Once the soup has finished cooking and before puréeing, lift out the chicken and place on a cutting board. Remove the skin and bones and shred by pulling the meat apart with two forks. Complete the recipe.

Make Ahead

This soup can be partially prepared before it is cooked. Complete Step 1. Cover and refrigerate for up to 2 days. When you're ready to cook, continue with recipe.

Mulligatawny, which means "pepper water" in Tamil, is an Anglo-Indian soup imported to England by seafaring merchants. This is a hearty and tasty soup that is suitable for many occasions, either as a first course or the focal point of a light meal. It is also a great way to use up leftover chicken.

- **Medium to large (3½ to 5 quart) slow cooker**
- **Blender or food processor**

2 tbsp	clarified butter or ghee	30 mL
2	onions, finely chopped	2
2	carrots, peeled and thinly sliced	2
4	stalks celery, thinly sliced	4
4	cloves garlic, minced	4
1 tbsp	minced gingerroot	15 mL
2 tsp	cumin seeds, toasted and ground (see Tips, page 73)	10 mL
1 tsp	coriander seed, toasted and ground	5 mL
½ tsp	sea salt	2 mL
½ tsp	cracked black peppercorns	2 mL
5 cups	chicken stock	1.25 L
2	medium potatoes, peeled and diced	2
2 tsp	curry powder (see Tips, page 41)	10 mL
1 cup	plain full-fat yogurt (see Tips, left), plus additional for drizzling, divided	250 mL
2 cups	cooked shredded chicken	500 mL
2 cups	cooked cauliflower florets, optional Finely chopped cilantro leaves	500 mL

1. In a large skillet, heat butter over medium heat for 30 seconds. Add onions, carrots and celery and cook, stirring, until vegetables are softened, about 7 minutes. Add garlic, ginger, toasted cumin and coriander, salt and peppercorns and cook, stirring, for 1 minute. Transfer to slow cooker stoneware. Add stock and stir to combine.

2. Stir in potatoes. Cover and cook on Low for 6 hours or on High for 3 hours, until vegetables are tender. Purée using an immersion blender. (If you don't have an immersion blender, do this in a blender or food processor, in batches, and return to stoneware.)

3. In a small bowl, place curry powder. Gradually add ¼ cup (60 mL) of the yogurt, beating until smooth. Add to stoneware along with remaining yogurt, chicken and cauliflower, if using. Cover and cook on High for 30 minutes, until chicken is heated through and flavors meld. When ready to serve, ladle into bowls and garnish with cilantro. Drizzle with additional yogurt, if desired.

Mexican-Style Chicken Soup

◆ Entertaining Worthy

Tips

If you prefer, substitute
2 tbsp (30 mL) chicken
demi-glace (page 59) for
the chicken stock and add
2 cups (500 mL) more water.

Make your own sour cream
or purchase it from a
trusted provider (not a mass
market brand) to ensure
that virtually all the lactose
has been eliminated in the
process of fermentation and
that it provides beneficial
bacterial cultures and does
not contain any additives.

To toast cumin seeds:
Place seeds in a dry skillet
over medium heat and
cook, stirring, until fragrant.
Transfer to a mortar or spice
grinder and grind.

Jalapeño or habanero
peppers are both used
widely in Mexican cuisine.
If you like a bit of heat,
either works well as a
finishing touch to this recipe,
although they have different
flavors and the "super hot"
habanero packs much
more heat.

*Here's a surprisingly simple, yet absolutely delicious soup that is light
and refreshing. Topped with avocado and a cumin-flavored crema, it is
distinctive enough to impress discriminating guests.*

- **Medium to large (3½ to 5 quart) slow cooker**
- **Sieve, lined with a double layer of cheesecloth**

Stock

2	onions, chopped	2
4	stalks celery, chopped (see Tips, page 39)	4
2	carrots, peeled and chopped	2
2	sprigs cilantro	2
10	whole peppercorns	10
2	half chicken breasts, each cut in half	2
3 cups	water	750 mL
2 cups	chicken stock (see Tips, left)	500 mL
	Sea salt	

Crema

½ cup	sour cream (see Tips, left and page 14)	125 mL
1 tbsp	toasted ground cumin (see Tips, left)	15 mL
2	small avocados, pitted and sliced	2
	Freshly squeezed lime juice	
	Finely chopped cilantro leaves	
	Minced seeded habanero or jalapeño chile pepper, optional	

1. *Stock:* In slow cooker stoneware, combine onions, celery, carrots, cilantro, peppercorns, chicken, water and chicken stock. Cover and cook on Low for 6 hours or on High for 3 hours, until chicken is falling off the bone. Lift out chicken and remove and discard skin and bones. Shred by pulling the meat apart with two forks. Set aside and keep warm.

2. Strain stock through prepared sieve. Discard solids. Season stock with salt to taste. Set aside and keep warm.

3. *Crema:* In a bowl, whisk sour cream and cumin until combined.

4. Ladle stock into warm bowls. Lay shredded chicken and avocado strips on top. Sprinkle with lime juice to taste. Top with a dollop of crema and garnish with cilantro and chile, if using. Serve immediately.

Southwestern Roasted Red Pepper Soup with Crab

◆ **Entertaining Worthy**
◆ **Can Be Halved**
(see Tips, below)

Tips

If you are halving this recipe, be sure to use a small (2 to 3½ quart) slow cooker.

For the best flavor, toast and grind cumin seeds yourself. *To toast seeds:* Place seeds in a dry skillet over medium heat and cook, stirring, until fragrant, about 3 minutes. Immediately transfer to a spice grinder or mortar and grind.

In the Paleo world, sweet corn is seriously misunderstood. It is a vegetable, not a grain, and is acceptable on a Paleo diet so long as it is organically grown. It is starchier field corn that is allowed to dry on the stalk that is actually a grain. Field corn is also problematic because most is grown from genetically modified seed.

Although the roots of this soup lie deep in the heart of Tex-Mex cuisine, it is elegant enough for even the most gracious occasion. You will also enjoy serving it as a deliciously different meal-in-a-bowl.

- Medium to large (3½ to 5 quart) slow cooker
- Blender

2 tbsp	extra virgin olive oil	30 mL
1	large onion, diced	1
6	cloves garlic, minced	6
1 tbsp	ground cumin (see Tips, left)	15 mL
1 tbsp	chopped rosemary, dried or fresh	15 mL
1	bay leaf	1
½ tsp	sea salt	2 mL
½ tsp	cracked black peppercorns	2 mL
6 cups	chicken stock, divided	1.5 L
1	dried New Mexico, ancho or guajillo chile pepper	1
1 cup	boiling water	250 mL
1	jalapeño pepper, seeded and coarsely chopped, optional	1
4 cups	sweet corn kernels, thawed if frozen (see Tips, left)	1 L
2	red bell peppers, roasted and cut into ½-inch (1 cm) cubes (see Tips, page 48)	2
1 cup	cooked crabmeat	250 mL
	Finely chopped parsley or cilantro leaves	

1. In a skillet, heat oil over medium heat. Add onion and cook, stirring, until softened, about 3 minutes. Add garlic, cumin, rosemary, bay leaf, salt and peppercorns and cook, stirring, for 1 minute. Add 1 cup (250 mL) of the stock and bring to a boil.

2. Transfer to slow cooker stoneware. Add remaining stock. Cover and cook on Low for 6 hours or on High for 3 hours.

3. About an hour before the soup has finished cooking, in a heatproof bowl, soak dried chile pepper in boiling water for 30 minutes, weighing down with a cup to ensure it remains submerged. Drain, discarding soaking liquid and stem, and chop coarsely. Transfer to a blender. Add 1 cup (250 mL) of stock from the soup and jalapeño pepper, if using, and purée.

4. Add chile mixture to stoneware and stir well. Add corn, roasted pepper and crab. Cover and cook on High for 30 minutes, until corn is tender. Discard bay leaf. Spoon into individual bowls and garnish with parsley.

Homemade Mushroom Stock

Makes about 12 cups (3 L)

Tips

If you have mushroom stems left over from another recipe, add them to the stoneware. However, make sure they are in good condition. When making stock of any kind you should never use vegetables that are passed their peak.

You can substitute the green part of leeks or scallions for all or part of the onions in this recipe. Use about 2 cups (500 mL) coarsely chopped and packed for each onion.

There are many advantages to making your own mushroom stock. You know exactly what is in it, you can control the quantity of salt and it is more economical than buying a prepared version. This makes a mildly flavored version, which I prefer. If a stronger mushroom flavor appeals to you, double the quantity of dried portobello mushrooms.

- **Large (minimum 5 quart) slow cooker**
- **Sieve, lined with a double layer of cheesecloth**

1	package ($\frac{1}{2}$ oz/14 g) dried portobello mushrooms, crumbled	1
1 cup	hot water	250 mL
1 tbsp	extra virgin olive oil or butter	15 mL
2	onions, coarsely chopped	2
4	stalks celery, coarsely chopped	4
4	cloves garlic, coarsely chopped	4
1 tsp	dried thyme	5 mL
1 tsp	cracked black peppercorns	5 mL
$\frac{1}{2}$ tsp	sea salt	2 mL
8	sprigs parsley	8
12 cups	water	3 L

1. In a bowl, combine dried mushrooms and hot water. Stir well and let stand for 30 minutes. Drain liquid into stoneware. Set solids aside.

2. Meanwhile, in a skillet, heat oil over medium heat. Add onions and celery and cook, stirring, until softened, about 5 minutes. Add garlic, thyme, peppercorns, salt, parsley and reserved reconstituted mushrooms and cook, stirring, for 1 minute. Transfer to slow cooker stoneware. Add water. Cover and cook on High for 6 hours. Strain through prepared sieve and discard solids. Refrigerate for up to 5 days or freeze in portions in airtight containers.

Vegetable Stock

**Makes about
8 cups (2 L)**

Tip

There are few firm rules about what vegetables to include in stock. Making stock is a good way to use up the parts of vegetables that are usually discarded, such as the green part of scallions or leeks, which can be substituted for onions (see Tips, page 57), or mushroom stems, which add depth and flavor. However, the vegetables must be in good condition. Do not use any that have passed their peak. Moreover, vegetables from the cruciferous family, which includes broccoli, cabbage and turnip, should not be used as their pungency will overpower the other ingredients.

This recipe produces a mildly flavored stock that will not overpower the taste of most vegetable recipes. If you prefer a stronger-tasting stock, after straining off the liquid, transfer to a stockpot and simmer, uncovered, for 30 minutes until it is reduced by about one-third or use Roasted or Enhanced Vegetable Stock (see Variations, below).

- **Medium to large (3½ to 5 quart) slow cooker**
- **Sieve, lined with a double layer of cheesecloth**

8 cups	water	2 L
4	stalks celery, coarsely chopped	4
4	carrots, scrubbed and coarsely chopped	4
2	onions, coarsely chopped	2
2	cloves garlic	2
4	sprigs parsley	4
2	bay leaves	2
½ tsp	sea salt	2 mL
8	black peppercorns	8

1. In slow cooker stoneware, combine water, celery, carrots, onions, garlic, parsley, bay leaves, salt and peppercorns. Cover and cook on Low for 8 hours or on High for 4 hours. Strain through prepared sieve and discard solids. Cover and refrigerate for up to 5 days or freeze in an airtight container.

Variations

Enhanced Vegetable Stock: To enhance 8 cups (2 L) Vegetable Stock, combine in a large saucepan over medium heat with 2 carrots, peeled and coarsely chopped, 3 tbsp (45 mL) minced reconstituted dried tomatoes (or 1 tbsp/15 mL tomato paste), 1 tsp (5 mL) celery seed, 1 tsp (5 mL) cracked black peppercorns, ½ tsp (2 mL) dried thyme, 4 parsley sprigs, 1 bay leaf and 1 cup (250 mL) white wine. Bring to a boil. Reduce heat to low and simmer, covered, for 30 minutes, then strain and discard solids.

Roasted Vegetable Stock: Preheat oven to 425°F (220°C). In a bowl, toss celery, carrots, onions and garlic in 1 tbsp (15 mL) extra virgin olive oil or melted butter. Spread on a baking sheet and roast, turning 3 or 4 times, for 20 minutes, until nicely browned. Transfer to slow cooker stoneware, add remaining ingredients and proceed with recipe.

Homemade Chicken Stock

Makes about 12 cups (3 L)

Tips

The more economical parts of the chicken, such as necks, backs, and wings, make the best stock.

You can easily reduce your consumption of sodium by making your own stock and not adding salt. One cup (250 mL) of this stock, with no salt added, contains 21 mg of sodium. The same quantity of a typical prepared stock likely contains more than 500 mg of sodium.

There's nothing quite like the flavor of homemade chicken stock. It is also very good for you — chicken soup, also known as "Jewish penicillin" is a tried and true remedy for many ailments. It's very easy to make — you can cook it overnight, strain it in the morning and refrigerate or freeze.

- **Large (approx. 5 quart) slow cooker**
- **Sieve, lined with a double layer of cheesecloth**

4 lbs	bone-in skin-on chicken parts (see Tips, left)	2 kg
3	onions, coarsely chopped (see Tips, page 57)	3
4	carrots, scrubbed and coarsely chopped	4
4	stalks celery, coarsely chopped	4
6	sprigs parsley	6
½	head garlic	½
3	bay leaves	3
10	black peppercorns	10
1 tsp	dried thyme	5 mL
	Sea salt, optional	
1 tbsp	white wine vinegar	15 mL
12 cups	water	3 L

1. In slow cooker stoneware, combine chicken, onions, carrots, celery, parsley, garlic, bay leaves, peppercorns, thyme, salt, if using, vinegar and water. Cover and cook on High for 8 hours. Strain through prepared sieve and discard solids. Refrigerate for up to 5 days or freeze in portions in airtight containers.

Chicken or Beef Demi-Glace

Demi-glace is intensely flavored stock that has been reduced to state of concentration. It is useful for adding a burst of flavor to dishes. I always like to have some in my freezer. After making stock, I often transfer about 2 cups (500 mL) of the finished product to a saucepan to make a portion of demi-glace. Bring the stock to a boil, reduce the heat and simmer until syrupy, about 1½ hours. Let cool then transfer to a shallow dish and refrigerate. After it has solidified, lift it out in 1 piece, place on a cutting board, then cut it into squares (each containing a volume of about 1 tbsp/15 mL). (You should get about 8 pieces.) Wrap individually in plastic and freeze. When frozen, place in resealable bags and label.

Hearty Beef Stock

Tips

The acid in the vinegar helps to draw nutrients, including important minerals such as magnesium and potassium, from the bones.

You can substitute the green part of leeks or scallions for all or part of the onions in this recipe. Use about 2 cups (500 mL) coarsely chopped and packed for each onion.

When you read about nurturing "bone broth," a hearty gelatin-rich beef stock is usually what the writer had in mind. Among other benefits, by binding with water, the gelatin in a homemade beef stock supports digestion. Traditionally, bone broth has also been used as an elixir — good for whatever ails you.

- **Large (approx. 6 quart) slow cooker**
- **Preheat oven to 375°F (190°C)**
- **Sieve, lined with a double layer of cheesecloth**

3	onions, quartered (see Tips, left)	3
3	carrots, cut into chunks	3
3	stalks celery	3
2 tbsp	extra virgin olive oil or melted butter	30 mL
3 lbs	beef bones	1.5 kg
4	sprigs parsley	4
3	sprigs fresh thyme	3
10	black peppercorns	10
1 tbsp	red wine vinegar	15 mL
12 cups	water	3 L

1. Place onions, carrots and celery in a roasting pan and toss well with oil. Add bones and toss again. Arrange in a single layer (as much as possible) in pan and roast in preheated oven until ingredients are browning nicely, about 1 hour. Transfer to slow cooker stoneware, along with accumulated juices.

2. Add parsley, thyme, peppercorns, vinegar and water. Cover and cook on Low for 12 hours or on High for 6 hours, until stock is a rich brown color and flavorful. Strain through prepared sieve and discard solids. Let cool slightly. Refrigerate for up to 5 days or freeze in portions in airtight containers.

Fish Stock

Tips

The fish bones used to make stock are a source of the mineral iodine.

Be sure not to use oily fish such as salmon, mackerel or tuna or your stock may be unpleasantly pungent.

The acid in the wine helps to draw nutrients from the bones, which intensifies the flavor of the stock, but feel free to omit it. Or substitute 1 tbsp (15 mL) white wine vinegar.

I do not recommend making fish stock on High because for best results the liquid should never boil.

Homemade fish stock is a great base for luscious fish soups and stews.

- **Large (approx. 5 quart) slow cooker**
- **Sieve, lined with a double layer of cheesecloth**

3 lbs	fish trimmings, including heads (see Tips, left)	1.5 kg
2	onions or well-washed green parts of 3 large leeks, coarsely chopped	2
1	carrot, coarsely chopped	1
1	stalk celery, coarsely chopped	1
4	sprigs parsley	4
2	sprigs fresh thyme	2
2	bay leaves	2
2 tsp	fennel seeds	10 mL
1 cup	dry white wine, optional (see Tips, left)	250 mL
12 cups	filtered water	3 L

1. In slow cooker stoneware, combine fish trimmings, onions, carrot, celery, parsley, thyme, bay leaves, fennel seeds, wine, if using, and water. Cover and cook on Low for 8 hours (see Tips, left). Strain through prepared sieve and discard solids. Refrigerate for up to 5 days or freeze in portions in airtight containers.

Chicken Provençal

Poultry

Chicken Provençal

◆ **Entertaining Worthy**
◆ **Can Be Halved**
(see Tips, below)

Tips

If you are halving this recipe, be sure to use a small (2 to 3 quart) slow cooker.

Chicken, duck and goose fats are all good choices when cooking poultry. About one-third of their fat is saturated; the remainder is varying degrees of unsaturated fat, including essential omega-3 fatty acids, the ratio of which can be increased depending upon how the poultry was fed. Free range birds that eat insects or have flax meal added to their diet will have a higher proportion of these very desirable fats.

If you prefer, substitute 1 cup (250 mL) chicken stock plus 1 tbsp (15 mL) lemon juice for the white wine.

Make Ahead

Complete Steps 2 and 3, adding bacon to tomato mixture before refrigerating. Cover and refrigerate mixture for up to 2 days (see Making Ahead, page 21). When you're ready to cook, complete the recipe.

The secret ingredient in this easy-to-make dish is herbes de Provence, a pungent blend of dried herbs — such as thyme, savory, sage, lavender and fennel — that provides great flavor with virtually no effort on your part. The black olives (see Variation, below) add a particularly pleasant bite, so long as you are not olive-averse.

• **Medium to large (3½ to 5 quart) slow cooker**

3 lbs	skinless bone-in chicken thighs (12 thighs)	1.5 kg
1 tbsp	extra virgin olive oil or chicken fat (see Tips, left)	15 mL
4 oz	chunk bacon, diced	125 g
2	onions, finely chopped	2
4	cloves garlic, minced	4
1½ tsp	herbes de Provence	7 mL
½ tsp	sea salt	2 mL
½ tsp	cracked black peppercorns	2 mL
1 cup	dry white wine (see Tips, left)	250 mL
1	can (14 oz/398 mL) tomatoes with juice, coarsely chopped (see page 13)	1

1. Arrange chicken evenly over bottom of slow cooker stoneware, overlapping as necessary.
2. In a skillet, heat oil over medium-high heat. Add bacon and cook, stirring, until nicely browned. Using a slotted spoon, remove bacon and drain on paper towels. Drain off all but 2 tbsp (30 mL) of the fat from the pan.
3. Add onions to pan and cook, stirring, until softened, about 3 minutes. Add garlic, herbes de Provence, salt and peppercorns and cook, stirring, for 1 minute. Add wine, bring to a boil and boil for 2 minutes. Add tomatoes with juice and bring to a boil. Add reserved bacon.
4. Transfer to slow cooker stoneware. Cover and cook on Low for 6 hours or High for 3 hours, until juices run clear when chicken is pierced with a fork.

Variation
Sprinkle ½ cup (125 mL) chopped pitted black olives evenly over the top of the chicken after it has finished cooking. Cover and cook on High about 5 minutes, until heated through.

French-Country Chicken

◆ **Entertaining Worthy**
◆ **Can Be Halved**
(see Tips, below)

Tips

If you are halving this recipe, be sure to use a small (2 to 3 quart) slow cooker.

If you prefer, substitute ½ cup (125 mL) chicken stock plus 2 tsp (10 mL) lemon juice for the white wine.

Make Ahead

Complete Steps 1 and 2, refrigerating bacon separately. Cover and refrigerate mixture for up to 2 days. When you're ready to cook, complete the recipe.

I love the bold flavors of this hearty country-style dish. There's nothing more satisfying on a chilly day. Accompany with a green salad and a robust red wine.

• **Medium to large (3½ to 5 quart) slow cooker**

2 oz	chunk bacon or pork belly, cut in ¼-inch (0.5 cm) cubes	60 g
2	onions, finely chopped	2
4	cloves garlic, minced	4
2 tsp	dried Italian seasoning	10 mL
1 tsp	cracked black peppercorns	5 mL
½ tsp	sea salt	2 mL
1	bay leaf	1
½ cup	dry white wine (see Tips, left)	125 mL
1	can (14 oz/398 mL) tomatoes with juice, coarsely chopped (see page 13)	1
3 lbs	skinless bone-in chicken thighs (about 12 thighs)	1.5 kg
½ cup	sliced pitted black olives	125 mL
½ cup	sliced pitted green olives	125 mL
	Finely chopped Italian flat-leaf parsley leaves	

1. In a skillet over medium-high heat, cook bacon until crisp. Drain on paper towels. Cover and refrigerate until ready to use. Drain all but 2 tbsp (30 mL) fat from the pan.

2. Reduce heat to medium. Add onions and cook, stirring, until softened, about 3 minutes. Add garlic, Italian seasoning, peppercorns, salt and bay leaf and cook, stirring, for 1 minute. Add wine, bring to a boil and boil for 2 minutes. Add tomatoes with juice and bring to a boil.

3. Arrange chicken evenly over bottom of slow cooker and cover with sauce. Cover and cook on Low for 6 hours or on High for 3 hours, until juices run clear when chicken is pierced with a fork. Add black and green olives and reserved bacon. Cover and cook on High for 15 minutes, until heated through. Discard bay leaf. Serve piping hot, garnished with parsley.

Tuscan Chicken with Sage

Serves 6

◆ **Can Be Halved**
(see Tips, below)

Tips

If you are halving this recipe, be sure to use a small (2 to 3 quart) slow cooker.

Chicken, duck and goose fats are all good choices when cooking poultry. About one-third of their fat is saturated; the remainder is varying degrees of unsaturated fat, including essential omega-3 fatty acids, the ratio of which can be increased depending upon how the poultry was fed. Free range birds that eat insects or have flax meal added to their diet will have a higher proportion of these very desirable fats.

For optimum results, make an effort to find fresh sage, which is usually available in the produce section of well-stocked supermarkets. If you can't locate it, dried sage is an acceptable substitute in this recipe.

Make Ahead

Complete Step 1. Cover and refrigerate mixture for up to 2 days. When you're ready to cook, complete the recipe.

This simple, yet delicious chicken gets its distinctive slightly peppery flavor from the addition of fresh sage, which has a pleasantly pungent flavor. In many ways, it's an Italian variation of coq au vin. *Serve with a robust green vegetable, such as broccoli or sautéed rapini.*

• **Medium to large (3½ to 5 quart) slow cooker**

2 tbsp	extra virgin olive oil or chicken fat (see Tips, left)	30 mL
2	onions, finely chopped	2
2	cloves garlic, minced	2
½ tsp	sea salt	2 mL
½ tsp	cracked black peppercorns	2 mL
½ cup	fresh sage leaves or 1 tsp (5 mL) dried sage (see Tips, left)	125 mL
2 cups	dry robust red wine, such as Chianti	500 mL
3 lbs	skinless bone-in chicken thighs (about 12 thighs)	1.5 kg

1. In a skillet, heat oil over medium heat. Add onions and cook, stirring, until softened, about 3 minutes. Add garlic, salt, peppercorns and sage and cook, stirring, for 1 minute. Add wine, bring to boil and cook, stirring, until sauce is reduced by one-third, about 5 minutes.

2. Arrange chicken evenly over bottom of slow cooker and cover with sauce. Cover and cook on Low for 6 hours or on High for 3 hours, until juices run clear when chicken is pierced with a fork. Serve immediately.

Poultry Fat

Schmaltz, which is rendered chicken fat, has traditionally been used in Jewish cooking, but the fat from ducks and geese is widely used as well, particularly in France. All are excellent fats to use in the kitchen because they are flavorful, very stable and the majority of their healthful fatty acids are unsaturated. Some butchers sell rendered poultry fat but you can easily make your own. Simply place cut-up poultry skin in a heavy saucepan with a small amount of water (about ⅓ cup/75 mL water per pound/500 g, according to chef and cookbook author Jennifer McLagan). Cook on very low heat until the fat melts, the water evaporates and the skin crisps, about 2 hours. Strain through a double layer of cheesecloth. Transfer to a clean container and store in the refrigerator for up to 2 months.

Saffron-Braised Chicken

◆ Entertaining Worthy
◆ Can Be Halved
  (see Tip, below)

Tip

If you are halving this recipe, be sure to use a small (2 to 3 quart) slow cooker.

Make Ahead

Complete Steps 1 and 2. Cover and refrigerate chicken and vegetable mixtures separately. When you're ready to cook, complete the recipe.

Superb flavor together with ease of preparation is a marriage made in heaven, which this dish provides. Don't balk at the generous hit of saffron — it really distinguishes the sauce. Add some steamed green beans for a delicious Mediterranean-themed dinner.

• **Large (approx. 5 quart) slow cooker**

Rub

2 tsp	finely grated garlic or garlic put through a press	10 mL
1 tsp	finely grated lemon zest	5 mL
1 tbsp	freshly squeezed lemon juice	15 mL
1 tsp	coarse sea salt	5 mL
½ tsp	saffron threads, crumbled	2 mL
1 tbsp	extra virgin olive oil	15 mL
3 lbs	skinless bone-in chicken thighs (about 12 thighs)	1.5 kg
1 tbsp	extra virgin olive oil or chicken fat, divided (see Tips, page 66)	15 mL
3	onions, thinly sliced on the vertical	3
1 tsp	dried oregano	5 mL
½ tsp	cracked black peppercorns	2 mL
4	bay leaves	4
1	piece (2 inches/5 cm) cinnamon stick	1
2 tbsp	brandy or cognac, optional	30 mL
2 cups	chicken stock	500 mL

1. *Rub:* In a bowl, combine garlic, lemon zest and juice, sea salt and saffron. Stir in olive oil. Spread evenly over chicken and rub mixture in. Cover and refrigerate for 2 hours or overnight. When you're ready to cook, arrange chicken evenly over bottom of slow cooker stoneware and drizzle with any residual juices.

2. In a skillet, heat olive oil over medium heat. Add onions and cook, stirring, until softened, about 3 minutes. Add oregano, peppercorns, bay leaves and cinnamon stick and cook, stirring, for 1 minute. Add brandy, if using, and cook until it evaporates, about 2 minutes. Stir in stock.

3. Transfer to slow cooker stoneware. Cover and cook on Low for 6 hours or on High for 3 hours, until juices run clear when chicken is pierced with a fork. Remove and discard bay leaves and cinnamon stick.

African-Style Chicken in Onion Gravy

◆ **Can Be Halved**
(see Tips, below)

Tips

If you are halving this recipe, be sure to use a small (2 to 3 quart) slow cooker.

Most fresh chile peppers will work in this recipe, and the quantity you use depends upon their heat quotient and your taste. In this dish, I prefer the flavor of habanero, Scotch bonnet or long red or green chiles. Although jalapeño peppers will provide heat, they have a Tex-Mex flavor that I don't think is appropriate for this dish.

If you are desperately seeking a break from the same old thing, try this take on yassa, *a traditional celebratory dish originating in Senegal. It's very simple — chicken braised in a blanket of onions and seasoned stock — but the results are seductive.*

• **Medium to large (3½ to 5 quart) slow cooker**

2 tsp	finely grated lime zest	10 mL
½ cup	freshly squeezed lime juice	125 mL
6	cloves garlic, minced	6
2 tbsp	gluten-free soy sauce or coconut aminos (see page 15)	30 mL
2 tsp	ground allspice	10 mL
1 tsp	cracked black peppercorns	5 mL
½ tsp	sea salt	2 mL
3 lbs	skinless bone-in chicken thighs (about 12 thighs)	1.5 kg
2 tbsp	extra virgin olive or coconut oil	30 mL
2	large Spanish or white onions, very thinly sliced on the vertical	2
2	carrots, peeled and diced	2
2 tbsp	minced gingerroot	30 mL
1 cup	chicken stock	250 mL
1 to 2	fresh chile peppers, seeded and minced (see Tips, left)	1 to 2

1. In a large bowl, combine lime zest and juice, garlic, soy sauce, allspice, peppercorns and salt. Pat chicken dry, add to mixture and toss until well coated. Cover and refrigerate for at least 4 hours or overnight.

2. Lift chicken from marinade and transfer to slow cooker stoneware. Set marinade aside.

3. In a skillet, heat oil over medium heat. Add onions and carrots and cook, stirring, until onions just begin to turn golden, about 10 minutes. Add ginger and cook, stirring, for 1 minute. Add reserved marinade and stock and bring to a boil.

4 Transfer to slow cooker stoneware. Cover and cook on Low for 6 hours or on High for 3 hours, until chicken is falling off the bone. Stir in chile peppers to taste and serve.

Spicy Chicken in Coconut Sauce

◆ **Entertaining Worthy**
◆ **Can Be Halved**
(see Tips, below)

Tips

If you are halving this recipe, be sure to use a small (2 to 3 quart) slow cooker.

Look for canned tomatoes that are organically grown, with no salt added, and come in glass jars or BPA (bisphenol-A) free cans. When using canned tomatoes (or any canned product) check to make sure they are gluten-free.

Check your curry powder to make sure it doesn't contain gluten. Some blends may contain wheat or are processed in a plant where wheat is present, thus being potentially contaminated.

If you don't have a fresh chile pepper, add $\frac{1}{4}$ tsp (1 mL) cayenne pepper along with the curry powder.

The flavor combinations in this dish stray ever so slightly from the beaten track. I love the combination of tomatoes and coconut milk and the hint of Indian curry powder rather than Thai curry paste, which would be a more traditional pairing with the coconut milk.

• **Medium to large ($3\frac{1}{2}$ to 5 quart) slow cooker**

3 lbs	skinless bone-in chicken thighs (12 thighs)	1.5 kg
	Zest and juice of 1 lemon	
1 tbsp	extra virgin olive oil	15 mL
2	onions, finely chopped	2
4	cloves garlic, minced	4
1 tbsp	minced gingerroot	15 mL
1 tsp	cracked black peppercorns	5 mL
$\frac{1}{2}$ tsp	sea salt	2 mL
1	piece (2 inches/5 cm) cinnamon stick	1
1	can (28 oz/796 mL) diced tomatoes with juice (see Tips, left)	1
1 cup	coconut milk, divided	250 mL
1 tsp	mild curry powder (see Tips, left)	5 mL
1	long red chile pepper, seeded and minced (see Tips, left)	1
$\frac{1}{4}$ cup	chopped cilantro leaves	60 mL

1. In a bowl, combine chicken and lemon zest and juice. Cover and set aside for 15 minutes. Drain, reserving liquid, and transfer chicken to slow cooker stoneware.

2. Meanwhile, in a skillet, heat oil over medium heat. Add onions and cook, stirring, until softened, about 3 minutes. Add garlic and ginger and cook, stirring, for 1 minute. Add peppercorns, salt and cinnamon stick and cook, stirring, for 1 minute. Add reserved marinade and bring to a boil. Stir in tomatoes with juice.

3. Transfer to slow cooker stoneware. Cover and cook on Low for 5 hours or on High for $2\frac{1}{2}$ hours, until juices run clear when chicken is pierced with a fork.

4. In a bowl, combine $\frac{1}{4}$ cup (60 mL) of the coconut milk and curry powder and mix until well blended. Add to slow cooker stoneware along with remaining coconut milk and chile pepper. Cover and cook on High for 15 minutes, until flavors meld and dish is heated through. Discard cinnamon stick. Garnish with cilantro and serve.

Island-Style Chicken Curry

◆ **Entertaining Worthy**
◆ **Can Be Halved**
  (see Tips, below)

Tips

If you are halving this recipe, be sure to use a small (1½ to 3 quart) slow cooker.

If you are using the outer stalks of celery, peel them before chopping; the top layer is very fibrous. The inner stalks (hearts) can be used without peeling.

Scotch bonnet and habanero peppers, which figure prominently in Caribbean cuisine, are among the world's hottest chiles, so be cautious when using them. A whole one would make this dish very spicy. I like their unique flavors, but other chiles, such as jalapeños or long red or green chiles, would also work well in this dish.

In this curry I've tried to capture some of my favorite Caribbean flavors. The allspice and Scotch bonnet pepper provide a definitely Jamaican spin, echoing jerk seasoning, which I love. Serve this in soup plates and finish the meal with a tossed salad.

● **Medium to large (3½ to 5 quart) slow cooker**

4	cloves garlic, grated or put through a press	4
4	green onions, white part only, minced	4
1 tbsp	minced gingerroot	15 mL
1 tsp	dried thyme	5 mL
1 tsp	ground allspice	5 mL
½ tsp	ground cloves	2 mL
	Finely grated zest and juice of 1 lime	
2 tbsp	gluten-free soy sauce or coconut aminos (see page 15)	30 mL
2 lbs	skinless bone-in chicken thighs (about 8 thighs)	1 kg
1 tbsp	extra virgin olive or coconut oil	15 mL
2	onions, thinly sliced on the vertical	2
2	stalks celery, diced (see Tips, left)	2
1 tsp	cracked black peppercorns	5 mL
1 tsp	ground turmeric	5 mL
½ tsp	sea salt	2 mL
2 cups	chicken stock	500 mL
½ to 1	Scotch bonnet or habanero pepper, seeded and diced (see Tips, left)	½ to 1
1 cup	coconut milk	250 mL
	Finely chopped cilantro leaves	

1. In a small bowl, combine garlic, green onions, ginger, thyme, allspice, cloves, lime zest and juice and soy sauce. Using a fork, poke holes in the chicken and rub marinade all over to thoroughly coat. Cover and refrigerate for at least 6 hours or overnight.

2. Arrange chicken evenly over bottom of slow cooker stoneware, reserving excess marinade.

3. In a skillet, heat oil over medium heat. Add onions and celery and cook, stirring, until softened, about 5 minutes. Add peppercorns, turmeric and salt and cook, stirring, for 1 minute. Add reserved marinade and boil for 1 minute. Add stock and bring to a boil.

4. Transfer to slow cooker stoneware. Cover and cook on Low for 5 hours or on High for 2½ hours, until juices run clear when chicken is pierced with a fork. Stir in chile pepper to taste and coconut milk. Cover and cook on High for 20 minutes, until flavors meld. Garnish with cilantro and serve.

Simple Chicken Curry

Serves 4

◆ **Entertaining Worthy**

◆ **Can Be Halved**
(see Tips, left)

Tips

If you are halving this recipe, be sure to use a small (1½ to 3 quart) slow cooker.

Garam masala is a spice blend used in Indian cooking that is available in Asian markets or, increasingly, well-stocked supermarkets. Be sure to check with the manufacturer to make sure that no products containing gluten have been added. It is usually used in the final stages of a dish, but in this recipe I have used it to add hints of coriander, cloves, cinnamon and cardamom to the aromatics.

This quantity of cayenne produces a nicely spicy result. If you're a heat seeker, increase the amount, but be cautious, as cayenne is very hot.

Make Ahead

Complete Step 1. Cover and refrigerate mixture for up to 2 days. When you're ready to cook, complete the recipe.

If you have a well-stocked spice cupboard, this luscious curry can be put together with ingredients you're likely to have on hand. Serve with a green vegetable and Cauliflower Mash (page 242) to soak up the sauce.

• **Medium to large (3½ to 5 quart) slow cooker**

1 tbsp	extra virgin olive or coconut oil or ghee	15 mL
2	onions, finely chopped	2
4	cloves garlic, minced	4
1 tbsp	minced gingerroot	15 mL
2 tsp	garam masala (see Tips, left)	10 mL
2 tsp	cumin seeds, toasted and ground (see Tips, page 73)	10 mL
1 tsp	fennel seeds, toasted and ground	5 mL
1 tsp	cracked black peppercorns	5 mL
1 tsp	ground turmeric	5 mL
½ tsp	sea salt	2 mL
1	can (14 oz/398 mL) diced tomatoes with juice (see page 13)	1
1 cup	chicken stock	250 mL
2 lbs	skinless bone-in chicken thighs (8 thighs)	1 kg
¼ tsp	cayenne pepper (see Tips, left)	1 mL
1 cup	plain full-fat yogurt (see page 14)	250 mL

1. In a skillet, heat oil over medium-high heat. Add onions and cook, stirring, until they begin to turn golden, about 5 minutes. Add garlic, ginger, garam masala, cumin, fennel, peppercorns, turmeric and salt and cook, stirring, for 1 minute. Add tomatoes with juice and stock and bring to a boil.

2. Arrange chicken evenly over bottom of slow cooker stoneware and add tomato mixture. Cover and cook on Low for 6 hours or on High for 3 hours, until juices run clear when chicken is pierced with a fork. In a bowl, combine cayenne and yogurt. Stir well. Add to chicken, stir well and cook on Low for 10 minutes to meld flavors.

Mellow Chicken Curry

Tips

If you are halving this recipe, be sure to use a small (2 to 3 quart) slow cooker.

Ghee is, basically, clarified butter. If you are using a commercially prepared version, check to make sure it doesn't contain additives.

For the best flavor, toast and grind cumin and coriander seeds yourself. *To toast seeds:* Place seeds in a dry skillet over medium heat and cook, stirring, until fragrant, about 3 minutes. Immediately transfer to a spice grinder or mortar and grind.

If you're using a mixture of light and dark meat, placing the dark meat on the bottom and the white on the top will help to maintain moisture. If you're cooking breasts, they will probably be done in 5 hours on Low. Overcooking will dry them out.

Make Ahead

Complete Step 1. Cover and refrigerate for up to 2 days. When you're ready to cook, complete the recipe.

By Indian standards, this is a simple chicken curry, but the results are delicious nonetheless. In Indian cooking it is customary for chicken to be cut up into fairly small pieces, which makes for a more elegant presentation.

• **Medium (approx. 4 quart) slow cooker**

1 tbsp	extra virgin coconut oil or ghee (see Tips, left)	15 mL
3	onions, thinly sliced	3
4	cloves garlic, minced	4
1 tbsp	minced gingerroot	15 mL
2 tsp	ground cumin (see Tips, left)	10 mL
1 tsp	ground coriander	5 mL
1 tsp	ground turmeric	5 mL
3	black or green cardamom pods	3
1	piece (2 inches/5 cm) cinnamon stick	1
$1/2$ tsp	sea salt	2 mL
$1/2$ tsp	cracked black peppercorns	2 mL
1	bay leaf	1
1 tbsp	freshly squeezed lemon juice	15 mL
1	can (28 oz/796 mL) tomatoes, drained and chopped (see page 13)	1
3 lbs	skinless boneless chicken pieces, cut into 1-inch (2.5 cm) cubes (see Tips, left)	1.5 kg
1 to 2	long red or green chiles, minced	1 to 2
1 cup	plain full-fat yogurt (see page 14)	250 mL

1. In a large skillet, heat oil over medium heat. Add onions and cook, stirring, until softened, about 3 minutes. Add garlic, ginger, cumin, coriander, turmeric, cardamom, cinnamon stick, salt, peppercorns and bay leaf and cook, stirring, for 1 minute. Add lemon juice and tomatoes and stir to combine.

2. Arrange chicken evenly over bottom of slow cooker stoneware and cover with sauce. Cover and cook on Low for 5 to 6 hours or on High for $2^1/2$ to 3 hours, until juices run clear when pierced with a fork. In a bowl, combine chile to taste and yogurt. Add to chicken. Cover and cook on High for 10 minutes to meld flavors. Discard cardamom pods, cinnamon stick and bay leaf.

Fruit-Spiked Chicken Curry

Tips

If you are halving this recipe, be sure to use a small (1½ to 3 quart) slow cooker.

For the best flavor, toast and grind cumin seeds yourself. *To toast seeds:* Place seeds in a dry skillet over medium heat and cook, stirring, until fragrant, about 3 minutes. Immediately transfer to a spice grinder or mortar and grind.

Curry powder should be simply a blend of spices, which are gluten-free, but some brands add wheat starch to the mixture so be sure to check the label.

If you don't have a fresh chile pepper, substitute ¼ tsp (1 mL) cayenne pepper.

Make Ahead

Complete Step 1. Cover and refrigerate mixture for up to 2 days. When you're ready to cook, complete the recipe.

If your taste in curry runs to mild and soothing, this is for you. The addition of apple, banana and currants lends appealingly exotic notes to the broth, and the coconut milk provides a pleasantly creamy finish.

• **Medium to large (3½ to 5 quart) slow cooker**

1 tbsp	extra virgin olive or coconut oil	15 mL
2	onions, finely chopped	2
2	stalks celery, diced (see Tips, page 71)	2
2	carrots, peeled and diced	2
4	cloves garlic, minced	4
1 tsp	cracked black peppercorns	5 mL
1 tsp	ground cumin (see Tips, left)	5 mL
½ tsp	sea salt	2 mL
4	whole black cardamom pods, crushed	4
1 tsp	curry powder (see Tips, left)	5 mL
1	firm apple, peeled and diced	1
1½ cups	chicken stock	375 mL
1½ lbs	skinless boneless chicken thighs, cut into 1-inch (2.5 cm) cubes	750 g
1 cup	coconut milk	250 mL
1	banana, peeled and chopped	1
¼ cup	currants	60 mL
1	long red or green chile pepper, minced (see Tips, left)	1

1. In a skillet, heat oil over medium heat. Add onions, celery and carrots and cook, stirring, until softened, about 7 minutes. Add garlic, peppercorns, cumin, salt, cardamom and curry powder and cook, stirring, for 1 minute. Add apple and toss until coated. Stir in stock.

2. Transfer to slow cooker stoneware. Stir in chicken. Cover and cook on Low for 5 hours or on High for 2½ hours. Add coconut milk, banana, currants and chile pepper. Cover and cook on High for 15 minutes to meld flavors. Remove and discard cardamom pods before serving.

The Captain's Curry

- **Entertaining Worthy**
- **Can Be Halved**
(see Tips, below)

Tips

If you are halving this recipe, be sure to use a small (2 to 3 quart) slow cooker.

This amount of curry powder and cayenne is based on using a mild curry powder and produces a nicely spicy result. Adjust the strength of the curry powder and the quantity of cayenne to suit your taste. If diners prefer different degrees of heat, consider mincing some fresh long red or green or Thai chiles and passing them at the table so heat seekers can satisfy themselves.

Curry powder should be simply a blend of spices, which are gluten-free, but some brands add wheat starch to the mixture so be sure to check the label.

Make Ahead

Complete Step 1. Cover and refrigerate for up to 2 days. When you're ready to cook, continue with the recipe.

This style of curry, made with a creamed curry sauce, was popular in the great American seaports during the 19th century. It gets its name from sea captains involved in the spice trade, who brought their wares to cities such as Charleston. Today, we associate coconut milk with our current interest in Asian foods. But citizens of the old South were quite familiar with this ingredient, which they made themselves using fresh coconuts from the West Indies.

- **Medium to large (3$\frac{1}{2}$ to 5 quart) slow cooker**

1 tbsp	extra virgin coconut oil or ghee	15 mL
2	onions, finely chopped	2
2	stalks celery, thinly sliced (see Tips, page 71)	2
4	cloves garlic, minced	4
6	whole allspice	6
$\frac{1}{2}$ tsp	freshly grated nutmeg	2 mL
1	piece (3 inches/7.5 cm) cinnamon stick	1
1	bay leaf	1
2 cups	chicken stock	500 mL
1$\frac{1}{2}$ lbs	skinless boneless chicken thighs or breasts, cut into 1-inch (2.5 cm) cubes (see Tips, page 73)	750 g
1 cup	coconut milk, divided	250 mL
1 tbsp	curry powder (see Tips, left)	15 mL
$\frac{1}{2}$ tsp	cayenne pepper	2 mL
	Toasted sliced almonds, optional	

1. In a skillet, heat oil over medium heat. Add onions and celery and cook, stirring, until celery is softened, about 5 minutes. Add garlic, allspice, nutmeg, cinnamon stick and bay leaf and cook, stirring, for 1 minute. Add stock. Bring to a boil and cook, stirring, until slightly thickened, about 5 minutes.

2. Arrange chicken evenly over bottom of stoneware and cover with vegetable mixture. Cover and cook on Low for 5 to 6 hours or on High for 2$\frac{1}{2}$ to 3 hours, until juices run clear when chicken is pierced with a fork.

3. In a small bowl, combine $\frac{1}{4}$ cup (60 mL) of the coconut milk with curry powder and cayenne. Mix well. Add to stoneware. Stir in remaining coconut milk and cook on High for 15 minutes, until heated through and flavors meld. Discard cinnamon stick and bay leaf. Garnish with almonds, if using.

Peppery Chicken in Coconut-Mushroom Gravy

Serves 4

◆ Entertaining Worthy
◆ Can Be Halved
(see Tip, below)

Tip

If you are halving this recipe, be sure to use a small (1½ to 3 quart) slow cooker.

Make Ahead

Complete Steps 1 and 2. Cover and refrigerate mixture for up to 2 days. When you're ready to cook, complete the recipe.

The flavors in this chicken are vaguely Thai but the shiitake mushrooms add a Chinese twist. There is a good hit of zesty ginger in the sauce and the coconut milk adds a creamy finish.

• **Medium to large (3½ to 5 quart) slow cooker**

1	package (½ oz/14 g) dried sliced shiitake mushrooms	1
1 cup	hot water	250 mL
1 tbsp	extra virgin coconut oil	15 mL
1	onion, diced	1
2	carrots, peeled and diced	2
4	cloves garlic, minced	4
2 tbsp	minced gingerroot	30 mL
½ tsp	sea salt	2 mL
½ tsp	cracked black peppercorns	2 mL
1 cup	chicken stock	250 mL
2 lbs	skinless bone-in chicken thighs (about 8 thighs)	1 kg
2 tbsp	freshly squeezed lime juice	30 mL
¼ tsp	cayenne pepper	1 mL
1 cup	coconut milk	250 mL
1	red bell pepper, seeded and diced	1
½ cup	chopped fresh cilantro leaves	125 mL

1. In a bowl, combine dried mushrooms and hot water. Let stand for 30 minutes. Drain through a fine sieve, reserving soaking liquid. Pat mushrooms dry with paper towel and set aside.

2. In a skillet, heat oil over medium heat. Add onion and carrots and cook, stirring, until carrots are softened, about 7 minutes. Add garlic, ginger, salt, peppercorns and reserved dried mushrooms and cook, stirring, for 1 minute. Add stock and reserved mushroom soaking liquid and bring to a boil.

3. Arrange chicken evenly over bottom of slow cooker stoneware and add vegetable mixture. Cover and cook on Low for 5 hours or on High for 2½ hours, until juices run clear when chicken is pierced with a fork.

4. In a bowl, combine lime juice and cayenne. Stir until cayenne dissolves. Add to slow cooker stoneware along with coconut milk and bell pepper. Stir well. Cover and cook on High for 20 minutes, until pepper is tender and mixture is hot. Garnish with cilantro.

Mexican-Style Chicken with Cilantro and Lemon

Tips

If you are halving this recipe, be sure to use a small (2 to 3 quart) slow cooker.

Buy seeds and nuts at a natural foods or bulk food store with high turnover, as they are likely to be much fresher than those in packages.

Lard is traditionally used for frying in Mexican cooking and properly made is a healthy fat (see page 12).

Make Ahead

Complete Steps 1 and 2. Cover and refrigerate puréed sauce for up to 2 days. When you're ready to cook, complete the recipe.

With a sauce of pumpkin seeds, cumin, oregano and cilantro, this dish reminds me of warm evening dinners in the courtyard of a charming Mexican hacienda. Mexicans have been thickening sauces with pumpkin seeds long before the Spanish arrived and, today, every cook has their own recipes for mole, one of the world's great culinary concoctions.

- Medium to large (3½ to 5 quart) slow cooker
- Food processor

¼ cup	raw pumpkin seeds (see Tips, left)	60 mL
2 tsp	cumin seeds	10 mL
1 tbsp	extra virgin olive oil or pure lard	15 mL
2	onions, thinly sliced	2
4	cloves garlic, minced	4
2 tbsp	tomato paste (see page 13)	30 mL
1 tsp	cracked black peppercorns	5 mL
1 tsp	dried oregano	5 mL
½ tsp	sea salt	2 mL
¼ tsp	ground cinnamon	1 mL
2 cups	cilantro, leaves and some stems, chopped	500 mL
1 tbsp	grated lemon zest	15 mL
2 tbsp	freshly squeezed lemon juice	30 mL
1 cup	chicken stock	250 mL
3 lbs	skinless bone-in chicken thighs (about 12 thighs)	1.5 kg
1 to 2	jalapeño peppers, minced	1 to 2
	Finely chopped cilantro and green onion	
	Grated lemon zest	

1. In a dry skillet over medium heat, toast pumpkin and cumin seeds, until pumpkin seeds are popping and cumin has released its flavor. Transfer to a mortar or spice grinder and grind. Set aside.

2. In same skillet, heat oil over medium heat. Add onions and cook, stirring, until softened, about 3 minutes. Add garlic, tomato paste, peppercorns, oregano, salt, cinnamon and cilantro and cook, stirring, for 1 minute. Transfer contents of pan to a food processor. Add lemon zest and juice, chicken stock, and reserved pumpkin and cumin seeds and process until smooth.

3. Arrange chicken evenly over bottom of slow cooker stoneware. Pour sauce over chicken. Cover and cook on Low for 6 hours or on High for 3 hours, until juices run clear when chicken is pierced with a fork. Stir in jalapeño pepper to taste. When ready to serve, garnish with cilantro, green onion and lemon zest.

Spicy Chinese Chicken

Serves 6

◆ **Can Be Halved**
(see Tips, below)

Tips

If you are halving this recipe, be sure to use a small (2 to 3 quart) slow cooker.

Arrowroot is a starch that has some degree of acceptance in the Paleo community. It is used here to thicken the sauce, but if you have problems digesting starch, skip this step.

Make Ahead

This dish can be assembled the night before it is cooked and, in fact, improves in flavor for marinating in the sauce overnight. Using a large bowl, complete Step 1. Add chicken and toss to coat. Cover and refrigerate overnight. The next day, complete the recipe.

I've been making variations of this basic recipe for more than twenty years and I still love it. This one is particularly good because the vinegar, coconut sugar and chile pepper add a nice complexity to the basic sauce.

• **Medium to large (3½ to 5 quart) slow cooker**

¾ cup	chicken stock	175 mL
3 tbsp	rice vinegar	45 mL
2 tsp	coconut sugar	10 mL
¼ cup	gluten-free soy sauce or coconut aminos (see page 15)	60 mL
4	green onions, including stems, cut into 2-inch (5 cm) pieces	4
4	cloves garlic, minced	4
1 tbsp	minced gingerroot	15 mL
1 tsp	cracked black peppercorns	5 mL
3 lbs	skinless bone-in chicken thighs (about 12 thighs)	1.5 kg
1	long red or green chile pepper or 2 Thai chiles, minced	1
1 tbsp	arrowroot, dissolved in 2 tbsp (30 mL) cold water, optional (see Tips, left)	15 mL

1. In a bowl, combine chicken stock, vinegar, coconut sugar and soy sauce, stirring well to ensure sugar is dissolved. Add green onions, garlic, ginger and peppercorns.

2. Arrange chicken evenly over bottom of slow cooker stoneware and cover with sauce. Cover and cook on Low for 6 hours or on High for 3 hours, until juices run clear when chicken is pierced with a fork.

3. With a slotted spoon, transfer chicken to a platter and keep warm. Strain liquid into a saucepan. Add chile pepper to taste and arrowroot solution. Simmer over low heat, stirring for about 3 minutes or until thickened and glossy. Pour over chicken.

Indonesian Chicken

Serves 4 to 6

◆ **Can Be Halved**
(see Tips, below)

Tips

If you are halving this recipe, be sure to use a small (2 to 3 quart) slow cooker.

Lemongrass, which has a unique woody-lemony flavor, is available in Asian markets and many supermarkets. Before adding lemongrass to a recipe, "smash" it with the flat side of a chef's knife, so it can release its flavor when it cooks.

Make Ahead

Complete Step 1. Cover and refrigerate mixture for up to 2 days. When you're ready to cook, complete the recipe.

Although this chicken dish is remarkably easy to make, its slightly sweet yet spicy coconut-milk sauce gives it an exotic flavor.

- Medium to large (3½ to 5 quart) slow cooker
- Food processor

1 tbsp	extra virgin coconut oil	15 mL
2	onions, sliced	2
4	cloves garlic, minced	4
1 tbsp	minced gingerroot	15 mL
1 tsp	ground coriander	5 mL
1 tsp	ground turmeric	5 mL
8	whole blanched almonds	8
1½ cups	chicken stock	375 mL
3 lbs	skinless bone-in chicken thighs (about 12 thighs)	1.5 kg
1	stalk lemongrass, bruised and cut into 2-inch (5 cm) pieces (see Tips, left)	1
1 cup	coconut milk	250 mL
2 tbsp	gluten-free soy sauce or coconut aminos	30 mL
1 tsp	minced red Thai chile pepper	5 mL
1 tsp	coconut sugar	5 mL
	Finely chopped cilantro leaves	

1. In a skillet, heat oil over medium heat. Add onions and cook, stirring, until softened, about 3 minutes. Add garlic, ginger, coriander, turmeric and almonds and cook, stirring, for 1 minute. Add chicken stock and stir. Transfer contents of pan to food processor and process until smooth.

2. Arrange chicken evenly over bottom of slow cooker and cover with sauce. Add lemongrass. Cover and cook on Low for 6 hours or on High for 3 hours, until juices run clear when chicken is pierced with a fork.

3. In a bowl, combine coconut milk, soy sauce, chile pepper and coconut sugar. Stir well. Pour over chicken. Cover and cook on High for 15 minutes, until heated through. Discard lemongrass. Garnish with cilantro.

Variation

If you enjoy the flavor of almonds and the added texture they provide, add whole blanched almonds, to taste, along with the coconut milk.

Turkey Meatballs in Tomato Sauce

◆ **Can Be Halved**
(see Tips, below)

Tips

If you are halving this recipe, be sure to use a small (1½ to 3 quart) slow cooker.

If you prefer, use 1 cup (250 mL) chicken stock or water combined with 1 tbsp (15 mL) lemon juice instead of the wine.

I like to use parchment when cooking this dish because the recipe doesn't contain much liquid. Creating a tight seal ensures that none evaporates and that the meatballs and sauce are well basted in their own juices.

Look for canned tomatoes that are organically grown, with no salt added, and come in glass jars or BPA (bisphenol-A) free cans. When using canned tomatoes (or any canned product) check to make sure they are gluten-free.

Served over spaghetti squash, this should satisfy any yen you might have for an old-fashioned pasta dish. Light and mildly flavored but providing all the satisfaction of its more robust relatives, this is sure to become a family favorite. It's skimpy on sauce, so I recommend topping the squash with a healthy dollop of butter or extra virgin olive oil before adding the meatballs.

- **Large (approx. 5 quart) slow cooker**
- **Large piece of parchment paper**

¼ cup	almond flour	60 mL
1 lb	ground turkey	500 g
½ cup	finely chopped red onion	125 mL
2 tsp	dried oregano	10 mL
½ tsp	sea salt	2 mL
½ tsp	cracked black peppercorns	2 mL
1	egg, beaten	1
2 tbsp	clarified butter	30 mL

Tomato Sauce

1	onion, finely chopped	1
2	stalks celery, diced (see Tips, page 71)	2
2	carrots, peeled and diced	2
4	cloves garlic, minced	4
2 tsp	dried Italian seasoning	10 mL
1 tsp	cracked black peppercorns	5 mL
½ tsp	sea salt	2 mL
1 cup	dry white wine or stock (see Tips, left)	250 mL
1	can (28 oz/796 mL) tomatoes with juice, coarsely chopped (see Tips, left and page 13)	1

1. In a large bowl, combine almond flour, turkey, red onion, oregano, salt, peppercorns and egg. Using your hands, mix until well combined. Form into 12 meatballs, each about 1½ inches (4 cm) in diameter.

2. In a skillet, heat clarified butter over medium-high heat. Add meatballs, in batches, and brown well, about 5 minutes per batch. Transfer to slow cooker stoneware. Reduce heat to medium.

3. *Tomato Sauce:* Add onion, celery and carrots to pan and cook, stirring, until carrots are softened, about 7 minutes. Add garlic, Italian seasoning, peppercorns and salt and cook, stirring, for 1 minute. Add wine, bring to a boil and boil for 2 minutes. Stir in tomatoes with juice.

Make Ahead

Complete Step 3, heating 1 tbsp (15 mL) oil in pan before softening the vegetables. Cover and refrigerate mixture for up to 2 days. When you're ready to cook, complete the recipe.

4. Transfer to slow cooker stoneware. Place a large piece of parchment over the mixture, pressing it down to brush the food and extending up the sides of the stoneware so it overlaps the rim. Cover and cook on Low for 6 hours or on High for 3 hours, until mixture is hot and bubbly and juices run clear when meatballs are pierced with a fork.

Variation

Chicken Meatballs in Tomato Sauce: Substitute an equal quantity of ground chicken for the turkey.

Clarified Butter

Clarified butter is butter from which the milk solids have been removed. It is excellent for use in dishes where true butter flavor is valued and also, because it has a high smoke point, for frying over high heat. I usually clarify about half a pound (250 g) of butter at a time and keep it in the refrigerator to have on hand. Clarified butter has become one of my favorite cooking fats.

To make clarified butter, melt unsalted butter over low heat (if you have a true simmer function on your stove top, this is a perfect time to use it). Foam will rise to the top and eventually it will begin to sputter. Continue to heat until it calms down, then remove from heat and spoon off the foam. Strain the remaining bright yellow liquid into a heatproof container (I use a large ramekin) through a sieve, lined with a double layer of cheesecloth.

Cover and refrigerate for up to 6 months. (Mine rarely lasts much longer than a week. Be aware that the volume of clarified butter you produce will be significantly less than the quantity of butter you began with.)

Tomato-Braised Turkey Breast

◆ Entertaining Worthy
◆ Can Be Halved
(see Tips, below)

Tips

If you are halving this recipe, be sure to use a small (2 to 3 quart) slow cooker.

If you prefer, substitute an extra cup (250 mL) of chicken or turkey stock plus 1 tbsp (15 mL) lemon juice for the white wine.

Arrowroot is a starch that has some degree of acceptance in the Paleo community. It is used here to thicken the gravy in the dish but if you have problems with digesting starch do not use it.

Make Ahead

Complete Step 2. Cover and refrigerate mixture for up to 2 days. When you're ready to cook, complete the recipe.

If you're tired of the same old thing, try this simple-to-make braised turkey. Add some steamed green beans for a perfect special meal.

- **Medium to large (3½ to 5 quart) slow cooker**
- **Instant-read thermometer**

2 tbsp	extra virgin olive oil or clarified butter (see page 83)	30 mL
1	turkey breast, skin on, 2 to 3 lbs (1 to 1.5 kg)	1
2	onions, thinly sliced on the vertical	2
2	anchovy fillets, minced	2
4	cloves garlic, minced	4
1 tsp	dried oregano	5 mL
1 tsp	cracked black peppercorns	5 mL
½ tsp	sea salt	2 mL
¼ cup	tomato paste (see Tips, page 52)	60 mL
1 cup	dry white wine (see Tips, left)	250 mL
2 cups	chicken or turkey stock	500 mL
1 tbsp	arrowroot, dissolved in 2 tbsp (30 mL) water, optional (see Tips, left)	15 mL
½ cup	finely chopped parsley leaves	125 mL

1. In a skillet, heat oil over medium-high heat. Add turkey, skin side down, and cook until nicely browned, about 3 minutes. Transfer to slow cooker stoneware, skin side up.

2. Add onions and anchovies to skillet and cook, stirring, until anchovies dissolve and onions begin to turn golden, about 7 minutes. Add garlic, oregano, peppercorns and salt and cook, stirring, for 1 minute. Stir in tomato paste and wine and cook, stirring and scraping up the brown bits from bottom of the pan, for 2 minutes. Stir in stock and bring to a boil.

3. Transfer to slow cooker stoneware. Cover and cook on Low for 6 hours or on High for 3 hours, until turkey is tender and no longer pink inside or an instant-read thermometer reads 160°F (71°C). Stir in arrowroot solution, if using. Cover and cook on High until mixture thickens, about 5 minutes. To serve, transfer to a deep platter, spoon sauce over turkey and garnish with parsley.

Variation

Tomato-Braised Turkey Legs: Substitute about 3 lbs (1.5 kg) skinless bone-in turkey thighs or legs for the breast. Skip Step 1 and arrange turkey over bottom of slow cooker stoneware. Add oil to skillet and continue with Steps 2 and 3.

Turkey Mole

◆ Can Be Halved
(see Tips, page 84)

Serves 6

Tips

Tomatillos are available in the Mexican food section of supermarkets. I have used canned tomatillos here for convenience but if you want to use fresh ones, combine 4 cups (1 L) fresh tomatillos with water to cover in a saucepan. Bring to a boil, reduce heat and simmer just until tender, about 10 minutes. Drain and cool slightly before adding to the food processor.

Serrano chiles are much milder than jalapeños, so choose according to your preference for heat.

Make Ahead

Complete Steps 2 and 4, heating 1 tbsp (15 mL) oil in pan before softening onions. Cover and refrigerate puréed sauces separately for up to 2 days, being aware that the chile mixture will lose some of its vibrancy if held for this long. When you're ready to cook, brown the turkey (Step 1) or remove skin from turkey, omit browning and place directly in stoneware. Continue with recipe.

In Mexico, no special occasion is complete without turkey cooked in mole poblano. The authentic version is quite a production. This mole has been greatly simplified but is still very good.

- **Medium to large (3½ to 5 quart) slow cooker**
- **Food processor**
- **Instant-read thermometer**

1 tbsp	extra virgin olive oil or pure lard	15 mL
1	turkey breast, skin on, about 2 to 3 lbs (1 to 1.5 kg), patted dry	1
2	onions, sliced	2
3	cloves garlic, sliced	3
4	whole cloves	4
1	piece (2 inches/5 cm) cinnamon stick	1
1 tsp	cracked black peppercorns	5 mL
½ tsp	sea salt	2 mL
1	can (28 oz/796 mL) tomatillos, drained	1
½ cup	whole blanched almonds	125 mL
½ oz	unsweetened chocolate, broken in pieces	15 g
1 cup	chicken or turkey stock, divided	250 mL
2	dried ancho chiles	2
½ cup	coarsely chopped cilantro, stems and leaves	125 mL
1 tbsp	chili powder (see Tips, page 172)	15 mL
1 to 2	jalapeño or serrano chiles, chopped	1 to 2

1. In a skillet, heat oil over medium heat. Add turkey, skin side down, and brown well, about 4 minutes. Transfer to slow cooker stoneware.

2. Add onions to pan and cook, stirring, until softened, about 3 minutes. Add garlic, cloves, cinnamon, pepper and salt and cook, stirring, for 1 minute. Transfer to a food processor. Add tomatillos, almonds, chocolate and ½ cup (125 mL) stock and process until smooth.

3. Pour sauce over turkey, cover and cook on Low for 6 hours or on High for 3 hours, until juices run clear when turkey is pierced with a fork or instant-read thermometer reads 160°F (71°C).

4. About an hour before turkey has finished cooking, in a heatproof bowl, soak dried chiles in boiling water for 30 minutes, weighing down with a cup to ensure they remain submerged. Drain, discarding soaking liquid and stems and chop coarsely. Transfer to a blender. Add cilantro, remaining ½ cup (125 mL) of the stock, chili powder and jalapeño pepper to taste and purée. Add to stoneware and stir gently to combine. Cover and cook on High for 30 minutes, until flavors meld.

Variations

Chicken Mole: Substitute 3 lbs (1.5 kg) skinless bone-in chicken thighs (about 12 thighs) for the turkey.

Zesty Seafood Chowder

Fish and Seafood

Zesty Seafood Chowder

Serves 6

◆ **Can Be Halved**
(see Tips, below)

Tips

If you are halving this recipe, be sure to use a small (2 to 3½ quart) slow cooker.

Some brands of Cajun seasoning contain gluten. Check the label.

The potato in this recipe has been used to add flavor and, more importantly, to replace cream, which is traditionally used to thicken chowder. If you are concerned about eating this starchy vegetable, the fat in the mayo and the bacon mitigate the glycemic response. However, if you cannot consume potatoes for other dietary reasons, omit it. The soup will be tasty but will lack a creamy consistency.

To clean clams, scrub thoroughly with a wire brush and soak in several changes of cold salted water.

Make Ahead

Complete Steps 1 and 2. Cover and refrigerate bacon and vegetable mixture separately for up to 2 days. When you're ready to cook, continue with the recipe.

This robust chowder is a lip-smacking meal-in-a-bowl. I love the hint of smokiness balanced by the heat of the jalapeño.

• **Medium to large (3½ to 5 quart) slow cooker**

4 oz	smoked bacon, diced	125 g
2	leeks, white part with just a hint of green, cleaned and thinly sliced (see Tips, page 90)	2
2	stalks celery, diced (see Tips, page 96)	2
2	cloves garlic, minced	2
1 tsp	Cajun seasoning (see Tips, left)	5 mL
1 tsp	dried thyme	5 mL
½ tsp	sea salt	2 mL
½ tsp	cracked black peppercorns	2 mL
1 cup	dry white wine (see Tips, page 89)	250 mL
2 cups	fish stock	500 mL
2	potatoes, peeled and shredded (see Tips, left)	2
3 lbs	small clams, cleaned (see Tips, left)	1.5 kg
1 lb	firm white fish fillets, cut into 1-inch (2.5 cm) cubes (see Tips, page 89)	500 g
1 cup	corn kernels, thawed if frozen (see Tip, page 56)	250 mL
1 to 2	jalapeño peppers, seeded and diced	1 to 2
	Paleo Mayo (page 238)	
	Finely chopped parsley leaves	

1. In a skillet, cook bacon over medium-high heat until crisp. Drain well on paper towel, cover and refrigerate until ready to use.

2. Reduce heat to medium. Add leeks and celery to pan and cook, stirring, until softened, about 5 minutes. Add garlic, Cajun seasoning, thyme, salt and peppercorns and cook, stirring, for 1 minute. Add wine, bring to a boil and boil for 2 minutes.

3. Transfer to slow cooker stoneware. Stir in fish stock and potatoes. Cover and cook on Low for 8 hours or on High for 4 hours, until potatoes are dissolving into the broth.

4. Discard any clams that are open. In a large saucepan over medium-high heat, bring 1 cup (250 mL) water to a rapid boil. Add clams, cover and cook, shaking the pot, until all the clams open. Discard any that do not open. Strain cooking liquid through a fine sieve into a bowl. Using a fork, remove clam meat from shells.

5. Add clam cooking liquid and meat to slow cooker, along with fish fillets, reserved bacon, corn and jalapeño to taste. Cover and cook on High for 10 minutes, until fish is cooked through and flavors meld. To serve, spoon about 1 tbsp (15 mL) Paleo Mayo into the bottom of each warmed bowl. Ladle soup into bowls and garnish with parsley.

Zuppa di Pesce

◆ **Entertaining Worthy**
◆ **Can Be Halved**
  (see Tips, below)

Tips

If you are halving this recipe, be sure to use a small (2 to 3½ quart) slow cooker.

To toast fennel seeds: Place seeds in a dry skillet over medium heat and cook, stirring, until fragrant, about 3 minutes. Immediately transfer to a mortar or a spice grinder and grind.

If you don't have Aleppo pepper, substitute 1 tsp (5 mL) sweet paprika mixed with a pinch of cayenne pepper.

Use firm white fish such as Pacific halibut or sea bass.

If you prefer, substitute an extra cup (250 mL) of water plus 1 tbsp (15 mL) lemon juice for the white wine.

For best results, when asking for trimmings, be sure to use non-oily fish, which means no salmon or tuna.

Make Ahead

Complete Steps 1 and 2. Cover and refrigerate fish and vegetable mixtures separately overnight. When you're ready to cook, complete the recipe.

This is a very simple Italian-style fish stew that is differentiated by an assortment of fish. It doesn't contain any seafood. Its simplicity demands a good-quality broth, which can easily be achieved by simmering fish trimmings with the other ingredients.

• **Large (approx. 5 quart) slow cooker**
• **Large square of cheesecloth**

3 tbsp	extra virgin olive oil, divided	45 mL
1 tbsp	freshly squeezed lemon juice	15 mL
1 tsp	fennel seeds, toasted and ground	5 mL
1 tsp	coarse sea salt	5 mL
1 tsp	mild chile powder, such as Aleppo (see Tips, left)	5 mL
2 lbs	assorted skinless fish fillets, cut into chunks (see Tips, left)	1 kg
2	onions, finely chopped	2
4	stalks celery, diced (see Tips, page 96)	4
4	cloves garlic, minced	4
2	bay leaves	2
1 tsp	dried oregano	5 mL
½ tsp	cracked black peppercorns	2 mL
1 cup	dry white wine (see Tips, left)	250 mL
1	can (28 oz/796 mL) tomatoes with juice, chopped	1
2 lbs	fish trimmings (see Tips, left)	1 kg
6 cups	water	1.5 L
	Roasted Garlic Aïoli or Anchovy Paleo Mayo, optional (Variations, page 238)	
½ cup	finely chopped flat-leaf parsley leaves	125 mL

1. In a bowl, combine 2 tbsp (30 mL) of the olive oil, lemon juice, fennel seeds, salt and chile powder. Mix well. Add fish and toss until coated. Cover and refrigerate for 2 hours or overnight, stirring occasionally.

2. In a skillet, heat remaining tbsp (15 mL) of olive oil over medium heat. Add onions and celery and cook, stirring, until softened, about 5 minutes. Add garlic, bay leaves, oregano and peppercorns and cook, stirring, for 1 minute. Add wine and bring to a boil. Boil for 2 minutes. Stir in tomatoes with juice. Transfer to stoneware.

3. In a large square of cheesecloth, tie fish trimmings. Add to stoneware along with water, ensuring trimmings are submerged. Cover and cook on Low for 8 hours or on High for 4 hours. Remove trimmings and discard. Increase heat to High. Add marinated fish and cook for about 15 minutes, until fish is tender. Remove and discard bay leaves.

4. To serve, ladle soup into warm bowls, or for a fancier version, place about 1 tbsp (15 mL) Roasted Garlic Aïoli in the bottom of each bowl and ladle the soup over it. Garnish with parsley.

Bistro Fish Soup

◆ **Entertaining Worthy**
◆ **Can Be Halved**
(see Tips, page 91)

Tips

Leeks can be gritty. *To clean leeks:* Split leeks in half lengthwise and submerge in a basin of water, swishing them around to remove all traces of dirt. Transfer to a colander and rinse under cold water.

To roast peppers: Preheat oven to 400°F (200°C). Place pepper(s) on a baking sheet and roast, turning two or three times, until skin on all sides is blackened, about 25 minutes. Transfer pepper(s) to a heatproof bowl. Cover with a plate and let stand until cool. Remove and, using a sharp knife, lift skins off. Discard skins and slice according to recipe instructions.

If you don't have a food processor, you can chop the roasted red pepper very finely and grate the garlic or put it through a press. Combine in a bowl with the mayonnaise and hot pepper sauce.

Make Ahead

Complete Step 1. Cover and refrigerate for up to 2 days. When you're ready to cook, complete the recipe.

Described as soupe de poisson *in France, where it is a mainstay of bistro culture, this ambrosial concoction makes a satisfying main course.*

• **Large (approx. 5 quart) slow cooker**

2 tbsp	extra virgin olive oil or clarified butter	30 mL
3	large leeks, white with a bit of green, cleaned and thinly sliced (see Tips, left)	3
1	onion, diced	1
1	bulb fennel, trimmed, cored and chopped	1
4	sprigs parsley or chervil	4
4	cloves garlic, minced	4
1 tsp	fennel seeds, crushed	5 mL
1/2 tsp	each sea salt and cracked black peppercorns	2 mL
1	can (28 oz/796 mL) tomatoes with juice, coarsely chopped	1
6 cups	vegetable stock	1.5 L
2 lbs	fish trimmings (non-oily fish)	1 kg
2	potatoes (about 1 lb/500 g), diced (see Tips, page 91)	2
1 tbsp	Pernod, optional	15 mL
1/2 cup	flat-leaf parsley leaves, finely chopped	125 mL

Rouille

1/4 cup	Paleo Mayo (page 238)	60 mL
1	roasted red pepper, peeled and chopped (see Tips, left)	1
2	cloves garlic, minced	2
	Hot Pepper Sauce (page 240)	
	Finely chopped flat-leaf parsley leaves	

1. In a skillet, heat oil over medium heat. Add leeks, onion and fennel and cook, stirring, until fennel is softened, about 6 minutes. Add parsley, garlic, fennel seeds, salt and peppercorns and cook, stirring, for 1 minute. Add tomatoes with juice and bring to a boil.

2. Transfer to slow cooker stoneware. Add stock, fish trimmings and potatoes and stir well. Cover and cook on Low for 6 hours or on High for 3 hours, until vegetables are very tender.

3. Place a sieve over a large bowl or saucepan. Working in batches, ladle the soup into the sieve, removing and discarding any visible bones. Using a wooden spoon, push the solids through sieve. Add Pernod, if using, to the strained soup. Add parsley and stir well.

4. *Rouille:* In a food processor fitted with the metal blade (a mini bowl attachment is ideal), process mayonnaise, red pepper, garlic, and hot pepper sauce, to taste, until smooth. To serve, ladle soup into individual bowls, garnish with parsley and top with a dollop of rouille.

Florida Fish Chowder

◆ **Can Be Halved**
(see Tips, below)

Tips

If you're halving this recipe, be sure to use a small (1½ to 3 quart) slow cooker.

If you prefer, substitute 1 cup (250 mL) fish stock plus 1 tbsp (15 mL) lemon juice for the white wine.

If you don't want to use potatoes, substitute 2 carrots and 2 stalks of celery.

Make Ahead

This dish can be partially prepared the night before it is served. Complete Step 1. Cover and refrigerate overnight. The next morning, continue cooking as directed in Step 2.

Served with salad, this simple fish chowder can be the basis of a delicious light meal.

• **Medium to large (3½ to 5 quart) slow cooker**

2 tbsp	extra virgin olive oil or butter	30 mL
2	large leeks, white part only, cleaned and coarsely chopped (see Tips, page 90)	2
4	stalks celery, peeled and diced	4
2	carrots, peeled and diced	2
2	cloves garlic, minced	2
½ tsp	dried thyme	2 mL
½ tsp	sea salt	2 mL
½ tsp	cracked black peppercorns	2 mL
1	can (28 oz/796 mL) tomatoes, including juice (see page 13)	1
1 tbsp	tomato paste (see page 13) or 2 tbsp (30 mL) minced reconstituted sun-dried tomatoes	15 mL
4 cups	fish stock	1 L
1 cup	dry white wine (see Tips, left)	250 mL
2	potatoes, peeled and diced, optional (see Tips, left)	2
1½ lbs	grouper fillets or other firm white fish (skinned), cut into 1-inch (2.5 cm) squares	750 g
1	green bell pepper, diced	1
1	chile pepper, seeded and finely chopped	1
	Finely chopped parsley leaves	

1. In a skillet, heat oil over medium heat. Add leeks, celery and carrots and cook, stirring, until softened. Add garlic, thyme, salt and peppercorns and cook, stirring, for 1 minute. Add tomatoes and tomato paste, breaking tomatoes up with a spoon, and bring to a boil.

2. Transfer mixture to slow cooker stoneware. Stir in fish stock, wine and potatoes. Cover and cook on Low for 8 hours or on High for 4 hours, until potatoes are tender. Add grouper, bell pepper and chile pepper. Cover and cook on High for 20 to 30 minutes, until fish is cooked through. Garnish with parsley and serve hot.

Variation

Bermuda Fish Chowder: Add 2 tbsp to ¼ cup (30 to 60 mL) peppered sherry along with the fish, depending on the amount of heat desired. To make peppered sherry, pour 1 cup (250 mL) sherry into a clean jar. Thoroughly wash 4 chile peppers, preferably Scotch bonnet and chop finely. Add with seeds to sherry. Cover and let steep for at least 24 hours. Strain the required amount into the chowder. Refrigerate the remainder and save for use in soups and stews, straining out the required amount as needed.

Braised Swordfish

◆ **Entertaining Worthy**
◆ **Can Be Halved**
(see Tips, below)

Tips

If you are halving this recipe, be sure to use a small (1½ to 3 quart) slow cooker.

If you can't find swordfish that is sustainably caught, that is line or harpooned, substitute another firm white fish such as mahi-mahi, grouper or Pacific halibut.

It is hard to be specific about the cooking time as it depends upon the configuration of the steaks (thickness and width). It may take up to 1½ hours.

This is a great dish for entertaining because you can assemble it just before your guests arrive and turn the slow cooker on when they come through the door. By the time everyone is enjoying drinks and nibblies, the conversation is flowing and you're thinking about moving to the table, the fish will be cooked. Serve with a big platter of sautéed spinach or rapini alongside. Add a good dessert and await the praise.

- **Medium to large (3 to 5 quart) oval slow cooker**
- **Large sheet of parchment paper**

2	large swordfish steaks (about 2½ lbs/1.25 kg) patted dry (see Tips, left)	2
1	sweet onion, such as Vidalia, very thinly sliced on the vertical	1
½ cup	finely chopped flat-leaf parsley leaves	125 mL
1 cup	pitted black olives, preferably kalamata, halved	250 mL
2	cloves garlic, minced	2
1 tsp	mild chile powder such as Aleppo, piment d'Espelette or hot paprika	5 mL
½ tsp	sea salt	2 mL
½ cup	extra virgin olive oil	125 mL
1½ cups	dry white wine	375 mL

1. Place swordfish in slow cooker stoneware. Sprinkle with onion, parsley, olives, garlic, chile powder and salt. Pour in olive oil, tipping the stoneware to ensure fish is coated. Pour wine evenly over fish. Place a large piece of parchment paper over the mixture, pressing it down to brush the food and extending up the sides of the stoneware so it overlaps the rim. (This ensures fish is well basted during the cooking process.) Cover and cook until fish flakes easily when pierced with a knife, about 1 hour (see Tips, left).

2. To serve, lift out the parchment and discard, being careful not to spill the accumulated liquid into the stoneware. Lift out fish and cut in half.

Poached Salmon

Serves 6 to 8 as
a main course
or 12 to 15 as
a buffet dish

◆ Entertaining Worthy

Tips

Make sure that the salmon is completely covered with the poaching liquid. If you do not have sufficient liquid, add water to cover.

When the salmon is cooked, it should feel firm to the touch and the skin should peel off easily.

Make Ahead

You can make the poaching liquid before you intend to cook. Cover and refrigerate for up to 2 days.

Although I love salmon cooked almost any way, poaching produces the moistest result. The problem is, successfully poaching a large piece of salmon used to require a fish poacher, a piece of kitchen equipment that was rarely used yet relatively costly and cumbersome to store. A large oval slow cooker is the ideal solution. It produces great results with little fuss. Serve poached salmon, warm or cold, as the focus of an elegant buffet or dinner, attractively garnished with sliced lemon and sprigs of parsley or dill and accompany with favorite sauce or a herb-spiked mayonnaise such as Chive, Tarragon or Dill Paleo Mayo (Variations, page 238).

• Large (minimum 5 quart) oval slow cooker

Poaching Liquid

6 cups	water	1.5 L
1	onion, chopped	1
2	stalks celery, chopped, or 1/2 tsp (2 mL) celery seeds	2
4	sprigs parsley	4
1/2 cup	white wine or freshly squeezed lemon juice	125 mL
8	whole black peppercorns	8
1	bay leaf	1

Salmon

1	fillet of salmon (about 3 lbs/1.5 kg)	1
	Lemon slices	
	Sprigs parsley or dill	
	Paleo Mayo (page 238)	

1. *Poaching Liquid:* In a saucepan over medium heat, combine water, onion, celery, parsley, wine, peppercorns and bay leaf. Bring to a boil and simmer for 30 minutes. Strain and discard solids.

2. *Salmon:* Preheat slow cooker on High for 15 minutes. Fold a 2-foot (60 cm) piece of foil in half lengthwise. Place on bottom and up sides of stoneware, allowing it to overhang the casing a bit. Lay salmon over foil strip. Return poaching liquid to a boil and pour over salmon (see Tips, left). Cover and cook on High for 1 hour. Remove stoneware from slow cooker. Let salmon cool in stoneware for 20 minutes. If serving cold, place stoneware in refrigerator and let salmon chill in liquid. When cold, lift out and transfer to a platter. If serving hot, lift out and transfer to a platter. Garnish with lemon slices and sprigs of parsley and serve with a small bowl of a herb-spiked Paleo Mayo alongside.

Poached Halibut

Serves 6 to 8

◆ Entertaining Worthy
◆ Can Be Halved
(see Tips, below)

Tips

If you are halving this recipe, be sure to use a small (2 to 3½ quart) slow cooker.

The cooking time depends upon the configuration of your fish. The thicker it is, the longer it will take. Start checking for doneness after 1 hour. I've made this using a thick chunk of halibut and it took close to 1½ hours.

This is an elegant dish, perfect for entertaining. The dill mayonnaise is a simple but effective finish.

• **Medium to large (3 to 5 quart) slow cooker**

Poaching Liquid

1	onion, chopped	1
2	stalks celery, including leaves, chopped	2
4	sprigs parsley	4
8	peppercorns	8
1 tsp	coarse sea or kosher salt	5 mL
2	bay leaves	2
6 cups	water	1.5 L
½ cup	white wine or lemon juice	125 mL

Halibut

2 lbs	Pacific halibut fillet	1 kg
	Dill Paleo Mayo (Variations, page 238)	

1. *Poaching Liquid:* In a saucepan, combine onion, celery, parsley, peppercorns, salt, bay leaves, water and wine. Bring to a boil, reduce heat and simmer for 30 minutes. Strain and discard solids.

2. *Halibut:* Preheat slow cooker on High for 15 minutes and add hot poaching liquid. Add halibut. Cover and cook on High about 1 hour and 15 minutes, until fish flakes easily when pierced with a knife (see Tips, left). Using a slotted spoon, transfer fish to a warm platter. Remove and discard bay leaves. Serve warm with Dill Paleo Mayo.

Creamy Coconut Grouper

◆ **Can Be Halved**
(see Tips, below)

Tips

If you are halving this recipe, be sure to use a small (2 to 3½ quart) slow cooker.

If you are using the outer stalks of celery, peel them before chopping; the top layer is very fibrous. The inner stalks (hearts) can be used without peeling.

The potato adds flavor and helps to thicken broth but if you don't eat potatoes, feel free to omit it.

If you prefer, substitute 1½ cups (375 mL) diced peeled butternut squash for the sweet potato.

Make Ahead

Complete Steps 1 and 2. Cover and refrigerate fish and vegetable mixtures separately overnight. When you're ready to cook, continue with the recipe.

The sweet potato (or squash, if you prefer; see Tips, below) in this tasty stew lends an appealing hint of sweetness that is nicely balanced by the spicy cayenne. If you like heat, add a fresh chile along with the coconut milk.

• **Medium to large (3½ to 5 quart) slow cooker**

1 cup	finely chopped cilantro leaves	250 mL
2 tbsp	freshly squeezed lime juice	30 mL
¼ tsp	cayenne pepper	1 mL
2 lbs	skinless grouper fillets, cut into 1-inch (2.5 cm) cubes	1 kg
1 tbsp	extra virgin olive or coconut oil	15 mL
2	onions, finely chopped	2
2	stalks celery, diced (see Tips, left)	2
4	cloves garlic, minced	4
1 tsp	cracked black peppercorns	5 mL
1 tsp	dried oregano	5 mL
½ tsp	sea salt	2 mL
1	can (28 oz/796 mL) diced tomatoes with juice (see page 13)	1
1	potato, peeled and shredded, optional (see Tips, left)	1
1	sweet potato, peeled and cubed (see Tips, left)	1
1 cup	fish or vegetable stock or water	250 mL
1	can (14 oz/400 mL) coconut milk	1
1	long red chile pepper, seeded and minced, optional	1

1. In a bowl, combine cilantro, lime juice, cayenne and grouper. Mix well. Cover and refrigerate until ready to use.

2. In a skillet, heat oil over medium heat. Add onions and celery and cook, stirring, until softened, about 5 minutes. Add garlic, peppercorns, oregano and salt and cook, stirring, for 1 minute. Add tomatoes with juice and bring to a boil.

3. Transfer to slow cooker stoneware. Add potato, if using, sweet potato and fish stock. Cover and cook on Low for 6 hours or on High for 3 hours, until sweet potato is tender. Add grouper mixture, coconut milk, and chile, if using. Cover and cook on High about 10 minutes, until fish flakes easily when pierced with a knife and mixture is hot and bubbly.

Basque-Style Tuna

◆ **Can Be Halved**
(see Tips, below)

Tips

If you are halving this recipe, be sure to use a small (1½ to 3 quart) slow cooker.

Vary the quantity of Espelette to suit your taste. If you don't have hot paprika or piment d'Espelette, try using an equal quantity of sweet paprika with a pinch or two of cayenne.

Look for canned tomatoes that are organically grown, with no salt added, and come in glass jars or BPA (bisphenol-A) free cans. When using canned tomatoes (or any canned product) check to make sure they are gluten-free.

Make Ahead

Complete Steps 1 and 2. Cover and refrigerate fish and vegetable mixtures separately overnight. When you're ready to cook, continue with the recipe.

Like many traditional fish dishes, this classic stew, known as marmitako, *originated with local fishermen, who prepared it on their boats using some of the day's catch. The classic Basque ingredients — tomatoes, garlic and peppers with a hint of piment d'Espelette, a mild red chile pepper from the Basque area of France — are among my favorite combinations.*

• **Medium to large (3½ to 5 quart) slow cooker**

3 tbsp	extra virgin olive oil, divided	45 mL
1 to 2 tsp	piment d'Espelette or hot paprika (see Tips, left)	5 to 10 mL
½ tsp	sea salt	2 mL
1½ lbs	yellowfin tuna, cut into 1-inch (2.5 cm) cubes	750 g
2	onions, thinly sliced on the vertical	2
6	cloves garlic, minced	6
1 tsp	cracked black peppercorns	5 mL
½ cup	dry white wine	125 mL
1	can (14 oz/398 mL) diced tomatoes with juice (see Tips, left)	1
2	potatoes, peeled and shredded (see Tips, page 96)	2
2 cups	fish stock	500 mL
1	green bell pepper, roasted, peeled and cut into strips	1
	Roasted Garlic Aïoli (Variations, page 238)	

1. In a bowl, combine 2 tbsp (30 mL) of the olive oil, piment d'Espelette to taste and salt. Mix well. Add fish and toss to coat. Refrigerate until ready to use.

2. In a skillet, heat remaining tbsp (15 mL) of oil over medium heat. Add onions and cook, stirring, until softened, about 3 minutes. Add garlic and peppercorns and cook, stirring, for 1 minute. Add wine, bring to a boil and boil for 1 minute. Add tomatoes with juice and bring to a boil.

3. Transfer to slow cooker stoneware. Add potatoes and fish stock. Cover and cook on Low for 6 hours or on High for 3 hours. Add reserved tuna and roasted pepper. Cover and cook on High for 5 minutes, until tuna is barely cooked through. To serve, place 1 tbsp (15 mL) Roasted Garlic Aïoli in each warmed bowl and ladle stew over top.

Caribbean Fish Stew

◆ **Entertaining Worthy**
◆ **Can Be Halved**
(see Tips, below)

Tips

If you are halving this recipe, be sure to use a small (2 to 3 quart) slow cooker.

One Scotch bonnet pepper is probably enough for most people, but if you're a heat seeker, use two. You can also use habanero peppers instead.

Because of concerns about the environmental sustainability of some fish and seafood, we recommend that you check reliable sites such as www. montereybayaquarium.org or the Environmental Defense Fund at www.edf.org for the latest information on these products before purchasing.

Make Ahead

Complete Steps 1 and 2. Cover and refrigerate for up to 2 days. When you're ready to cook, complete the recipe.

I love the combination of flavors in this tasty stew. The allspice and the Scotch bonnet peppers add a distinctly island tang. For a distinctive and delicious finish, be sure to include the dill. Serve this with a fresh green salad and some crisp white wine.

• **Medium to large (3½ to 5 quart) slow cooker**

2 tsp	cumin seeds	10 mL
6	whole allspice	6
1 tbsp	extra virgin olive oil	15 mL
2	onions, finely chopped	2
4	cloves garlic, minced	4
2 tsp	dried thyme, crumbled	10 mL
1 tsp	ground turmeric	5 mL
1 tbsp	grated orange or lime zest	15 mL
½ tsp	cracked black peppercorns	2 mL
1	can (28 oz/796 mL) tomatoes with juice, coarsely chopped (see page 13)	1
2 cups	fish stock	500 mL
	Sea salt	
1 to 2	Scotch bonnet peppers, minced (see Tips, left)	1 to 2
2 cups	sliced okra (¼ inch/0.5 cm) (see Tips, page 110)	500 mL
1½ lbs	firm white fish fillets, such as Pacific halibut, turbot or haddock, cut into bite-size pieces (see Tips, left)	750 g
8 oz	shrimp, cooked, peeled and deveined	250 g
½ cup	finely chopped dill fronds, optional	125 mL

1. In a large dry skillet over medium heat, toast cumin seeds and allspice, stirring, until fragrant, about 3 minutes. Immediately transfer to a mortar or a spice grinder and grind. Set aside.

2. In same skillet, heat oil over medium heat. Add onions and cook, stirring, until softened, about 3 minutes. Add garlic, thyme, turmeric, orange zest, peppercorns and reserved cumin and allspice and cook, stirring, for 1 minute. Add tomatoes with juice and fish stock and bring to a boil. Season with salt to taste. Transfer to slow cooker stoneware.

3. Cover and cook on Low for 6 hours or on High for 3 hours. Add chile peppers to taste, okra, fish fillets and shrimp. Cover and cook on High for 20 minutes, until fish flakes easily with a fork and okra is tender. Stir in dill, if using.

Indian-Spiced Salmon with Spinach

Tips

If you are halving this recipe, be sure to use a small (1½ to 3 quart) slow cooker.

For the best flavor, toast and grind cumin and coriander seeds yourself. *To toast seeds:* Place seeds in a dry skillet over medium heat and cook, stirring, until fragrant, about 3 minutes. Using a mortar and pestle or a spice grinder, pound or grind as finely as you can.

Make Ahead

Complete Steps 1 and 2. Cover and refrigerate fish and vegetable mixtures separately overnight. When you're ready to cook, continue with the recipe.

If you're fond of salmon but, like me, in a bit of a rut about how to prepare it, here's a dish that will jolt you out of the doldrums. Salmon marinated in gentle spicing is poached with spinach in a light but flavorful tomato sauce. It's so easy to make you can serve it on weekdays, although it's tasty enough to serve to guests.

- Medium (approx. 3½ quart) slow cooker

2 tbsp	freshly squeezed lemon juice	30 mL
1 tsp	garam masala (see Tips, page 72)	5 mL
¼ tsp	cayenne pepper	1 mL
1½ lbs	salmon fillet, skin removed	750 g
1 tbsp	extra virgin olive oil or ghee	15 mL
2	onions, finely chopped	2
4	cloves garlic, minced	4
1 tbsp	minced gingerroot	15 mL
1 tbsp	ground cumin (see Tips, left)	15 mL
2 tsp	ground coriander	10 mL
1 tsp	salt	5 mL
1 tsp	cracked black peppercorns	5 mL
½ tsp	ground turmeric	2 mL
1	can (28 oz/796 mL) diced tomatoes with juice	1
4 cups	packed chopped spinach leaves	1 L

1. In a bowl, combine lemon juice, garam masala and cayenne. Stir well. Add salmon and toss until well coated with mixture. Cover and refrigerate until ready to use.

2. In a skillet, heat oil over medium heat. Add onions and cook, stirring, until softened, about 3 minutes. Add garlic, ginger, cumin, coriander, salt, peppercorns and turmeric and cook, stirring, for 1 minute. Add tomatoes with juice and bring to a boil.

3. Transfer to slow cooker stoneware. Cover and cook on Low for 6 hours or on High for 3 hours. Working in batches, stir in spinach. Cover and cook on High for 10 minutes. Add reserved salmon with juices. Cover and cook on High about 7 minutes, until fish flakes easily with a fork.

Mediterranean-Style Mahi-Mahi

I love the vibrant flavors of the gremolata used to finish this dish. This is another recipe that is great for entertaining because you can time starting the slow cooker so that the fish will be cooked when your guests are ready to eat. I like to serve this with spinach or Swiss chard.

• **Medium to large (3 to 5 quart) oval slow cooker**

2 lbs	mahi-mahi steaks, patted dry	1 kg
1 tsp	dried oregano	5 mL
1	lemon, thinly sliced	1
1	can (28 oz/796 mL) tomatoes with juice, coarsely chopped (see page 13)	1
½ cup	dry white wine	125 mL
¼ cup	extra virgin olive oil, divided	60 mL
½ tsp	sea salt	2 mL
	Freshly ground black pepper	

Gremolata

½ cup	finely chopped flat-leaf parsley leaves	125 mL
3 tbsp	capers, drained and minced	45 mL
2	whole anchovies, rinsed and finely chopped	2
	Freshly ground black pepper	
	Chopped black olives, optional	

1. Place fish in slow cooker stoneware. Sprinkle with oregano and lay lemon slices evenly over top. In a bowl, combine tomatoes with juice, wine, 2 tbsp (30 mL) of the olive oil, salt and pepper to taste. Pour over fish. Cover and cook on High for 1 hour (see Tips, left), until fish flakes easily when pierced with a knife.

2. *Gremolata:* Meanwhile, in a bowl, combine parsley, capers, anchovies, remaining 2 tbsp (30 mL) of olive oil and pepper to taste. Mix well and set aside in refrigerator until fish is cooked.

3. To serve, transfer fish and tomato sauce to a warm platter. Spoon gremolata evenly over and garnish with olives, if using.

Anchovy-Spiked Peppery Fish Stew

Serves 6

◆ **Entertaining Worthy**
◆ **Can Be Halved**
(see Tips, below)

Tips

If you are halving this recipe, be sure to use a small (2 to 3 quart) slow cooker.

If you prefer, substitute an extra cup (250 mL) of water plus 1 tbsp (15 mL) lemon juice for the white wine.

Look for canned tomatoes that are organically grown, with no salt added, and come in glass jars or BPA (bisphenol-A) free cans. When using canned tomatoes (or any canned product) check to make sure they are gluten-free.

Make Ahead

Complete Step 1. Cover and refrigerate for up to 2 days. When you're ready to cook, complete the recipe.

This is a simple fish stew with an in-your-face finish built around olives, a jalapeño pepper and anchovies. It has great flavor and is different enough to charm jaded taste buds.

• **Medium to large (3½ to 5 quart) slow cooker**

1 tbsp	extra virgin olive oil	15 mL
2	onions, finely chopped	2
1	bulb fennel, cored and diced	1
4	cloves garlic, minced	4
2 tsp	dried Italian seasoning	10 mL
1 tsp	cracked black peppercorns	5 mL
½ tsp	sea salt	2 mL
1 cup	dry white wine (see Tips, left)	250 mL
1	can (28 oz/796 mL) diced tomatoes with juice	1
2 cups	fish stock	500 mL
1½ lbs	firm white fish fillets, such as Pacific halibut, turbot or haddock, cut into bite-size pieces (see Tips, page 98)	750 g
½ cup	black olives, pitted and chopped	125 mL
1	jalapeño pepper, seeded and diced	1
	Anchovy Paleo Mayo (Variations, page 238)	

1. In a skillet, heat oil over medium heat. Add onions and fennel and cook, stirring, until softened, about 5 minutes. Add garlic, Italian seasoning, peppercorns and salt and cook, stirring, for 1 minute. Add wine, bring to a boil and boil for 2 minutes. Add tomatoes with juice and bring to a boil.

2. Transfer to slow cooker stoneware. Add fish stock. Cover and cook on Low for 6 hours or on High for 3 hours. Add fish, olives and jalapeño and stir well. Cover and cook on High about 7 minutes, until fish is cooked through.

3. To serve, place about 1 tbsp (15 mL) Anchovy Paleo Mayo in the bottom of each warmed soup plate. Ladle stew into soup plates and serve.

Spanish-Style Fish Stew

Serves 6

• **Entertaining Worthy**
• **Can Be Halved**
  (see Tips, below)

Tips

If you are halving this recipe, be sure to use a small (1½ to 3 quart) slow cooker.

My butcher uses only naturally raised meat and makes his sausage on-site so I know it doesn't contain gluten or any undesirable additives. If you are using commercially prepared sausage, check the label. Some brands contain gluten.

Chorizo comes in various degrees of spiciness. I prefer the hot version in this recipe, but use the one that suits your taste.

If you prefer, substitute an extra cup (250 mL) of water plus 1 tbsp (15 mL) lemon juice for the white wine.

The potatoes add flavor and help to thicken broth but if you don't eat potatoes, feel free to omit them.

Make Ahead

Complete Step 1. Cover mixture, ensuring it cools promptly (see Making Ahead, page 21), and refrigerate for up to 2 days. When you're ready to cook, complete the recipe.

Enlivened by the addition of spicy chorizo sausage and oh-so-good-for-you kale, this dish is easy to make but has the impact of a special occasion dish.

• **Medium to large (3½ to 5 quart) slow cooker**

1 tbsp	extra virgin olive oil	15 mL
1 lb	soft chorizo sausage, removed from casings (see Tips, left)	500 g
2	onions, thinly sliced on the vertical	2
2	stalks celery, diced	2
4	cloves garlic, minced	4
1 tsp	cracked black peppercorns	5 mL
½ tsp	sea salt	2 mL
2	bay leaves	2
1 cup	dry white wine (see Tips, left)	250 mL
4 cups	fish stock	1 L
2	potatoes, peeled and shredded, optional (see Tips, left)	2
1 tsp	smoked paprika	5 mL
4 cups	coarsely chopped kale	1 L
1½ lbs	firm white fish fillets, such as Pacific halibut, turbot or haddock, cut into bite-size pieces (see Tips, page 98)	750 g
	Rouille (page 106) or Roasted Garlic Aïoli (Variation, page 238), optional	

1. In a skillet, heat oil over medium heat. Add chorizo, onions and celery and cook, stirring, until meat is cooked, about 7 minutes. Add garlic, peppercorns, salt and bay leaves and cook, stirring, for 1 minute. Add wine, bring to a boil and boil for 2 minutes. Transfer to slow cooker stoneware.

2. Add fish stock and potatoes, if using. Cover and cook on Low for 6 hours or on High for 3 hours, until potatoes are almost dissolving into the sauce. Stir in paprika and kale.

3. Cover and cook on High for 15 minutes. Stir in fish. Cover and cook on High about 7 minutes, until cooked through. Remove and discard bay leaves. Ladle stew into warmed soup plates and serve immediately. If using rouille or aïoli, place 1 tbsp (15 mL) in the bottom of each warmed soup plate and ladle the soup over it.

Manhattan Clam Chowder

◆ Can Be Halved
(see Tips, below)

Tips

If you are halving this recipe, be sure to use a small (1½ to 3 quart) slow cooker.

If you prefer, substitute an extra cup (250 mL) of water plus 1 tbsp (15 mL) lemon juice for the white wine.

To clean clams, scrub thoroughly with a wire brush and soak in several changes of cold salted water.

Make Ahead

This dish can be partially prepared before it is cooked. Complete Steps 1 and 2. Cover and refrigerate broth for up to 2 days. When you're ready to cook, continue with the recipe.

Manhattan clam chowder is appealing because it is a lighter alternative to traditional New England-style chowder, which is loaded with dairy. However, I find that its tomato-based broth often seems harsh. The solution is to add a touch of creaminess with the addition of mayonnaise. This creates a chowder with the zest of Manhattan and the creamy smoothness of New England — the best of both worlds.

• Medium to large (3½ to 6 quart) slow cooker

4	slices bacon	4
2	onions, finely chopped	2
2	stalks celery, thinly sliced	2
1	can (28 oz/796 mL) tomatoes, including juice, chopped	1
2 cups	fish stock	500 mL
1 cup	dry white wine (see Tips, left)	250 mL
2	potatoes, diced	2
2½ lbs	clams, cleaned	1.25 kg
	Finely chopped flat-leaf parsley leaves	
	Paleo Mayo (page 238)	

1. In a skillet, cook bacon over medium-high heat until crisp. Drain well on paper towel and crumble. Cover and refrigerate until ready to use.

2. Reduce heat to medium. Add onions and celery to pan and cook, stirring, until softened, about 5 minutes. Add tomatoes with juice, fish stock and wine and bring to boil. Transfer to slow cooker stoneware.

3. Add potatoes and stir well. Cover and cook on Low for 6 hours or on High for 3 hours, until potatoes are tender.

4. Discard any clams that are open. In a large saucepan over medium-high heat, bring ½ cup (125 mL) water to a rapid boil. Add clams, cover and cook, shaking the pot until all the clams open. Discard any that do not open. Strain cooking liquid through a fine sieve into a bowl. Using a fork, remove clam meat from shells.

5. Add clam cooking liquid and meat to slow cooker along with reserved bacon. Cover and cook on High for 15 minutes, until heated through. Ladle soup into bowls and garnish liberally with parsley. Top each bowl with a dollop of Paleo Mayo.

New World Bouillabaisse

◆ **Entertaining Worthy**
◆ **Can Be Halved**
(see Tips, below)

Tips

If you're halving this recipe, be sure to use a small (1½ to 3 quart) slow cooker.

To toast fennel seeds: Place seeds in a dry skillet over medium heat, stirring, until fragrant, about 3 minutes. Immediately transfer to a mortar or a spice grinder and grind.

If you don't want to use potatoes, substitute 2 additional diced carrots and 2 stalks of celery, thinly sliced.

If you don't have fresh thyme, you can use ½ tsp (2 mL) dried thyme. Add it to the recipe in Step 2, along with the garlic.

Traditional bouillabaisse contains a wide variety of Mediterranean fish, which leads many to conclude that it can only be made in proximity to the Mediterranean Sea. But in my opinion, this elevates the dish to a status that defies its origins. Bouillabaisse was originally a one-pot meal fishermen made from their daily catch. This simple stew is distinguished by the inclusion of saffron, and a rapid reduction of the broth, which intensifies the flavor and emulsifies the olive oil. Serve this delicious meal-in-a bowl in soup plates followed by a simple salad and fresh fruit for dessert.

- **Large (minimum 5 quart) slow cooker**
- **Large square of cheesecloth**
- **Food processor**

3 tbsp	extra virgin olive oil, divided	45 mL
1 tsp	fennel seeds, toasted and ground (see Tips, left)	5 mL
1 lb	medium shrimp, peeled and deveined	500 g
1 lb	halibut, cut into 1-inch (2.5 cm) cubes	500 g
2	onions, chopped	2
2	carrots, peeled and diced	2
1	large bulb fennel, cored and thinly sliced on the vertical	1
6	cloves garlic, minced	6
½ tsp	sea salt	2 mL
½ tsp	cracked black peppercorns	2 mL
1	can (28 oz/796 mL) diced tomatoes with juice (see page 13)	1
2	potatoes, peeled and diced (see Tips, left)	2
4 cups	water	1 L
2 cups	dry white wine	500 mL
2 lbs	fish trimmings (non oily fish)	1 kg
4	sprigs parsley	4
2	sprigs thyme (see Tips, left)	2
2	bay leaves	2
1 tsp	saffron threads dissolved in 1 tbsp (15 mL) boiling water	5 mL
24	mussels, cleaned	24

Rouille

¼ cup	Paleo Mayo (page 238)	60 mL
1	roasted red pepper, peeled and chopped (see Tip, right)	1
2	cloves garlic, minced	2
Pinch	cayenne pepper	Pinch

Tip

To roast peppers: Preheat oven to 400°F (200°C). Place pepper(s) on a baking sheet and roast, turning two or three times, until skin on all sides is blackened, about 25 minutes. Transfer pepper(s) to a heatproof bowl. Cover with a plate and let stand until cool. Remove and, using a sharp knife, lift skins off. Discard skins and slice according to recipe instructions.

Make Ahead

Complete Steps 1 and 2. Cover and refrigerate fish and tomato mixtures separately overnight. The next morning, continue with the recipe. You can also make the rouille the night before you plan to cook.

1. In a bowl, combine 2 tbsp (30 mL) of the olive oil and toasted fennel. Add shrimp and halibut and toss until coated. Cover and refrigerate, stirring occasionally, for 2 hours or overnight.

2. In a skillet, heat remaining oil over medium heat. Add onions, carrots and fennel and cook, stirring, until carrots are softened, about 7 minutes. Add garlic, salt and peppercorns and cook, stirring, for 1 minute. Add tomatoes with juice and bring to a boil.

3. Transfer to slow cooker stoneware. Add potatoes, water and wine and stir well. In a large square of cheesecloth, tie fish trimmings, parsley, thyme and bay leaves. Place in stoneware, ensuring all or most is submerged in the sauce. Cover and cook on Low for 8 hours or on High for 4 hours, until vegetables are very tender. Remove package of fish trimmings and discard.

4. Place a colander over a large saucepan and add the soup. Transfer solids to food processor and purée. Bring liquids in saucepan to a boil over medium-high heat and cook until reduced by about one-third, about 10 minutes. Add dissolved saffron and mussels and cook for 5 minutes, until mussels open. Discard any mussels that do not open. Add marinated shrimp and halibut and cook until fish is tender. Add reserved puréed solids and heat until heated through.

5. *Rouille:* In a food processor fitted with the metal blade (a mini bowl attachment is ideal), process mayonnaise, red pepper, garlic and cayenne until smooth. To serve, place about 1 tbsp (15 mL) rouille in the bottom of each warmed soup plate and ladle the soup over it.

Portuguese Pork and Clams

Serves 6

◆ Entertaining Worthy
◆ Can Be Halved
(see Tips, below)

Tips

If you are halving this recipe, use a small (approx. 2 to 3 quart) slow cooker.

If you can't find acceptable chorizo (gluten-free), substitute 1 lb (500 g) trimmed pork shoulder or blade (butt) cut into 1-inch (2.5 cm) cubes and patted dry. Add minced seeded chile pepper, to taste, along with the bell pepper.

Scrub clams thoroughly with a wire brush and soak in several changes of cold salted water. Discard any clams that are open.

To cook shrimp: Immerse shrimp, in shells, in a large pot of boiling salted water. Cook over high heat, until the shells turn pink, 2 to 3 minutes. Let cool, then peel and devein.

Make Ahead

Complete Step 1. Cover and refrigerate for up to 2 days. When you're ready to cook, continue with the recipe.

This robust Portuguese-inspired dish is easy to make, yet produces impressive results. I like to serve this with a big green salad and a crisp white wine.

• Large (approx. 5 quart) slow cooker

1 lb	fresh chorizo sausage, removed from casings (see Tips, left)	500 g
4	stalks celery, thinly sliced	4
1	onion, finely chopped	1
4	cloves garlic, minced	4
1 tsp	saffron threads, soaked in 1 tbsp (15 mL) boiling water, optional	5 mL
1/4 tsp	sea salt	1 mL
1/4 tsp	cracked black peppercorns	1 mL
1	can (14 oz/398 mL) diced tomatoes with juice (see page 13)	1
2 cups	dry white wine	500 mL
1/2 cup	water	125 mL
12	small clams, cleaned (see Tips, left)	12
1	green bell pepper, finely chopped	1
1 lb	medium shrimp, cooked, peeled and deveined (see Tips, left)	500 g
1 tsp	sweet, hot or smoked paprika	5 mL
	Finely chopped flat-leaf parsley leaves	

1. In a skillet over medium heat, cook chorizo, celery and onion, stirring and breaking meat up with a spoon, until sausage is no longer pink, about 10 minutes. Add garlic, saffron, if using, salt and peppercorns and cook, stirring, for 1 minute. Using a slotted spoon, transfer to slow cooker stoneware.

2. Stir in tomatoes with juice, wine and water. Cover and cook on Low for 6 hours or on High for 3 hours, until hot and bubbly.

3. About 40 minutes before you intend to serve this dish, scoop out about 1/2 cup (125 mL) of cooking liquid from stew. Place in a large saucepan over medium-high heat and bring to a rapid boil. Add clams, cover and cook, shaking the pot until all open. Discard any that do not open.

4. Meanwhile, stir bell pepper, shrimp and paprika into stoneware. Cover and cook on High for 20 minutes, until peppers are softened and shrimp are heated through. Add hot clams with liquid and stir well. Ladle into large bowls and garnish with parsley.

Coconut Shrimp Curry

Serves 4

◆ **Can Be Halved**
(see Tips, below)

Tips

If you are halving this recipe, be sure to use a small (1½ to 3 quart) slow cooker.

For the best flavor, toast and grind coriander and cumin seeds yourself. *To toast seeds:* Place seeds in a dry skillet over medium heat and cook, stirring, until fragrant, about 3 minutes. Using a mortar and pestle or a spice grinder, pound or grind as finely as you can.

To make shrimp stock: In a saucepan, combine shrimp shells, 1 cup (250 mL) white wine and 1 cup (250 mL) water. Bring to a boil, reduce heat and simmer for 15 minutes. Strain, pushing the shells against the sieve to extract as much flavor as possible. Measure 1 cup (250 mL). Freeze excess.

Make Ahead

Complete Steps 1 and 2. Cover and refrigerate shrimp, stock and vegetable mixtures separately overnight. When you're ready to cook, continue with the recipe.

This is one of my favorite Friday night dinners.

- **Medium (approx. 3½ quart) slow cooker**

1 lb	shrimp, peeled and deveined, shells set aside	500 g
2 tbsp	freshly squeezed lemon juice	30 mL
2 tsp	ground coriander (see Tips, left)	10 mL
1 tsp	ground cumin	5 mL
½ tsp	coarse sea salt	2 mL
½ tsp	ground turmeric	2 mL
¼ tsp	cayenne pepper	1 mL
1 tbsp	extra virgin olive or coconut oil	15 mL
2	onions, finely chopped	2
2	stalks celery, diced	2
4	cloves garlic, minced	4
2 tbsp	minced gingerroot	30 mL
1 tsp	cracked black peppercorns	5 mL
½ tsp	sea salt	2 mL
1	can (14 oz/398 mL) crushed tomatoes (see page 13)	1
1 cup	shrimp stock (see Tips, left)	250 mL
1 cup	coconut milk	250 mL
1	green bell pepper, seeded and diced	1
1	long red or green chile pepper, seeded and minced, optional	1
1 to 2 tbsp	clarified butter	15 to 30 mL

1. In a small bowl, combine shrimp, lemon juice, coriander, cumin, salt, turmeric and cayenne. Stir well, cover and refrigerate. Make shrimp stock (see Tips, left).

2. In a skillet, heat oil over medium heat. Add onions and celery and cook, stirring, until softened, about 5 minutes. Add garlic, ginger, peppercorns and salt and cook, stirring, for 1 minute. Add tomatoes and bring to a boil.

3. Transfer to slow cooker stoneware. Stir in shrimp stock. Cover and cook on Low for 6 hours or on High for 3 hours, until hot and bubbly. Stir in coconut milk, bell pepper, and chile pepper, if using. Cover and cook on High for 15 minutes, until pepper is tender.

4. Meanwhile, in a large skillet over medium-high heat, heat 1 tbsp (15 mL) clarified butter. Add shrimp and marinade, in batches, if necessary, and sauté until shrimp turn pink and seize up, about 3 minutes, adding more butter as necessary. Transfer to slow cooker stoneware. Cover and cook on High for 5 minutes, to meld flavors.

Down-Home Shrimp

Serves 4

◆ **Entertaining Worthy**
◆ **Can Be Halved**
(see Tips, below)

Tips

If you are halving this recipe, be sure to use a small (1½ to 3 quart) slow cooker.

Okra, a tropical vegetable, has a great flavor but it becomes unpleasantly sticky when overcooked. Choose young okra pods, 2 to 4 inches (5 to 10 cm) long, that don't feel sticky to the touch. (If sticky they are too ripe.) Gently scrub the pods and cut off the top and tail before slicing.

To make shrimp stock:
In a saucepan, combine shrimp shells, white wine and water. Bring to a boil, reduce heat and simmer for 15 minutes. Strain, pushing the shells against the sieve to extract as much flavor as possible. Measure 1 cup (250 mL) and set aside. Freeze excess.

Make Ahead

Complete Steps 1 and 2. Cover and refrigerate shrimp, shrimp stock and vegetable mixture separately, overnight. When you're ready to cook, continue with the recipe.

Here's a dish, Cajun-inspired, that packs just a hint of heat and yields a great sense of freshness. It makes a great one-pot meal.

• **Medium (approx. 3½ quart) slow cooker**

1 lb	shrimp, peeled and deveined, shells reserved	500 g
2 tbsp	freshly squeezed lemon juice	30 mL
¼ tsp	cayenne pepper	1 mL
1 cup	dry white wine	250 mL
1 cup	water	250 mL
2 tbsp	extra virgin olive oil	30 mL
1	onion, finely chopped	1
2	stalks celery, peeled and diced	2
1 tsp	cracked black peppercorns	5 mL
½ tsp	sea salt	2 mL
½ tsp	dried thyme	2 mL
2	bay leaves	2
1	can (14 oz/398 mL) diced tomatoes with juice (see page 13)	1
1 cup	shrimp stock (see Tips, left)	250 mL
2 cups	thinly sliced okra (see Tips, left)	500 mL
1 cup	corn kernels (see page 15)	250 mL
1	red or green bell pepper, seeded and diced	1
2 tbsp	clarified butter	30 mL
2	cloves garlic, minced	2

1. In a small bowl, combine shrimp, lemon juice and cayenne. Stir well, cover and refrigerate until ready to use.

2. In a skillet, heat oil over medium heat. Add onion and celery and cook, stirring, until softened, about 5 minutes. Add peppercorns, salt, thyme and bay leaves and cook, stirring, for 1 minute. Add tomatoes with juice and bring to a boil.

3. Transfer to slow cooker stoneware. Stir in shrimp stock. Cover and cook on Low for 6 hours or on High for 3 hours. Stir in okra, corn and bell pepper. Cover and cook on High for 20 minutes, until okra is tender. Remove and discard bay leaves.

4. When you are ready to serve, heat 1 tbsp (15 mL) of the clarified butter in a small skillet over medium heat. Add garlic and cook, stirring, for 1 minute. Increase heat to medium-high. Using a slotted spoon, immediately add reserved shrimp, in batches, and cook, stirring, until they turn pink, adding remaining butter as necessary. Transfer to slow cooker as completed. Add marinade juices to pan and cook, stirring, for 1 minute. Add to slow cooker, stir well and serve.

Red Chowder with Fennel

◆ **Can Be Halved**
(see Tips, below)

Tips

If you are halving this recipe, be sure to use a small (1½ to 3 quart) slow cooker.

The fennel flavor in this chowder is pleasantly light. If you prefer a stronger licorice hit, add ½ tsp (2 mL) crushed fennel seeds along with the peppercorns.

The potato adds flavor and thickness to the broth but if you don't eat potatoes, feel free to omit it.

To clean clams, scrub thoroughly with a wire brush and soak in several changes of cold salted water.

Make Ahead

Complete Steps 1 and 2. Cover and refrigerate bacon and vegetable mixtures separately for up to 2 days. When you're ready to cook, complete the recipe.

This is a particularly tasty spin on classic Manhattan clam chowder, a little lighter on tomato than the norm and enhanced with the addition of fennel (see Tips, left). It makes a great weeknight dinner served with a simple salad.

• **Medium to large (3½ to 5 quart) slow cooker**

4 oz	chunk bacon, diced	125 g
2	onions, diced	2
1	bulb fennel, cored and diced (see Tips, left)	1
2	cloves garlic, minced	2
1 tsp	dried thyme	5 mL
½ tsp	sea salt	2 mL
½ tsp	cracked black peppercorns	2 mL
2	bay leaves	2
1 cup	dry white wine (see Tips, page 104)	250 mL
1	can (28 oz/796 mL) diced tomatoes with juice (see page 13)	1
2 cups	Fish Stock (page 61) or Vegetable Stock (page 58)	500 mL
1	potato, peeled and shredded, optional (see Tips, left)	1
3 lbs	small clams, cleaned (see Tips, left)	1.5 kg
½ cup	finely chopped flat-leaf parsley leaves	125 mL

1. In a skillet, cook bacon over medium-high heat until crisp. Drain well on paper towel, cover and refrigerate until ready to use. Reduce heat to medium. Add onions and fennel to pan and cook, stirring, until softened, about 5 minutes. Add garlic, thyme, salt, peppercorns and bay leaves and cook, stirring, for 1 minute. Add wine, bring to a boil and boil for 2 minutes. Add tomatoes with juice and return to a boil.

2. Transfer to slow cooker stoneware. Stir in stock and potato, if using. Cover and cook on Low for 6 hours or on High for 3 hours, until potato is almost falling apart.

3. Discard any clams that are open. In a large saucepan over medium-high heat, bring 1 cup (250 mL) water to a rapid boil. Add clams, cover and cook, shaking the pot, until all the clams open. Discard any that do not open. Strain cooking liquid through a fine sieve into a bowl. Using a fork, remove clam meat from shells. Add clam cooking liquid and meat to slow cooker, along with reserved bacon. Cover and cook on High for 15 minutes, until heated through. Remove and discard bay leaves. Ladle soup into bowls and garnish with parsley.

Caribbean Pepper Pot

◆ **Can Be Halved**
(see Tips, below)

Tips

If you are halving this recipe, be sure to use a small (2 to 3½ quart) slow cooker.

Callaloo, also known as pigweed or amaranth leaves, is becoming increasingly available in greengrocers. Also look for it in farmers' markets.

To cook shrimp: Immerse shrimp, in shells, in a large pot of boiling salted water. Cook over high heat, until the shells turn pink, 2 to 3 minutes. Let cool, then peel and devein.

If you are using large shrimp, chop them into bite-size pieces before adding to the stew.

Only use a second habanero pepper if you are a true heat seeker.

Make Ahead

Complete Step 1. Cover and refrigerate for up to 2 days. When you're ready to cook, continue with the recipe.

There are two dishes known as pepper pot — one that apparently originated during the American revolutionary war and a Caribbean version. Although both are traditionally based on ingredients the cook has on hand, the results are very different. The original version of Philadelphia pepper pot included tripe and black peppercorns, but in the islands the dish contains a hodgepodge of local ingredients, including incendiary Scotch bonnet peppers and leafy green callaloo. It is often finished with coconut milk, producing a nicely spicy and lusciously creamy stew.

• **Large (approx. 5 quart) slow cooker**

1 tbsp	extra virgin olive or coconut oil	15 mL
3	onions, thinly sliced on the vertical	3
4	cloves garlic, minced	4
2 tbsp	minced gingerroot	30 mL
1 tsp	cracked black peppercorns	5 mL
1 tsp	ground allspice	5 mL
½ tsp	sea salt	2 mL
½ tsp	dried thyme	2 mL
2	bay leaves	2
1	can (14 oz/398 mL) diced tomatoes with juice (see page 13)	1
2 cups	chicken stock	500 mL
4 cups	cubed (1 inch/2.5 cm) butternut squash (about 1)	1 L
1 lb	skinless boneless chicken thighs, cut into 1-inch (2.5 cm) cubes	500 g
4 cups	chopped kale or callaloo (see Tips, left)	1 L
1 lb	cooked, peeled deveined shrimp (see Tips, left)	500 g
1 to 2	diced habanero or Scotch bonnet chile peppers (see Tips, left)	1 to 2
1 cup	coconut milk	250 mL

1. In a skillet, heat oil over medium heat. Add onions and cook, stirring, until softened, about 3 minutes. Add garlic, ginger, peppercorns, allspice, salt, thyme and bay leaves and cook, stirring, for 1 minute. Stir in tomatoes with juice and stock and bring to a boil. Boil for 1 minute.

2. Transfer to slow cooker stoneware. Stir in squash and chicken. Cover and cook on Low for 6 hours or on High for 3 hours, until chicken is no longer pink. Working in batches, stir in kale. Add shrimp, chile peppers to taste and coconut milk. Cover and cook on High for about 20 minutes, until kale is wilted and flavors meld. Remove and discard bay leaves.

South American-Style Shrimp Chowder

◆ **Entertaining Worthy**
◆ **Can Be Halved**
(see Tips, below)

Tips

If you are halving this recipe, be sure to use a small (1½ to 3 quart) slow cooker.

This is fairly substantial chowder, but you could serve small bowls as a prelude to a special meal.

If you are using large shrimp, cut them into thirds after peeling. Smaller shrimp should be halved.

If you are using the outer stalks of celery, peel them before chopping; the top layer is very fibrous. The inner stalks (hearts) can be used without peeling.

The potato adds flavor and a bit of heft to the broth but if you don't eat potatoes, feel free to omit it.

Although I've taken more than a few liberties with the concept, this hearty and delicious meal-in-a-bowl was inspired by chupe, *a Peruvian shrimp chowder.*

• **Medium to large (3½ to 5 quart) slow cooker**

1 lb	peeled deveined shrimp, shells reserved (see Tips, left)	500 g
2 tbsp	freshly squeezed lime juice	30 mL
1 tbsp	chili powder (see Tip, page 172)	15 mL
1 tsp	coarse sea salt	5 mL
1 tsp	cracked black peppercorns	5 mL
1½ cups	dry white wine	375 mL
1½ cups	water	375 mL
2 tbsp	extra virgin olive oil or coconut oil, divided	30 mL
2	onions, finely chopped	2
2	stalks celery, diced (see Tips, left)	2
4	cloves garlic, minced	4
2 tsp	finely grated lime zest	10 mL
½ tsp	sea salt	2 mL
2 tbsp	tomato paste (see page 13) or ¼ cup (60 mL) chopped reconstituted sun-dried tomatoes	30 mL
1	can (14 oz/398 mL) diced tomatoes with juice (see page 13)	1
1	potato, peeled and shredded, optional (see Tips, left)	1
2	roasted red peppers, diced	2
1	jalapeño pepper, seeded and diced	1
2 cups	sweet corn kernels (see page 15)	500 mL
1 cup	coconut milk	250 mL
	Finely chopped cilantro leaves	

1. In a bowl, combine shrimp, lime juice, chile powder, salt and peppercorns. Stir well. Cover and refrigerate until ready to use.

2. Meanwhile, make shrimp stock. In a saucepan, combine shrimp shells, white wine and water. Bring to a boil, reduce heat and simmer for 15 minutes. Strain, pushing the shells against the sieve to extract as much flavor as possible. Measure 2 cups (500 mL) and set aside. Freeze excess.

Make Ahead

Complete Steps 1, 2 and 3. Cover and refrigerate shrimp, shrimp stock and vegetable mixtures separately overnight. When you're ready to cook, continue with the recipe.

3. In a skillet, heat 1 tbsp (15 mL) of the oil over medium heat. Add onions and celery and cook, stirring, until softened, about 5 minutes. Add garlic, lime zest and salt and cook, stirring, for 1 minute. Stir in tomato paste. Add tomatoes with juice and bring to a boil.

4. Transfer to slow cooker stoneware. Add potato, if using, and reserved shrimp stock. Cover and cook on Low for 6 hours or on High for 3 hours, until hot and bubbly. Stir in red peppers, jalapeño, corn kernels and coconut milk. Cover and cook on High for 15 minutes, until corn is tender.

5. Meanwhile, in a skillet, heat remaining oil over medium-high heat. Add shrimp, in batches, if necessary, and cook, stirring, until they turn pink. Add to stoneware and stir well. Serve chowder garnished with cilantro.

Coconut Oil

Coconut oil is a stable fat that is good for cooking over relatively high heat. It does have a pronounced coconut taste, so I save it for dishes with complementary flavor profiles. For decades, coconut oil was dismissed as unhealthy because of its high saturated fat content. However, researchers are now beginning to recognize that coconut oil has many health benefits, including the ability to boost HDL (good) cholesterol. The saturated fat in coconut oil is known as a medium-chain triglyceride, which means it is less likely to be stored in the body as fat. Coconut oil also contains lauric acid (a component of mother's milk), which has many healthful properties.

Mussels in Lemongrass Tomato Broth

Serves 4 as a main course or 6 as a starter

◆ Entertaining Worthy
◆ Can Be Halved
(see Tips, below)

Tips

If you are halving this recipe, be sure to use a small (1½ to 3 quart) slow cooker.

Farmed mussels are very clean and only need to be thoroughly rinsed under water before use in this recipe. If the mussels are not farmed, they will need to be carefully scrubbed with a wire brush under cold running water. Any fibrous beard should be trimmed with a sharp knife. The mussels should be tightly closed, or they should close when you tap them. If not, discard before cooking. Discard any that do not open after they are cooked.

Make Ahead

This dish can be partially prepared before it is cooked. Complete Step 1. Cover and refrigerate broth for up to 2 days. When you're ready to cook, continue with the recipe.

This is a variation of a recipe that appeared in New World Noodles *by Bill Jones and Stephen Wong. I particularly enjoy the unusual and slightly Indonesian flavors of the delicious broth. This works equally well as the centerpiece of a light meal or as a dramatic first course.*

• **Medium to large (3½ to 6 quart) slow cooker**

1 tbsp	extra virgin coconut oil	15 mL
1	onion, finely chopped	1
2	cloves garlic, minced	2
1 tsp	gingerroot, minced	5 mL
1 tsp	whole coriander seeds	5 mL
1	piece (2 inches/5 cm) cinnamon stick	1
1	stalk lemongrass, coarsely chopped	1
½ tsp	sea salt	2 mL
½ tsp	whole black peppercorns	2 mL
1	can (28 oz/796 mL) tomatoes, including juice, chopped	1
2 cups	fish or vegetable stock	500 mL
3 lbs	mussels, cleaned (see Tips, left)	1.5 kg
	Finely chopped cilantro	
	Hot Pepper Sauce (page 240), optional	

1. In a skillet, heat oil over medium heat for 30 seconds. Add onion and cook, stirring, until softened, about 3 minutes. Add garlic, ginger, coriander seeds, cinnamon stick, lemongrass, salt and peppercorns and cook, stirring, for 1 minute. Add tomatoes with juice and fish stock and bring to a boil. Transfer to slow cooker stoneware.

2. Cover and cook on Low for 6 to 8 hours or on High for 3 to 4 hours, until broth is flavorful. Strain broth through a fine-mesh strainer into a large saucepan, pressing out liquid with a wooden spoon. Discard solids.

3. Bring broth to a boil. Add mussels, cover and cook until mussels open. Discard any that do not open. Ladle mussels and broth into bowls, garnish with cilantro and serve. Pass hot pepper sauce, if desired.

Southwestern Brisket

Beef and Veal

Southwestern Brisket

Serves 6 to 8

◆ **Entertaining Worthy**
◆ **Can Be Halved**
(see Tips, below)

Tips

If you are halving this recipe, be sure to use a small (2 to 3½ quart) slow cooker. Reduce cooking time to about 6 hours on Low or 3 hours on High.

If the whole piece of brisket won't fit in your slow cooker, cut it in half and lay the two pieces on top of each other.

If you are using the outer stalks of celery, peel them before slicing to remove the fibrous exterior.

For the best flavor, toast and grind cumin seeds yourself. *To toast cumin:* Place seeds in a dry skillet over medium heat and cook, stirring, until fragrant, about 3 minutes. Immediately transfer to a spice grinder or mortar and grind.

Add the jalapeño peppers, if you like heat.

Make Ahead

Complete Step 2. Cover and refrigerate mixture for up to 2 days. When you're ready to cook, complete the recipe.

Juicy and full of flavor, brisket is tender and delicious and lends itself to a wide variety of sauces and seasonings. This version, which relies on New Mexico chiles for its rich, tangy taste, is mildly piquant.

• **Large (approx. 5 quart) slow cooker**
• **Blender**

2 tbsp	clarified butter, beef tallow or pure lard, divided	30 mL
4 lbs	double beef brisket, trimmed (see Tips, left)	2 kg
2	onions, thinly sliced	2
6	stalks celery, thinly sliced (see Tips, left)	6
6	cloves garlic, minced	6
1 tbsp	dried oregano	15 mL
1 tbsp	ground cumin (see Tips, left)	15 mL
1 tbsp	cracked black peppercorns	15 mL
½ tsp	sea salt	2 mL
2	bay leaves	2
2 cups	tomato sauce (see page 13)	500 mL
1 cup	beef stock	250 mL
¼ cup	coconut sugar	60 mL
2 tbsp	red wine vinegar (see page 15)	30 mL
2	dried New Mexico chile peppers	2
2 cups	boiling water	500 mL
1 to 2	jalapeño pepper, quartered, optional (see Tips, left)	1 to 2
2	green bell peppers, thinly sliced	2
½ cup	finely chopped flat-leaf parsley leaves	125 mL

1. In a large skillet, heat 1 tbsp (15 mL) of the clarified butter over medium-high heat. Brown brisket on both sides and place in slow cooker stoneware.

2. Reduce heat to medium and add remaining tbsp (15 mL) of butter to the pan. Add onions and celery and cook, stirring, until softened, about 5 minutes. Add garlic, oregano, cumin, peppercorns, sea salt and bay leaves and cook, stirring, for 1 minute. Add tomato sauce, stock, coconut sugar and vinegar and stir well.

3. Transfer to stoneware. Cover and cook on Low for 8 hours or on High for 4 hours, until brisket is very tender.

4. About an hour before you're ready to serve, in a heatproof bowl, soak New Mexico chiles in boiling water for 30 minutes. Drain, discarding soaking liquid and stems. Transfer to a blender and add approximately 1 cup (250 mL) of the brisket cooking liquid along with jalapeño peppers, if using. Purée. Add to brisket along with bell peppers. Cover and cook on High for an additional 30 minutes, until bell peppers are tender. Discard bay leaves. To serve, slice brisket thinly and place on a deep platter. Spoon sauce over and garnish liberally with parsley.

Braised Brisket with Chile Gravy

Serves 8

◆ **Can Be Halved**
(see Tips, below)

Tips

If you are halving this recipe, be sure to use a small (2½ to 3½ quart) slow cooker. Reduce cooking time to about 6 hours on Low or 3 hours on High.

Vary the quantity of chiles to suit your level of tolerance for heat. They are all on the mild end of the Scoville scale.

Many people feel that brisket improves in flavor if it is made ahead and reheated. If you prefer to follow this method, complete Steps 1 through 3. Cover and refrigerate overnight or for up to 2 days. Skim off accumulated fat, slice brisket and place in Dutch oven. Spoon off about 1 cup (250 mL) of the liquid and place in a blender. Add cilantro and chiles and purée. Add to Dutch oven along with remaining sauce. Reheat on stove top over medium-low heat until hot and bubbly. Serve immediately.

Make Ahead

Complete Step 2. Cover and refrigerate for up to 2 days. When you're ready to cook, complete the recipe.

Brisket with Mexican overtones is a marriage made in heaven.

- **Large (approx. 5 quart) slow cooker**
- **Blender**

2 tbsp	clarified butter or pure lard, divided	30 mL
4 to 5 lbs	double beef brisket, trimmed (see Tips, page 120)	2 to 2.5 kg
2	onions, thinly sliced on the vertical	2
4	stalks celery, diced (see Tips, 120)	4
6	cloves garlic, minced	6
1 tbsp	ground cumin (see Tips, page 120)	15 mL
2 tsp	dried oregano	10 mL
1	piece (2 inches/5 cm) cinnamon stick	1
1 tsp	cracked black peppercorns	5 mL
½ tsp	sea salt	2 mL
1	can (28 oz/796 mL) tomatoes with juice	1
1 cup	chicken stock	250 mL
3 to 4	dried ancho, New Mexico or guajillo chiles (see Tips, left)	3 to 4
2 cups	boiling water	500 mL
1 cup	cilantro, stems and leaves	250 mL
1	jalapeño pepper, seeded and diced, optional	1
1	green bell pepper, diced	1

1. In a large skillet, heat 1 tbsp (15 mL) of the butter over medium-high heat. Add brisket and brown well on both sides, about 6 minutes. Transfer to slow cooker stoneware.

2. Reduce heat to medium. Add remaining tbsp (15 mL) of butter to pan. Add onions and celery and cook, stirring, until softened, about 5 minutes. Add garlic, cumin, oregano, cinnamon stick, peppercorns and sea salt and cook, stirring, for 1 minute. Add tomatoes with juice and stock. Bring to a boil, stirring and scraping up brown bits from bottom of pan.

3. Transfer to slow cooker stoneware. Cover and cook on Low for 8 hours or on High for 4 hours, until beef is very tender.

4. About 1 hour before you are ready to serve, soak chiles in boiling water for 30 minutes, weighing down with a cup to ensure they remain submerged. Drain, discarding soaking liquid and stems. Transfer to a blender and add cilantro, jalapeño, if using, and approximately 1 cup (250 mL) of the brisket cooking liquid. Purée and add to slow cooker along with bell pepper. Cover and cook on High for 20 minutes, until pepper is tender.

Short Ribs with Horseradish Cream

◆ Entertaining Worthy
◆ Can Be Halved
(see Tips, below)

Tips

If you are halving this recipe, be sure to use a small (2 to 3½ quart) slow cooker.

People differ on how well cooked they like short ribs to be. I prefer mine to be falling off the bone, but if you like a firmer result, or if your slow cooker cooks particularly quickly, reduce the cooking time.

Puréeing the vegetables (Step 3) is a technique for thickening the sauce without adding starch to the recipe.

Make Ahead

Complete Step 2. Cover and refrigerate for up to 2 days. When you're ready to cook, complete the recipe.

This combination of flavors is classic. Serve it for a special Sunday dinner.

- Large (approx. 5 quart) slow cooker
- Blender or food processor

4 to 5 lbs	beef short ribs	2 to 2.5 kg
1 tbsp	extra virgin olive oil or beef tallow (see page 144)	15 mL
3	onions, finely chopped	3
2	carrots, peeled and diced	2
2	stalks celery, diced (see Tips, page 120)	2
4	cloves garlic, minced	4
1 tsp	dried thyme	5 mL
1 tsp	cracked black peppercorns	5 mL
½ tsp	sea salt	2 mL
2	bay leaves	2
2 tbsp	tomato paste or ¼ cup (60 mL) minced reconstituted sun-dried tomatoes (see page 13)	30 mL
1 cup	dry red wine	250 mL
2 cups	chicken stock	500 mL
	Sea salt and freshly ground black pepper	

Horseradish Cream

3 tbsp	Homemade Horseradish (page 240)	45 mL
½ cup	sour cream or crème fraîche (see page 14)	125 mL

1. Position broiler rack 6 inches (15 cm) from heat source. Broil ribs on both sides, turning once, for 10 minutes per side. Drain on paper towels. Separate ribs if in strips and place in stoneware.

2. In a large skillet, heat oil over medium heat. Add onions, carrots and celery and cook, stirring, until softened, about 7 minutes. Add garlic, thyme, peppercorns, sea salt and bay leaves and cook, stirring, for 1 minute. Stir in tomato paste and wine and cook, stirring, for 2 minutes. Stir in stock and bring to a boil.

3. Transfer vegetable mixture to stoneware. Cover and cook on Low for 8 hours or on High for 4 hours, until ribs are falling off the bone. Transfer ribs to a large serving dish and keep warm. Remove and discard bay leaves. Using an immersion blender or food processor, purée the sauce and adjust seasoning (see Tips, left). Pour over short ribs.

4. *Horseradish Cream:* Meanwhile, in a small serving bowl, combine horseradish and sour cream. Refrigerate for at least 1 hour to allow flavors to meld. Pass at the table and allow guests to serve themselves.

Short Ribs in Rich Mushroom Gravy

◆ **Entertaining Worthy**
◆ **Can Be Halved**
(see Tips, below)

Tips

If you are halving this recipe, be sure to use a small (2 to $3\frac{1}{2}$ quart) slow cooker.

People differ on how well cooked they like short ribs to be. I prefer mine to be falling off the bone, but if you like a firmer result, or if your slow cooker cooks particularly quickly, reduce the cooking time.

Beef tallow is rendered beef fat. It is a very stable fat, only about half of which is saturated, although nutritionists are now recognizing that the adverse effects of saturated fats have been overstated and that saturated fats actually play a significant role in keeping us healthy.

Make Ahead

Complete Steps 1 and 3. Cover and refrigerate for up to 2 days. When you're ready to cook, complete the recipe.

This is real stick-to-your-ribs cold-weather cooking — and exceptionally delicious, to boot. It's so good you'll want to invite friends.

• **Large (approx. 5 quart) slow cooker**

1	package ($\frac{1}{2}$ oz/14 g) dried porcini mushrooms	1
1 cup	hot water	250 mL
4 lbs	beef short ribs	2 kg
1 tbsp	extra virgin olive oil or beef tallow (see Tips, left and page 144)	15 mL
2	onions, finely chopped	2
2	carrots, peeled and diced	2
2	stalks celery, diced	2
6	cloves garlic, minced	6
1 tsp	dried thyme	5 mL
1 tsp	cracked black peppercorns	5 mL
$\frac{1}{2}$ tsp	sea salt	2 mL
2	bay leaves	2
1 cup	dry red wine	250 mL
1	can (14 oz/398 mL) tomatoes with juice (see page 13)	1
8 oz	cremini mushrooms, trimmed and quartered	250 g

1. In a bowl, soak dried mushrooms in hot water for 30 minutes. Strain through a fine sieve, reserving liquid. Chop mushrooms finely and set aside.

2. Meanwhile, position broiler rack 6 inches (15 cm) from heat source. Broil ribs on both sides, turning once, until well browned, about 10 minutes per side. Drain on paper towels. Separate ribs if in strips and place in slow cooker stoneware.

3. In a large skillet, heat oil over medium heat. Add onions, carrots and celery and cook, stirring, until softened, about 7 minutes. Add garlic, thyme, peppercorns, sea salt, bay leaves and reserved dried mushrooms and cook, stirring, for 1 minute. Add wine, bring to a boil and cook, stirring and scraping up brown bits from bottom of pan, for 2 minutes. Stir in reserved mushroom liquid and tomatoes with juice and bring to a boil.

4. Transfer to stoneware. Stir in cremini mushrooms. Cover and cook on Low for 8 hours or on High for 4 hours, until ribs are falling off the bone (see Tips, left). Remove and discard bay leaves.

Short Ribs with Orange Gremolata

Serves 4 to 6

◆ Entertaining Worthy
◆ Can Be Halved
   (see Tips, below)

Tips

If you are halving this recipe, be sure to use a small (2 to 3½ quart) slow cooker.

I love short ribs but they are very fatty. Browning them under the broiler before cooking renders much of the fat.

Make Ahead

This dish can be partially prepared before it is cooked. Complete Step 2. Cover and refrigerate for up to 2 days. When you're ready to cook, brown the ribs (Step 1) and continue with the recipe.

These delicious Italian-inspired ribs are classy enough for the most discriminating guest yet homey enough for a family dinner. Serve with steamed broccoli spears or rapini for a scrumptious Italian-themed meal.

- **Large (minimum 5 quart) slow cooker**
- **Preheat broiler**

4 to 5 lbs	beef short ribs (see Tips, left)	2 to 2.5 kg
1 tbsp	extra virgin olive oil	15 mL
2	onions, finely chopped	2
2	large carrots, peeled and thinly sliced	2
4	stalks celery, thinly sliced	4
4	cloves garlic, minced	4
1 tsp	cracked black peppercorns	5 mL
½ tsp	sea salt	2 mL
2	whole sprigs fresh thyme or ½ tsp (2 mL) dried thyme	2
1 tbsp	tomato paste or 2 tbsp (30 mL) reconstituted sun-dried tomatoes (see page 13)	15 mL
½ cup	dry red wine	125 mL
½ cup	beef stock	125 mL

Orange Gremolata

½ cup	flat-leaf parsley leaves, finely chopped	125 mL
1	clove garlic, minced	1
	Zest of 1 orange, finely chopped	

1. Position broiler rack 6 inches (15 cm) from heat source. Broil ribs on both sides, turning once, until well browned, about 10 minutes per side. Drain on paper towels. Separate ribs if in strips and place in slow cooker stoneware.

2. In a skillet, heat oil over medium heat. Add onions, carrots and celery and cook, stirring, until softened, about 7 minutes. Add garlic, peppercorns, sea salt and thyme and cook, stirring, for 1 minute. Add tomato paste and wine, bring to a boil and boil for 2 minutes. Stir in stock.

3. Pour sauce over ribs and stir to combine. Cover and cook on Low for 8 hours or on High for 4 hours, until ribs are tender and falling off the bone.

4. *Orange Gremolata:* Combine parsley, garlic and orange zest in a small bowl just before serving and pass at the table.

Chile-Spiced Short Ribs

- ◆ Entertaining Worthy
- ◆ Can Be Halved
  (see Tips, below)

Tips

If you are halving this recipe, be sure to use a small (2 to 3 1/2 quart) slow cooker.

The ancho chile powder is only mildly hot but adds pleasant depth and complexity to the sauce.

Chipotle chiles in adobo sauce lend a great smoky flavor as well as heat to this dish. They are very hot, so unless you are a heat seeker, use only 1 in this recipe. If you prefer not to use a canned product that has been prepared, substitute 2 minced jalapeño chile peppers. Not all brands of chipotle peppers in adobo sauce are gluten-free so if you are using this product be sure to check the label.

Make Ahead

Complete Step 2. Cover and refrigerate for up to 2 days. When you're ready to cook, complete the recipe.

Here's a short rib recipe that is delectably different yet fairly easy to make. The secret is ancho chile powder and chipotle pepper in adobo sauce, which add incredible depth of flavor with very little effort on the part of the cook. I like to serve this with steamed runner beans as an accompaniment.

- **Large (approx. 5 quart) slow cooker**

4 to 5 lbs	beef short ribs	2 to 2.5 kg
1 tbsp	extra virgin olive oil or beef tallow (see page 144)	15 mL
2	onions, finely chopped	2
2	stalks celery, diced	2
2	carrots, peeled and diced	2
4	cloves garlic, minced	4
1	piece (4 inches/10 cm) cinnamon stick	1
1 tsp	dried thyme	5 mL
1 tsp	cracked black peppercorns	5 mL
1/2 tsp	sea salt	2 mL
2 tbsp	tomato paste or 1/4 cup (60 mL) minced reconstituted sun-dried tomatoes (see page 13)	30 mL
1 cup	dry red wine	250 mL
2 cups	chicken or vegetable stock	500 mL
1 tbsp	ancho chile powder (see Tips, left)	15 mL
1 to 2	chipotle chiles in adobo sauce, minced (see Tips, left)	1 to 2
	Finely chopped cilantro leaves	

1. Position broiler rack 6 inches (15 cm) from heat source. Broil ribs on both sides, turning once, until well browned, about 10 minutes per side. Drain on paper towels. Separate ribs if in strips and place in slow cooker stoneware.

2. In a skillet, heat oil over medium heat. Add onions, celery and carrots and cook, stirring, until softened, about 7 minutes. Add garlic, cinnamon stick, thyme, peppercorns and sea salt and cook, stirring, for 1 minute. Stir in tomato paste and wine and bring to a boil. Boil rapidly for 2 minutes.

3. Transfer to slow cooker stoneware. Stir in stock. Cover and cook on Low for 8 hours or on High for 4 hours, until ribs are tender and falling off the bone (see Tips, page 123). Stir in chile powder and chipotle chile with adobo sauce. Cover and cook on High for 30 minutes, until flavors meld. Garnish liberally with cilantro.

Savory Short Ribs

Tip

To toast fennel seeds:
Place seeds in a dry skillet over medium heat and cook, stirring, until fragrant, about 3 minutes. Using a mortar and pestle or a spice grinder, grind.

Make Ahead

After refrigerating the ribs to marinate, complete Step 3. Cover and refrigerate mixture overnight. The next morning, complete the recipe, but don't add the olives. Cover and refrigerate the cooked ribs for up to 2 days. Thirty minutes before you're ready to serve the ribs, preheat oven to 350°F (180°C). Skim the fat off the ribs and discard. Transfer meat and sauce to a large oven-to-table serving dish. Cover loosely with foil and heat for 20 minutes. Stir in olives. Return to oven and continue heating until sauce is hot and bubbly, about 10 minutes.

These robust short ribs are delicious and make a great casual dinner with friends. Add a tossed green salad and some robust red wine to finish the meal.

• **Large (minimum 5 quart) slow cooker**

1 tbsp	cracked black peppercorns	15 mL
1 tbsp	dried thyme	15 mL
1 tbsp	fennel seeds, toasted and ground (see Tip, left)	15 mL
2 tbsp	extra virgin olive oil	30 mL
4 to 5 lbs	beef short ribs	2 to 2.5 kg
4 oz	bacon, diced	125 g
2	onions, finely chopped	2
2	carrots, peeled and finely chopped	2
4	cloves garlic, minced	4
4	anchovy fillets, finely chopped	4
1 tsp	sea salt	5 mL
1/2 tsp	cracked black peppercorns	2 mL
1 tbsp	red wine vinegar	15 mL
1 cup	robust red wine	250 mL
1	can (28 oz/796 mL) diced tomatoes, including juice (see page 13)	1
1	bouquet garni	1
1 cup	chopped pitted black olives	250 mL

1. In a baking dish large enough to accommodate the short ribs, combine peppercorns, thyme, toasted fennel and oil. Add ribs, in batches, turning until evenly coated. Cover and refrigerate overnight.

2. Preheat broiler and position broiler rack 6 inches (15 cm) from the heat source. Broil ribs on both sides, turning once, until well browned, about 10 minutes per side. Drain on paper towels. Separate ribs if in strips and place in slow cooker stoneware.

3. In a skillet, cook bacon over medium-high heat, stirring, until brown on all sides. Using a slotted spoon, transfer to slow cooker stoneware. Reduce heat to medium. Add onions and carrots and cook, stirring, until carrots are softened, about 7 minutes. Add garlic, anchovies, sea salt and 1/2 tsp (2 mL) peppercorns and cook, stirring, for 1 minute. Add vinegar and wine and cook, stirring, for 2 minutes. Add tomatoes with juice and bouquet garni and transfer to slow cooker stoneware.

4. Cover and cook on Low for 8 hours or on High for 4 hours, until ribs are tender and falling off the bone. Stir in olives.

Wine-Braised Oxtails with Mushrooms

Serves 6 to 8

◆ **Can Be Halved**
(see Tips, below)

Tips

If you are halving this recipe, be sure to use a small (2 to 3½ quart) slow cooker.

For best results, cook this overnight or a day ahead and chill. Spoon off the fat that rises to the surface and reheat, covered, in a 350°F (180°C) oven until hot and bubbly, about 30 minutes.

If you prefer a richer tomato flavor, you may want to add 1 tbsp (15 mL) tomato paste or 2 tbsp (30 mL) minced reconstituted sun-dried tomatoes along with the tomatoes.

Make Ahead

Complete Step 2. Cover and refrigerate for up to 2 days. When you're ready to cook, complete the recipe.

This hearty dish will more than satisfy the meat lovers in your circle. Cooked on the bone, the beef is particularly succulent and the sauce is deep and rich.

• **Large (approx. 5 quart) slow cooker**

2 tbsp	clarified butter or beef tallow (see page 144), divided	30 mL
4 lbs	oxtails, cut into 2-inch (5 cm) pieces, and patted dry	2 kg
2	onions, finely chopped	2
2	carrots, peeled and diced	2
2	stalks celery, diced (see Tips, page 120)	2
4	cloves garlic, minced	4
1 tsp	dried thyme leaves	5 mL
½ tsp	sea salt	2 mL
½ tsp	cracked black peppercorns	2 mL
2	bay leaves	2
1½ cups	dry red wine	375 mL
1	can (28 oz/796 mL) tomatoes with juice, coarsely chopped (see page 13)	1
12 oz	mushrooms, trimmed and quartered	375 g
½ cup	finely chopped flat-leaf parsley leaves	125 mL

1. In a skillet, heat 1 tbsp (15 mL) of the butter over medium-high heat. Add oxtails, in batches, and cook, stirring, until lightly browned on all sides, about 4 minutes per batch. Transfer to slow cooker stoneware as completed. Drain off all the fat from the pan.

2. Reduce heat to medium. Add remaining tbsp (15 mL) of butter to pan. Add onions, carrots and celery and cook, stirring, until vegetables are softened, about 7 minutes. Add garlic, thyme, sea salt, peppercorns and bay leaves and cook, stirring, for 1 minute. Add wine, bring to a boil and boil, stirring and scraping up brown bits from bottom of pan, for 2 minutes. Stir in tomatoes with juice.

3. Transfer to slow cooker stoneware. Add mushrooms and stir well. Cover and cook on Low for 8 to 10 hours or on High for 4 to 5 hours, until meat is falling off the bone (see Tips, page 129). Remove and discard bay leaves. Garnish with parsley.

Roman-Style Oxtails with Celery

Serves 6 to 8

◆ **Entertaining Worthy**
◆ **Can Be Halved**
(see Tips, below)

Tips

If you are halving this recipe, be sure to use a small (2 to 3½ quart) slow cooker.

If you prefer, substitute an extra cup (250 mL) of chicken stock plus 1 tbsp (15 mL) lemon juice for the white wine.

Be aware that these cooking times are general estimates. Not only do cooking times vary substantially among slow cookers (see Cooking Times, page 18), but people have different preferences with regard to how well they like their meat done. The oxtails should be very tender when cooked within this time frame.

Make Ahead

Complete Steps 1 and 3. Add cooked pancetta to onion mixture. Cover and refrigerate (see Making Ahead, page 21) for up to 2 days. When you're ready to cook, continue with the recipe.

This is one of my favorite recipes for oxtails. The sauce is much lighter than most and the abundance of blanched celery adds beautiful flavor.

• **Large (approx. 5 quart) slow cooker**

2 tbsp	clarified butter, beef tallow or pure lard (approx.), divided	30 mL
4 oz	pancetta, diced	125 g
4 lbs	oxtails, cut into 2-inch (5 cm) pieces, and patted dry	2 kg
1	onion, diced	1
2	stalks celery, diced (see Tips, page 120)	2
2	cloves garlic, minced	2
1 tsp	sea salt	5 mL
1 tsp	cracked black peppercorns	5 mL
1 cup	dry white wine (see Tips, left)	250 mL
¼ cup	tomato paste or ½ cup (125 mL) crushed tomatoes	60 mL
2 cups	chicken stock	500 mL
6 cups	sliced celery (cut into 1-inch/2.5 cm pieces) (see Tips, page 120)	1.5 L
½ cup	finely chopped parsley leaves	125 mL

1. In a skillet, heat 1 tbsp (15 mL) clarified butter over medium-high heat. Add pancetta and cook, stirring, until nicely browned, about 4 minutes. Transfer to slow cooker stoneware.

2. Add oxtails, in batches, and brown on all sides, about 4 minutes per batch, adding more butter, if necessary. Transfer to slow cooker stoneware as completed. Drain off all the fat from pan.

3. Reduce heat to medium. Add remaining tbsp (15 mL) of butter to pan. Add onion, diced celery, garlic, sea salt and peppercorns and cook, stirring, until onions begin to turn golden, about 8 minutes. Add wine, bring to a boil and boil, stirring and scraping up brown bits from bottom of pan, for 2 minutes. Stir in tomato paste and stock.

4. Transfer to slow cooker stoneware. Cover and cook on Low for 8 to 10 hours or on High for 4 to 5 hours, until meat is falling off the bone.

5. When oxtails are almost cooked, bring a large pot of salted water to a boil. Add sliced celery and return to a boil. Reduce heat and simmer until celery is tender, about 5 minutes. Drain and add to oxtails. Cover and cook on High for 10 minutes, until flavors meld. Garnish with parsley and serve immediately.

Braised Beef Niçoise

If you're feeling the need for some robust winter fare, try this hearty French-inspired stew.

- **Medium to large (3½ to 5 quart) slow cooker**
- **Large sheet of parchment paper**

2 tbsp	clarified butter or beef tallow (see page 144), divided	30 mL
2 lbs	trimmed stewing beef, cut into 1-inch (2.5 cm) cubes, and patted dry	1 kg
2	onions, finely chopped	2
2	carrots, peeled and diced	2
1	bulb fennel, cored and thinly sliced on the vertical (see Tips, left)	1
4	cloves garlic, minced	4
1 tsp	dried thyme leaves, or 1 sprig fresh thyme, including stem	5 mL
1 tsp	cracked black peppercorns	5 mL
½ tsp	sea salt	2 mL
2	bay leaves	2
2 tbsp	red wine vinegar (see page 15)	30 mL
1 cup	dry red wine	250 mL
1	can (28 oz/796 mL) tomatoes with juice (see Tips, page 142)	1
½ cup	pitted black olives, chopped	125 mL
¼ cup	finely chopped flat-leaf parsley leaves	60 mL

1. In a skillet, heat 1 tbsp (15 mL) of the clarified butter over medium-high heat. Add beef, in batches, and cook, stirring, until lightly browned on all sides, about 4 minutes per batch. Transfer to slow cooker stoneware as completed.

2. Reduce heat to medium. Add remaining tbsp (15 mL) of clarified butter to pan. Add onions, carrots and fennel and cook, stirring, until softened, about 7 minutes. Add garlic, thyme, peppercorns, sea salt and bay leaves and cook, stirring, for 1 minute. Add vinegar and wine, bring to a boil and boil, scraping up brown bits from bottom of pan, for 2 minutes. Stir in tomatoes with juice.

3. Transfer to slow cooker stoneware. Place a large piece of parchment paper over the mixture, pressing it down to brush the food and extending up the sides of the stoneware so it overlaps the rim. Cover and cook on Low for 8 hours or on High for 4 hours, until beef is very tender. Lift out and discard parchment, being careful not to spill the accumulated liquid into the stoneware. Remove and discard bay leaves. Garnish with olives, parsley, and fennel fronds, if desired (see Tips, left).

Pot Roast in Barolo

◆ Entertaining Worthy
◆ Can Be Halved
(see Tips, below)

Tips

If you are halving this recipe, be sure to use a small (2½ to 3½ quart) slow cooker. Reduce cooking time to 6 hours on Low or 3 hours on High.

Once the roast is in slow cooker, if possible, turn halfway through cooking.

If you have fresh rosemary on hand, substitute 1 stalk, stem and all, for the dried. Remove and discard stem before puréeing the sauce.

Make Ahead

Complete Steps 1 and 3, using the fat from the pancetta to soften the vegetables. Use the extra virgin olive oil when you brown the beef, adding more oil, if necessary. Cover and refrigerate pancetta and vegetable mixture separately for up to 2 days. When you're ready to cook, complete the recipe.

This Italian classic makes a perfect Sunday dinner. Use Barolo to be authentic, but any full-bodied dry red wine will do. I like to finish the meal with a platter of sautéed rapini.

- Large (approx. 5 quart) slow cooker

2 tbsp	clarified butter, pure lard or beef tallow (see page 144), divided	30 mL
2 oz	pancetta, diced	60 g
1	boneless rump or chuck roast, about 4 lbs (2 kg), patted dry	1
2	onions, finely chopped	2
2	carrots, peeled and diced	2
2	stalks celery, diced (see Tips, page 120)	2
4	cloves garlic, minced	4
1 tsp	dried rosemary leaves (see Tips, left)	5 mL
2	bay leaves	2
1	piece (2 inches/5 cm) cinnamon stick	1
½ tsp	sea salt	2 mL
½ tsp	cracked black peppercorns	2 mL
2 tbsp	tomato paste or ¼ cup (60 mL) minced reconstituted sun-dried tomatoes (see page 13)	30 mL
3 cups	dry robust red wine, such as Barolo	750 mL
	Sea salt and freshly ground black pepper	

1. In a skillet, heat 1 tbsp (15 mL) of the clarified butter over medium-high heat. Add pancetta and cook, stirring, until browned, about 3 minutes. Using a slotted spoon, transfer to slow cooker stoneware.

2. Add beef to pan and brown on all sides, about 8 minutes. Transfer to stoneware.

3. Reduce heat to medium. Add remaining tbsp (15 mL) of clarified butter to pan. Add onions, carrots and celery and cook, stirring, until vegetables are tender, about 7 minutes. Add garlic, rosemary, bay leaves, cinnamon stick, sea salt and peppercorns and cook, stirring, for 1 minute. Stir in tomato paste. Add wine, bring to a boil, stirring and scraping up brown bits from bottom of pan. Cook, stirring, until slightly reduced and thickened, about 5 minutes.

4. Transfer to slow cooker stoneware. Cover and cook on Low for 8 hours or on High for 4 hours, until meat is very tender.

5. Transfer meat to a platter or cutting board, tent with foil and keep warm. Remove and discard bay leaves. Using an immersion blender, purée sauce (see Tips, page 133). Season with sea salt and pepper to taste. Slice meat thickly, transfer to a warm platter and smother in sauce.

Mom's Sunday Pot Roast

Tips

If you are halving this recipe, be sure to use a small (2½ to 3½ quart) slow cooker. Reduce cooking time to 6 hours on Low or 3 hours on High.

If you prefer, substitute an additional cup (250 mL) of beef stock for the red wine. Add all at once, bring to a boil and cook, stirring, until the sauce thickens.

To ensure robust flavor in the sauce, I recommend adding the steak sauce if you don't use red wine.

Puréeing the vegetables in the sauce is a technique for thickening it.

Make Ahead

Complete Step 2. Cover and refrigerate for up to 2 days. When you're ready to cook, complete the recipe.

It doesn't get much more traditional than this. It's the kind of pot roast I grew up with — with a simple but delicious beef gravy served over mounds of mashed potatoes. Unlike my mother, I've included a bit of red wine to enrich the flavor, but if you prefer, make it with all beef stock and, if you don't mind using a prepared product, stir in some steak sauce for added flavor.

- Large (approx. 5 quart) slow cooker

2 tbsp	clarified butter or beef tallow (see page 144), divided	30 mL
1	beef pot roast, about 4 lbs (2 kg), patted dry	1
2	onions, thinly sliced on the vertical	2
2	carrots, peeled and diced	2
2	stalks celery, diced (see Tips, 120)	2
4	cloves garlic, minced	4
1 tsp	dried thyme	5 mL
½ tsp	sea salt	2 mL
½ tsp	cracked black peppercorns	2 mL
1 tbsp	tomato paste or 2 tbsp (30 mL) minced reconstituted sun-dried tomatoes (see page 13)	15 mL
1 cup	dry red wine (see Tips, left)	250 mL
1 cup	beef stock	250 mL
2 tbsp	steak sauce, optional (see Tips, left)	30 mL
¼ cup	finely chopped parsley leaves	60 mL

1. In a skillet, heat 1 tbsp (15 mL) of the clarified butter over medium-high heat. Add roast and brown on all sides, about 10 minutes. Transfer to slow cooker stoneware.

2. Add remaining tbsp (15 mL) of butter to pan. Add onions, carrots and celery and cook, stirring, until vegetables are softened, about 7 minutes. Add garlic, thyme, sea salt and peppercorns and cook, stirring, for 1 minute. Stir in tomato paste and cook for 1 minute. Add wine, bring to a boil and boil, scraping up brown bits from bottom of pan, for 2 minutes. Add stock and return to a boil.

3. Transfer to slow cooker stoneware. Cover and cook on Low for 8 hours or on High for 4 hours, until meat is very tender. Transfer meat to a platter or cutting board, tent with foil and keep warm. Using an immersion blender, purée sauce (see Tips, left). Stir in steak sauce, if using. Season with sea salt and pepper to taste. Slice meat thinly and place on a warm platter. Cover with sauce and garnish with parsley.

Zesty Braised Beef

◆ **Can Be Halved**
(see Tips, below)

Tips

If you are halving this recipe, be sure to use a small (2 to 3½ quart) slow cooker.

Because it's important to bring the potatoes to a boil in order to ensure they cook in the slow cooker, I do not recommend making part of this dish ahead of time.

If you prefer, substitute 3 cups (750 mL) diced peeled yellow squash for the potatoes.

It's hard to believe that this simple combination of ingredients can taste so luscious. I like to serve this with a big platter of roasted carrots. Save leftovers and enjoy in a bowl like a hearty soup.

• **Medium to large (3½ to 5 quart) slow cooker**

2 tbsp	clarified butter, beef tallow or pure lard, divided	30 mL
2 oz	chunk pancetta, preferably hot pancetta, diced	60 g
2 lbs	trimmed stewing beef, cut into 1-inch (2.5 cm) cubes and patted dry	1 kg
2	onions, finely chopped	2
4	cloves garlic, minced	4
1 tsp	dried thyme	5 mL
1 tsp	cracked black peppercorns	5 mL
½ tsp	sea salt	2 mL
½ cup	dry white wine (see Tips, page 129)	125 mL
2 cups	chicken stock	500 mL
2 lbs	small new potatoes, scrubbed and thinly sliced (about 30 tiny ones) (see Tips, left)	1 kg
¼ tsp	cayenne pepper, dissolved in 1 tbsp (15 mL) freshly squeezed lemon juice	1 mL
	Finely chopped parsley leaves	

1. In a skillet, heat 1 tbsp (15 mL) of the clarified butter over medium-high heat. Add pancetta and cook, stirring, until nicely browned, about 3 minutes. Transfer to slow cooker stoneware. Add beef to skillet, in batches, and cook, stirring, until browned, about 4 minutes per batch. Transfer to stoneware as completed.

2. Reduce heat to medium. Add remaining tbsp (15 mL) of butter to pan. Add onions and cook, stirring, until softened, about 3 minutes. Add garlic, thyme, peppercorns and sea salt and cook, stirring, for 1 minute. Add wine, bring to a boil and boil, stirring and scraping up brown bits from bottom of pan, for 2 minutes. Add stock and potatoes and bring to a boil. Simmer for 2 minutes.

3. Transfer to stoneware. Cover and cook on Low for 8 hours or on High for 4 hours, until potatoes are tender. Stir in cayenne solution. Cover and cook on High for 10 minutes to meld flavors and to thicken. Transfer to a serving dish and garnish with parsley.

Beef with Beets and Horseradish Cream

Serves 6

◆ **Can Be Halved**
(see Tips, below)

Tips

If you are halving this recipe, be sure to use a small (2 to 3½ quart) slow cooker.

Be aware that these cooking times are general estimates. Not only do cooking times vary substantially among slow cookers (see Cooking Times, page 18), but people have different preferences with regard to how well they like their meat done. If you prefer fork-tender results, start checking after the food has cooked for 6 hours on Low.

Make Ahead

Complete Step 2, heating 1 tbsp (15 mL) of the butter in pan before softening vegetables. Cover and refrigerate mixture for up to 2 days. When you're ready to cook, continue with the recipe.

While not a traditional combination, beef cooked with beets and topped with horseradish cream makes for a hearty and delicious change.

- **Medium to large (3½ to 5 quart) slow cooker**
- **Cheesecloth**

2 tbsp	clarified butter or beef tallow (see page 144),	30 mL
2 lbs	trimmed stewing beef, cut into 1-inch (2.5 cm) cubes and patted dry	1 kg
2	onions, finely chopped	2
2	stalks celery, diced	2
4	cloves garlic, minced	4
½ tsp	sea salt	2 mL
½ tsp	cracked black peppercorns	2 mL
1	bay leaf	1
8	whole allspice	8
4	whole cloves	4
1 cup	dry red wine	250 mL
3 cups	beef stock	750 mL
1 tbsp	red wine vinegar	15 mL
1 tbsp	coconut sugar	15 mL
4	medium beets, peeled and cut into ½-inch (1 cm) cubes	4
½ cup	crème fraîche or sour cream (see page 14)	125 mL
2 tbsp	Homemade Horseradish (page 240)	30 mL

1. In a skillet, heat clarified butter over medium-high heat. Add beef, in batches, and cook, stirring, until lightly browned on all sides, about 4 minutes per batch. Transfer to slow cooker stoneware as completed.

2. Reduce heat to medium. Add onions and celery to pan and cook, stirring, until softened, about 5 minutes. Add garlic, sea salt, peppercorns and bay leaf and cook, stirring, for 1 minute. Tie allspice and cloves in a piece of cheesecloth, creating a spice bag, and add to pan. Add wine, bring to a boil and boil for 2 minutes. Add stock, vinegar and coconut sugar and return to a boil.

3. Transfer to slow cooker stoneware. Stir in beets. Cover and cook on Low for 8 hours or on High for 4 hours, until beets and beef are tender. Remove and discard bay leaf, allspice and cloves.

4. In a small bowl, combine crème fraîche and horseradish. Stir well. Serve with beef.

Classic Beef Stew

When I was growing up, one of my favorite dishes was my mother's beef stew. There was nothing fancy about it but the house always smelled wonderful while it was cooking. This is the stew I've tried to capture in this recipe. That said, even Mom's stew can be improved upon with the addition of mushrooms cooked in Madeira or a dollop of Slow-Roasted Garlic (see Variations, below).

• **Medium to large (3½ to 5 quart) slow cooker**

2 tbsp	extra virgin olive oil	30 mL
2 lbs	stewing beef, cut into 1-inch (2.5 cm) cubes and patted dry	1 kg
2	onions, finely chopped	2
4	stalks celery, thinly sliced	4
2	large carrots, peeled and diced	2
2	cloves garlic, minced	2
1 tsp	dried thyme	5 mL
1 tsp	sea salt	5 mL
½ tsp	cracked black peppercorns	2 mL
2	bay leaves	2
½ cup	dry red wine or additional beef stock	125 mL
1 cup	beef stock	250 mL
1 tbsp	Beef Demi-Glace (page 59)	15 mL
	Finely chopped flat-leaf parsley leaves	

1. In a skillet, heat oil over medium heat. Add beef, in batches, and brown, about 4 minutes per batch. Using a slotted spoon, transfer to slow cooker stoneware.

2. Add onions, celery and carrots and cook, stirring, until vegetables are softened, about 7 minutes. Add garlic, thyme, sea salt, peppercorns and bay leaves and cook, stirring, for 1 minute. Add wine and cook, stirring and scraping brown bits up from the bottom of the pan for 1 minute. Add stock and bring to a boil. Add demi-glace.

3. Transfer to stoneware and stir well. Cover and cook on Low for 6 to 8 hours or on High for 3 to 4 hours, until beef is very tender. Discard bay leaves. Just before serving, garnish liberally with parsley.

Variations

Beef Stew with Madeira Mushrooms: In a skillet, melt 2 tbsp (30 mL) butter over medium-high heat. Add 12 oz (375 g) sliced button mushrooms and sauté until mushrooms release their liquid, about 7 minutes. Season with salt and pepper to taste. Stir in ¼ cup (60 mL) Madeira or port wine and bring to a boil. Cook for 2 minutes. Just before serving, stir into stew, then garnish with parsley.

Beef Stew with Roasted Garlic: Mash 6 cloves roasted garlic (see Tips, left) and stir into stew before garnishing with parsley.

Boeuf Bourguignon

Tip

If you are halving this recipe, be sure to use a small (2 to 3 quart) slow cooker.

Make Ahead

Complete Steps 1 and 3, stirring browned mushrooms into wine mixture. Cover and refrigerate mixture overnight. The next morning, brown beef (Step 2), or if you're pressed for time, skip this step and place beef directly in stoneware. Complete the recipe.

To the French, this is comfort food — a long-simmered dish that evokes warm memories of childhood. To North Americans, it's great bistro food — flavorful and hearty, perfectly suited to a full-bodied red wine and lively evenings with friends. Either way, it's perfect for the slow cooker and great as a leftover since it's even better reheated.

• Medium to large (3½ to 5 quart) slow cooker

1 tbsp	clarified butter, beef tallow or pure lard	15 mL
4 oz	chunk of bacon or pork belly, cut into ½-inch (1 cm) cubes	125 g
2 lbs	stewing beef, cut into 1-inch (2.5 cm) cubes and patted dry	1 kg
1 lb	cremini mushrooms, trimmed and halved	500 g
2	onions, thinly sliced	2
3	carrots, peeled and thinly sliced	3
2	cloves garlic, minced	2
1 tsp	dried thyme or 2 sprigs fresh thyme	5 mL
1	bay leaf	1
½ tsp	sea salt	2 mL
½ tsp	cracked black peppercorns	2 mL
2 cups	dry red wine	500 mL
½ cup	beef stock	125 mL
	Zest of 1 orange	
	Chopped flat-leaf parsley leaves	

1. In a large skillet, heat clarified butter over medium-high heat. Add bacon and cook, stirring, until crisp. Using a slotted spoon, transfer to paper towel to drain. Drain off all but 2 tbsp (30 mL) fat in pan.

2. Add beef to pan, in batches, and brown, about 4 minutes per batch. Transfer to slow cooker stoneware.

3. Add mushrooms to pan and cook until tops are lightly browned, about 4 minutes. Transfer to stoneware. Reduce heat to medium. Add onions and carrots to pan and cook, stirring, until softened, about 7 minutes. Add garlic, thyme, bay leaf, sea salt and peppercorns and cook, stirring, for 1 minute. Add wine and beef stock, bring to a boil and cook, stirring and scraping up brown bits from bottom of pan, until slightly reduced, about 5 minutes.

4. Transfer to stoneware. Stir in bacon and orange zest. Cover and cook on Low for 8 hours or on High for 4 hours, until beef is very tender. Discard bay leaf. Just before serving, garnish liberally with parsley.

Italian-Style Goulash

Tips

If you are halving this recipe, be sure to use a small (2 to 3 quart) slow cooker.

If you prefer, omit the potatoes and serve this over Roasted Spaghetti Squash (page 243).

Be sure to dice your potatoes into 1/2-inch (1 cm) cubes rather than slicing them. Otherwise they are not likely to be cooked at the same time as the meat.

This amount of hot paprika produces a slightly spicy result. Use a bit more or less, depending upon your level of heat tolerance. If you like a hint of smoke, substitute smoked paprika for some or all of the hot paprika.

Make Ahead

Complete Step 2. Cover and refrigerate mixture for up to 2 days. When you're ready to cook, complete the recipe.

This version of goulash, known as golas, *is from the Friuli region of Italy. Not only does it have great depth of flavor, it also contains its own starch in the form of potatoes, so you don't need to add the traditional noodles. I like to serve this with a big bowl of steamed green beans and a robust red wine.*

• **Medium to large (3 1/2 to 5 quart) slow cooker**

2 tbsp	clarified butter or beef tallow, divided	30 mL
2 lbs	trimmed stewing beef, cut into 1-inch (2.5 cm) cubes and patted dry	1 kg
2	onions, diced	2
2	stalks celery, diced (see Tips, page 120)	2
1	carrot, peeled and diced	1
2	cloves garlic, minced	2
2 tsp	dried oregano	10 mL
1 tsp	dried rosemary or 1 sprig fresh rosemary	5 mL
1/2 tsp	sea salt	2 mL
1/2 tsp	cracked black peppercorns	2 mL
1/4 cup	tomato paste or 1/2 cup (125 mL) chopped reconstituted sun-dried tomatoes (see page 13)	60 mL
1 cup	dry red wine	250 mL
2	potatoes, peeled and diced (see Tips, left)	2
2 cups	beef stock	500 mL
1 tbsp	sweet paprika	15 mL
1 tsp	hot paprika (see Tips, left)	5 mL
2 tbsp	water	30 mL

1. In a skillet, heat 1 tbsp (15 mL) of the butter over medium-high heat. Add beef, in batches, and cook, stirring, until lightly browned on all sides, about 4 minutes per batch. Transfer to stoneware as completed.

2. Reduce heat to medium. Add remaining tbsp (15 mL) of butter to pan. Add onions, celery and carrot and cook, stirring, until vegetables are softened, about 7 minutes. Add garlic, oregano, rosemary, sea salt and peppercorns and cook, stirring, for 1 minute. Stir in tomato paste and wine. Bring to a boil and cook, stirring and scraping up brown bits from bottom of pan, for 2 minutes.

3. Transfer to slow cooker stoneware. Stir in potatoes and stock. Cover and cook on Low for 8 hours or on High for 4 hours, until meat is very tender and potatoes are cooked through.

4. In a small bowl, dissolve sweet and hot paprika in water. Add to stoneware and stir well. Cover and cook on High for 15 minutes, until flavors meld.

Moroccan-Spiced Beef Stew

Serves 6 to 8

◆ **Entertaining Worthy**
◆ **Can Be Halved**
(see Tips, below)

Tips

If you are halving this recipe, be sure to use a small (approx. 1½ to 3 quart) slow cooker.

Harissa is a spice paste indigenous to North Africa, which is useful for adding heat and complexity to soups and stews. It is available in specialty stores, but if you prefer, you can make your own (page 239).

Make Ahead

Complete Steps 1 and 3. Cover and refrigerate mixtures for up to 2 days. When you're ready to cook, continue with recipe.

This delicious mélange is easy to make and so good you'll want to share it with friends. All you need to add is a simple green vegetable such as steamed beans.

• **Medium to large (3½ to 5 quart) slow cooker**

1 tbsp	cumin seeds	15 mL
2 tbsp	clarified butter or beef tallow, divided	30 mL
2 lbs	stewing beef, cut into 1-inch (2.5 cm) cubes	1 kg
2	onions, thinly sliced on the vertical	2
4	cloves garlic, minced	4
1 tbsp	minced gingerroot	15 mL
1	piece (2 inches/5 cm) cinnamon stick	1
½ tsp	freshly grated nutmeg	2 mL
½ tsp	cracked black peppercorns	2 mL
4	whole cloves	4
1	can (14 oz/398 mL) diced tomatoes with juice (see page 13)	1
2 cups	beef stock	500 mL
2 cups	sliced peeled carrots	500 mL
½ cup	finely chopped flat-leaf parsley leaves	125 mL
1 tsp to 1 tbsp	harissa, optional (see Tips, left)	5 to 15 mL

1. In a skillet over medium heat, cook cumin seeds, stirring, until fragrant and seeds just begin to brown, about 3 minutes. Using a mortar and pestle or a spice grinder, pound or grind as finely as you can. Set aside.

2. In same skillet, heat 1 tbsp (15 mL) of the clarified butter over medium-high heat. Add beef, in batches, and cook, stirring, until lightly browned on all sides, about 4 minutes per batch. Transfer to slow cooker stoneware as completed.

3. Reduce heat to medium. Add remaining tbsp (15 mL) of butter to pan. Add onions and cook, stirring, until softened, about 3 minutes. Add garlic, ginger, cinnamon stick, nutmeg, peppercorns, cloves and reserved cumin and cook, stirring, for 1 minute. Add tomatoes with juice, stock and carrots. Bring to a boil and cook, stirring and scraping up brown bits from bottom of pan, for 2 minutes.

4. Transfer to slow cooker stoneware. Cover and cook on Low for 8 hours or on High for 4 hours, until beef and carrots are tender. Stir in harissa, if using, 1 tsp (5 mL) at a time, tasting after each addition, until desired spiciness is achieved. Cover and cook on High for 10 minutes, until flavors meld.

Coconut Beef Curry

◆ **Entertaining Worthy**
◆ **Can Be Halved**
(see Tips, below)

Tips

If you are halving this recipe, be sure to use a small (approx. 1½ to 3 quart) slow cooker.

I recommend using a smaller slow cooker to make this dish because it cooks in a small amount of liquid and some of the meat may not be completely covered during the cooking process. If your meat is not completely covered by liquid, stir it once or twice during cooking to ensure the meat doesn't oxidize, or cover with a large piece of parchment paper, pressing it down to brush the food and extending up the sides of the stoneware so it overlaps the rim.

For best results, toast and grind whole coriander and whole cumin seeds yourself. Place in a dry skillet over medium heat and cook, stirring, until fragrant, about 3 minutes. Using a mortar and pestle or a spice grinder, pound or grind as finely as you can.

Make Ahead

Complete Step 2. Cover and refrigerate mixture for up to 2 days. When you're ready to cook, complete the recipe.

This aromatic curry is a bit of a hybrid, borrowing from both Indian and Thai cuisines and adding French mustard to complete the mix. While the combination of beef and coconut milk isn't common, it is the basis of massaman curry, an elaborate special occasion dish in Thailand. This much simpler recipe is slightly sweet, with an abundance of ginger and a hint of cardamom. Vary the quantity of chiles to suit your taste.

- **Medium (3½ to 4 quart) slow cooker (see Tips, left)**

2 tbsp	extra virgin coconut oil, divided	30 mL
2 lbs	trimmed stewing beef, cut into ½-inch (1 cm) cubes and patted dry	1 kg
2	onions, finely chopped	2
4	cloves garlic, minced	4
2 tbsp	minced gingerroot	30 mL
2 tsp	ground coriander (see Tips, left)	10 mL
1 tsp	ground cumin	5 mL
1 tsp	ground turmeric	5 mL
1 tsp	sea salt	5 mL
1 tsp	cracked black peppercorns	5 mL
2	black cardamom pods, crushed	2
1	piece (3 inches/7.5 cm) cinnamon stick	1
1 cup	beef, chicken or vegetable stock or water	250 mL
2	long red chiles, seeded and minced	2
1 tsp	Dijon mustard (see Tips, page 151)	5 mL
1 cup	coconut milk	250 mL
	Finely chopped cilantro	

1. In a skillet, heat 1 tbsp (15 mL) of the oil over medium-high heat. Add beef, in batches, and cook, stirring, until lightly browned on all sides, about 4 minutes per batch. Transfer to slow cooker stoneware as completed.

2. Add remaining tbsp (15 mL) of oil to pan. Add onions and cook, stirring, until they begin to turn golden, about 5 minutes. Add garlic, ginger, coriander, cumin, turmeric, sea salt, peppercorns, cardamom and cinnamon stick and cook, stirring, for 1 minute. Add stock and bring to a boil.

3. Transfer to slow cooker stoneware and stir well. Cover and cook on Low for 8 hours or on High for 4 hours, until meat is very tender.

4. In a small bowl, combine chiles, mustard and coconut milk, stirring well to combine. Stir into meat. Cover and cook on High for 30 minutes, until flavors meld. Garnish with cilantro.

Country Stew with Fennel

◆ **Entertaining Worthy**
◆ **Can Be Halved**
(see Tips, below)

Tips

If you are halving this recipe, be sure to use a small (approx. 1½ to 3 quart) slow cooker.

Look for canned tomatoes that are organically grown, with no salt added, and come in glass jars or BPA (bisphenol-A) free cans. When using canned tomatoes (or any canned product) check to make sure they are gluten-free.

Make Ahead

This dish can be partially prepared before it is cooked. Complete Step 1. Complete Step 3, heating 1 tbsp (15 mL) oil in pan before softening onions. Cover and refrigerate for up to 2 days. When you're ready to cook, either brown the beef as outlined in Step 2 or add it to the stoneware without browning. Stir well and continue with Step 4.

Full of character, this robust beef stew, which is rooted in French country cooking, is the perfect antidote to a bone-chilling night. Don't worry if you're not a fan of anchovies — they add depth to the sauce and their taste is negligible in the finished dish.

- Medium to large (3½ to 5 quart) slow cooker

½ tsp	fennel seeds	2 mL
2 tbsp	clarified butter or beef tallow (approx.)	30 mL
1½ lbs	stewing beef, trimmed of fat, cut into 1-inch (2.5 cm) cubes and patted dry	750 g
2	onions, finely chopped	2
4	stalks celery, thinly sliced	4
1	bulb fennel, trimmed, cored and thinly sliced on the vertical	1
4	cloves garlic, minced	4
4	anchovy fillets, minced	4
1 tsp	dried thyme	5 mL
½ tsp	sea salt	2 mL
½ tsp	cracked black peppercorns	2 mL
1	can (28 oz/796 mL) tomatoes, including juice, coarsely chopped (see Tips, left)	1
2	bay leaves	2
½ cup	chopped pitted black olives	125 mL

1. In a dry skillet over medium heat, toast fennel seeds, stirring, until fragrant, about 3 minutes. Immediately transfer to a mortar or a spice grinder and grind. (Or place the seeds on a cutting board and crush, using the bottom of a bottle or cup.) Set aside.

2. In same skillet, heat clarified butter over medium-high heat. Add beef, in batches, and cook, stirring, adding more butter, if necessary, until lightly browned, about 4 minutes per batch. Using a slotted spoon, transfer to slow cooker stoneware.

3. Reduce heat to medium. Add onions, celery and bulb fennel to pan and cook, stirring, until celery is softened, about 5 minutes. Add garlic, anchovies, thyme, sea salt, peppercorns and reserved fennel seeds and cook, stirring, for 1 minute. Add tomatoes with juice and bring to a boil. Cook, stirring, just until mixture begins to thicken, about 2 minutes. Add bay leaves and stir well.

4. Transfer to slow cooker stoneware. Cover and cook on Low for 8 hours or on High for 4 hours, until beef is tender. Discard bay leaves. Stir in olives and serve.

Saucy Swiss Steak

Serves 6

◆ **Can Be Halved**
(see Tips, below)

Tips

If you are halving this recipe, be sure to use a small (approx. 2 quart) slow cooker.

While round steak is traditionally used for this dish, an equally successful version can be made with "simmering steak," which is cut from the blade or cross rib.

I have included Worcestershire sauce in this recipe because it is a very easy way to dramatically enhance the flavor of this dish. If you object to using a prepared sauce, substitute 2 tsp (10 mL) balsamic vinegar and 1 tsp (5 mL) minced anchovies.

Make Ahead

Complete Step 2. Cover and refrigerate mixture for up to 2 days. When you're ready to cook, complete the recipe.

Here's a retro dish that channels the 1950s. Back then it required a fair bit of muscle to pound the steak with a mallet. Today, you can avoid all that dreary work by using the slow cooker. This is so good, you'll want seconds.

• **Medium (approx. 3½ quart) slow cooker**

2 tbsp	clarified butter or beef tallow, divided	30 mL
2 lbs	round steak or "simmering" steak, patted dry (see Tips, left)	1 kg
2	medium onions, finely chopped	2
1	small carrot, peeled and thinly sliced, about ¼ cup (60 mL)	1
1	small stalk celery, thinly sliced, about ¼ cup (60 mL)	1
½ tsp	sea salt	2 mL
½ tsp	cracked black peppercorns	2 mL
1	bay leaf	1
1	can (28 oz/796 mL) diced tomatoes, drained and ½ cup (125 mL) juice reserved (see page 13)	1
1 tbsp	gluten-free Worcestershire sauce (see Tips, left)	15 mL

1. In a skillet, heat 1 tbsp (15 mL) of the clarified butter over medium-high heat. Add steak, in pieces, if necessary, and brown on both sides. Transfer to slow cooker stoneware.

2. Reduce heat to medium and add remaining tbsp (15 mL) of butter to pan. Add onions, carrot and celery to pan and cook, stirring, until softened, about 5 minutes. Stir in sea salt, peppercorns and bay leaf. Add tomatoes and reserved juice. Bring to a boil, stirring, until slightly thickened.

3. Pour tomato mixture over steak and cook on Low for 8 hours or on for High 4 hours, until meat is tender. Stir in Worcestershire sauce. Discard bay leaf and serve.

Beef Tallow

Beef tallow is rendered beef fat. It is a very stable fat, only about half of which is saturated, although saturated fats play a significant role in keeping us healthy by performing functions such as boosting immunity and promoting bone health. Beef tallow is excellent for frying. Among other benefits, it is a source of palmitoleic acid, an omega-7 fatty acid, which appears to have a beneficial effect on certain health conditions.

Boatmen's Braised Steak

Serves 4 to 6

◆ **Can Be Halved**
(see Tips, below)

Tips

If you are halving this recipe, be sure to use a small (approx. 1½ to 3 quart) slow cooker.

If you prefer, substitute 1 cup (250 mL) chicken stock plus 1 tbsp (15 mL) lemon juice for the white wine.

Be aware that these cooking times are general estimates. Not only do cooking times vary substantially among slow cookers (see Cooking Times, page 18), but people have different preferences with regard to how well they like their meat done. If you prefer fork-tender results, start checking after the food has cooked for 6 hours on Low.

Make Ahead

Complete Step 2. Cover and refrigerate mixture for up to 2 days. When you're ready to cook, complete the recipe.

This is a traditional French recipe that originated with the men who ran barges on the Rhône River, a transport route for goods coming inland from the Mediterranean Sea. It is hearty and very warming, and on the boats it was served directly from the pan. Its enthusiastic flavors cry out for some robust red wine.

• **Medium (approx 3½ quart) slow cooker**

2 tbsp	clarified butter or beef tallow, divided	30 mL
2 to 3 lbs	braising steak, such as round, blade or cross-rib steak, patted dry	1 to 1.5 kg
2	onions, thinly sliced on the vertical	2
4	cloves garlic, minced	4
1 tsp	cracked black peppercorns	5 mL
1 tsp	dried thyme	5 mL
½ tsp	sea salt	2 mL
1	bay leaf	1
1 cup	dry white wine (see Tips, left)	250 mL
2 tbsp	red wine vinegar	30 mL
1 tbsp	drained capers	15 mL
4	anchovy fillets, finely chopped	4
4	gherkins, diced	4

1. In a skillet, heat 1 tbsp (15 mL) of the clarified butter over medium-high heat. Add steak, in pieces, if necessary, and brown on both sides, about 4 minutes. Transfer to slow cooker stoneware.

2. Reduce heat to medium. Add remaining tbsp (15 mL) of butter to pan. Add onions and cook, stirring, until softened, about 3 minutes. Add garlic, peppercorns, thyme, sea salt and bay leaf and cook, stirring and scraping up brown bits from bottom of pan, for 1 minute. Add wine, bring a boil and boil for 2 minutes. Stir in vinegar. Pour over steak.

3. Cover and cook on Low for 6 to 8 hours or on High for 4 to 5 hours, until meat is very tender. Transfer meat to a deep platter and keep warm. Transfer sauce to a saucepan and bring to a boil over medium-high heat. Reduce heat and simmer until slightly thickened and reduced, about 10 minutes. Remove and discard bay leaf. Stir in capers, anchovies and gherkins. Pour over steak and serve.

Steak in Pizzaiola Sauce

◆ **Can Be Halved**
(see Tips, below)

Tips

If you are halving this recipe, be sure to use a small (approx. 2 to 3½ quart) slow cooker.

Even if you aren't a fan of anchovies, be sure to use them here. They really enhance the flavor of tomatoes and add depth to the sauce. Their own taste completely disappears in the mix.

Use any variety of hot red pepper to suit your taste, from the usual cayenne to more exotic varieties such as Syrian Aleppo.

Be aware that these cooking times are general estimates. Not only do cooking times vary substantially among slow cookers (see Cooking Times, page 18), but people have different preferences with regard to how well they like their meat done. If you prefer fork-tender results, start checking after the food has cooked for 6 hours on Low.

Make Ahead

Complete Step 2. Cover and refrigerate mixture for up to 2 days. When you're ready to cook, continue with the recipe.

In Italy, pizzaiola sauce (so named because it is traditionally used on pizza) is often served with pasta, chicken, fish or seafood. Here it provides a simple but sumptuous topping for a chewy cut of steak, which becomes meltingly tender in the slow cooker. Steamed spinach makes a perfect accompaniment.

• **Medium (approx. 3½ quart) slow cooker**

2 tbsp	clarified butter or beef tallow, divided	30 mL
2 to 3 lbs	braising steak, such as round, blade or cross-rib steak, patted dry	1 to 1.5 kg
4	cloves garlic, minced	4
4	anchovy fillets, chopped (see Tips, left)	4
2 tbsp	chopped parsley leaves	30 mL
1 tbsp	dried oregano, crumbled	15 mL
½ tsp	sea salt	2 mL
½ tsp	cracked black peppercorns	2 mL
1	can (28 oz/796 mL) tomatoes with juice, coarsely chopped (see page 13)	1
1 tsp	crushed hot red pepper (see Tips, left)	5 mL

1. In a skillet, heat 1 tbsp (15 mL) clarified butter over medium-high heat. Add steak, in pieces, if necessary, and brown on both sides, about 4 minutes. Transfer to slow cooker stoneware.

2. Reduce heat to medium. Add remaining tbsp (15 mL) clarified butter to pan. Add garlic, anchovies, parsley, oregano, sea salt and peppercorns and cook, stirring and scraping up brown bits from the bottom of the pan, until anchovies dissolve. Stir in tomatoes with juice and bring to a boil.

3. Transfer to slow cooker stoneware. Cover and cook on Low for 6 to 8 hours or on High for 3 to 4 hours, until meat is tender. Stir in crushed red pepper and cook on High for 10 minutes, until flavors meld.

Ranch House Chicken Fried Steak

◆ **Can Be Halved**
(see Tips, below)

Tips

If you are halving this recipe, be sure to use a small (approx. 2 quart) slow cooker.

While round steak is traditionally used for this dish, an equally successful version can be made with "simmering steak," which is cut from the blade or cross rib.

If you are using the outer stalks of celery, peel them before slicing to remove the fibrous exterior.

Make Ahead

Complete Step 2. Cover and refrigerate mixture for up to 2 days. When you're ready to cook, complete the recipe.

There's no chicken in it, so where did this classic cowboy dish get its name? Frankly, who cares? Making it in the slow cooker eliminates the traditional tasks of pounding the meat and watching the frying pan. It also produces melt-in-your-mouth results. The rich, spicy pan gravy served over mashed potatoes is a marriage made in heaven.

• **Medium (approx. 3½ quart) slow cooker**

1 tbsp	clarified butter or beef tallow (see page 144)	15 mL
2 lbs	round steak or "simmering" steak, patted dry (see Tips, left)	1 kg
2	onions, thinly sliced	2
2	stalks celery, thinly sliced (see Tips, left)	2
3	cloves garlic, minced	3
1 tsp	cracked black peppercorns	5 mL
½ tsp	sea salt	2 mL
1 cup	chicken stock	250 mL
1 tsp	sweet paprika	5 mL
¼ tsp	cayenne pepper	1 mL
¼ cup	sour cream, divided (see page 14)	60 mL
1 to 2	jalapeño peppers, finely chopped	1 to 2

1. In a skillet, heat clarified butter over medium-high heat. Add steak, in pieces, if necessary, and brown on both sides. Transfer to slow cooker stoneware.

2. Reduce heat to medium. Add onions and celery to skillet and cook, stirring, until softened, about 5 minutes. Add garlic, peppercorns and sea salt and cook, stirring, for 1 minute. Add stock, bring to a boil and cook, stirring and scraping up brown bits from the bottom of pan.

3. Transfer to stoneware. Cover and cook on Low for 8 hours or on High for 4 hours, until meat is tender.

4. In a small bowl, combine paprika, cayenne pepper and 2 tbsp (30 mL) of the sour cream, mixing until blended. Add to stoneware along with remaining sour cream and jalapeño pepper to taste. Cover and cook on High for 15 minutes to meld flavors.

Down-Home Smothered Steak

◆ **Can Be Halved**
(see Tips, below)

Tips

If you are halving this recipe, be sure to use a small (approx. 2 quart) slow cooker.

While round steak is traditionally used for this dish, an equally successful version can be made with "simmering steak," which is cut from the blade or cross rib.

If you are using the outer stalks of celery, peel them before slicing to remove the fibrous exterior.

Be aware that these cooking times are general estimates. Not only do cooking times vary substantially among slow cookers (see Cooking Times, page 18), but people have different preferences with regard to how well they like their meat done. If you prefer fork-tender results, start checking after the food has cooked for 6 hours on Low.

Make Ahead

Complete Step 2. Cover and refrigerate mixture for up to 2 days. When you're ready to cook, complete the recipe.

This traditional favorite from the Deep South is usually cooked on top of the stove, where it requires a fair bit of watching. Not only does the slow cooker do away with that tedious work, it produces outstanding results. Serve the rich gravy over mashed yellow squash.

• **Medium (approx. 3½ quart) slow cooker**

2 tbsp	clarified butter or beef tallow (see page 144), divided	30 mL
2 lbs	round steak or "simmering" steak, patted dry (see Tips, left)	1 kg
1	onion, thinly sliced	1
2	stalks celery, thinly sliced (see Tips, left)	2
½ tsp	sea salt	2 mL
½ tsp	cracked black peppercorns	2 mL
2 cups	beef stock	500 mL
2	green bell peppers, cut into thin strips	2

1. In a skillet, heat 1 tbsp (15 mL) of the clarified butter over medium-high heat. Add steak, in pieces, if necessary, and brown on both sides. Transfer to slow cooker stoneware.

2. Reduce heat to medium and add remaining tbsp (15 mL) of butter to pan. Add onion and celery and cook, stirring, until softened, about 5 minutes. Add sea salt and peppercorns. Add stock and bring to a boil, stirring to scrape up brown bits from bottom of pan.

3. Pour over meat. Cover and cook on Low for 8 hours or on High for 4 hours, until meat is tender.

4. Stir in bell peppers. Cover and cook on High for 20 minutes, until peppers are tender. Serve piping hot.

Steak Smothered in Mushroom Onion Gravy

Serves 6 to 8

◆ **Can Be Halved**
(see Tips, below)

Tips

If you are halving this recipe, be sure to use a small (2 to 3½ quart) slow cooker.

Be aware that these cooking times are general estimates. Not only do cooking times vary substantially among slow cookers (see Cooking Times, page 18), but people have different preferences with regard to how well they like their meat done. If you prefer fork-tender results, start checking after the food has cooked for 6 hours on Low.

While round steak is traditionally used for this dish, an equally successful version can be made with steak that is cut from the blade or cross rib, sometimes identified as "simmering steak." It is available at many supermarkets. If the whole piece won't fit in your slow cooker or skillet, cut it in half.

Make Ahead

Complete Step 3. Cover and refrigerate for up to 2 days. When you're ready to cook, continue with the recipe.

I don't know why — perhaps there is a Proust moment lurking in the background — but this dish reminds me of growing up. The closest my mother came to this was sautéing sliced white mushrooms in butter as an accompaniment to steak. This is a much more delicious version of that meal — the rich gravy and succulent meat are a real treat.

• **Medium to large (3½ to 5 quart) slow cooker**

1	package (½ oz/14 g) dried porcini mushrooms	1
1 cup	hot water	250 mL
2 tbsp	clarified butter or beef tallow, divided	30 mL
2 to 3 lbs	braising steak, such as round, blade or cross-rib steak, patted dry (see Tips, left)	1 to 1.5 kg
3	onions, thinly sliced on the vertical	3
2	cloves garlic, minced	2
1 tsp	dried thyme	5 mL
½ tsp	sea salt	2 mL
½ tsp	cracked black peppercorns	2 mL
1	bay leaf	1
1 tbsp	tomato paste or 2 tbsp (30 mL) minced reconstituted sun-dried tomatoes (see page 13)	15 mL
½ cup	dry sherry	125 mL
8 oz	cremini mushrooms, trimmed and sliced	250 g

1. In a bowl, combine dried mushrooms and hot water. Let stand for 30 minutes, then strain through a fine sieve, reserving liquid. Pat mushrooms dry with paper towel and chop finely. Set liquid and mushrooms aside separately.

2. In a skillet, heat 1 tbsp (15 mL) of the clarified butter over medium-high heat. Add steak and brown, in pieces, if necessary, on both sides, about 4 minutes. Transfer to slow cooker stoneware.

3. Reduce heat to medium. Add remaining tbsp (15 mL) of butter to pan. Add onions and cook, stirring, until they begin to turn golden, about 7 minutes. Add garlic, thyme, sea salt, peppercorns, bay leaf and reserved dried mushrooms and cook, stirring and scraping up brown bits from bottom of pan, for 1 minute. Stir in tomato paste. Add sherry and cook, stirring, for 1 minute. Stir in reserved mushroom liquid and 1 cup (250 mL) water. Bring to a boil and cook, stirring, until slightly thickened, about 3 minutes.

4. Transfer to slow cooker. Stir in cremini mushrooms. Cover and cook on Low for 6 to 8 hours or on High for 3 to 4 hours, until meat is very tender. Discard bay leaf.

Sloppy Joes

◆ **Can Be Halved**
(see Tips, below)

Tips

If you are halving this recipe, be sure to use a small (approx. 1½ to 3 quart) slow cooker.

For best results, toast and grind whole cumin seeds yourself. *To toast cumin seeds:* Place seeds in a dry skillet over medium heat and cook, stirring, until fragrant, about 3 minutes. Using a mortar and pestle or a spice grinder, pound or grind as finely as you can.

Dijon mustard is a robust blend of mustard seeds, white wine, herbs and seasoning and it should not contain gluten. However, gluten has made its way into many condiments, so check the label.

Make Ahead

Complete Steps 1 and 2. Cover and refrigerate meat and vegetable mixtures separately for up to 2 days. When you're ready to cook, complete the recipe.

This American classic is a great dish for those evenings when everyone is coming and going at different times. Just leave Roasted Eggplant (or Zucchini) Boats ready to be reheated and the fixin's for salad. People can scoop up a serving of this delicious mélange and enjoy a satisfying and nutritious meal.

• **Small to medium (2 to 4 quart) slow cooker**

2 tbsp	clarified butter or beef tallow, divided	30 mL
1 lb	lean ground beef	500 g
2	onions, finely chopped	2
2	stalks celery, diced (see Tips, 148)	2
2	cloves garlic, minced	2
2 tsp	ground cumin (see Tips, left)	10 mL
2 tsp	dried oregano	10 mL
½ tsp	sea salt	2 mL
½ tsp	cracked black peppercorns	2 mL
1	can (14 oz/398 mL) diced tomatoes with juice	1
1 tbsp	tomato paste or 2 tbsp (30 mL) minced reconstituted sun-dried tomatoes (see page 13)	15 mL
1 tbsp	balsamic vinegar	15 mL
1 tbsp	coconut sugar	15 mL
1 tbsp	Dijon mustard (see Tips, left)	15 mL
1	green bell pepper, seeded and diced	1
1	jalapeño pepper, seeded and diced	1
	Roasted Eggplant Boats (page 243)	

1. In a skillet, heat 1 tbsp (15 mL) of the clarified butter over medium-high heat. Add beef and cook, stirring, until meat is no longer pink, about 5 minutes. Transfer to slow cooker stoneware.

2. Reduce heat to medium. Add remaining tbsp (15 mL) of clarified butter to pan. Add onions and celery and cook, stirring and scraping up brown bits from bottom of pan, until softened, about 5 minutes. Add garlic, cumin, oregano, sea salt and peppercorns and cook, stirring, for 1 minute. Stir in tomatoes with juice, tomato paste, vinegar, coconut sugar and mustard and bring to a boil.

3. Transfer to slow cooker stoneware. Cover and cook on Low for 6 hours or on High for 3 hours, until hot and bubbly. Stir in bell and jalapeño peppers. Cover and cook on High for 20 minutes, until peppers are tender. Serve over Roasted Eggplant Boats.

Hot Italian Meatballs

Serves 4 to 6

◆ **Can Be Halved**
(see Tips, below)

Tips

If you are halving this recipe, be sure to use a small (approx. 2 to 3 quart) slow cooker.

Hot banana peppers, which are long, thin, yellow peppers ending in a sharp point, are available in most supermarkets or greengrocers. Although they are fiery and should, therefore, be used with discretion, they are far more subdued than their chile pepper relatives.

Everyone loves these zesty meatballs, which make a great weeknight dinner or weekend lunch. If you're certain that everyone likes the same degree of hotness, add the roasted banana peppers to the sauce just before serving. To play it safe, serve the peeled, chopped peppers in a separate dish so that people can help themselves. Serve over Grilled Eggplant (see Variations, page 153) or Zucchini Noodles (page 153).

• **Medium to large (3½ to 5 quart) slow cooker**

Meatballs

1 lb	lean ground beef	500 g
¼ cup	grated onion	60 mL
2	cloves garlic, minced	2
2 tbsp	finely chopped flat-leaf parsley leaves	30 mL
¼ cup	almond flour	60 mL
½ tsp	freshly grated nutmeg	2 mL
½ tsp	sea salt	2 mL
½ tsp	freshly ground black pepper	2 mL
1 tbsp	clarified butter or beef tallow	15 mL

Tomato Sauce

1	onion, finely chopped	1
2	stalks celery, peeled and thinly sliced	2
2	cloves garlic, minced	2
2 tsp	dried oregano	10 mL
½ tsp	sea salt	2 mL
½ tsp	cracked black peppercorns	2 mL
6	whole cloves	6
1	can (28 oz/796 mL) tomatoes, drained and chopped	1
½ cup	dry red wine	125 mL
2 to 4	hot banana peppers, roasted, peeled and cut into ½-inch (1 cm) slices (see Tips, left and right)	2 to 4
	Grilled Eggplant, optional (see Variations, page 153)	

1. *Meatballs:* In a bowl, combine beef, onion, garlic, parsley, almond flour, nutmeg, sea salt and pepper. Mix well. Form into 8 balls of uniform size.

2. In a skillet, heat clarified butter over medium-high heat. Add meatballs, in batches, if necessary, and brown on all sides, about 4 minutes per batch. Transfer to slow cooker stoneware.

Tip

To roast peppers: Preheat oven to 400°F (200°C). Place pepper(s) on a baking sheet and roast, turning two or three times, until skin on all sides is blackened, about 25 minutes. Transfer pepper(s) to a heatproof bowl. Cover with a plate and let stand until cool. Remove and, using a sharp knife, lift skins off. Discard skins and slice according to recipe instructions.

3. *Tomato Sauce:* Reduce heat to medium. Add onion and celery to pan and cook, stirring, until softened, about 5 minutes. Add garlic, oregano, sea salt, peppercorns and cloves and cook, stirring, for 1 minute. Stir in tomatoes and wine, bring to a boil and cook, stirring, until mixture is reduced by one-third, depending upon the size of your pan, about 5 minutes. Pour over meatballs, cover and cook on Low for 6 hours or on High for 3 hours, until meatballs are cooked through. Serve over Grilled Eggplant, if using, or Zucchini Noodles.

Variations

Substitute an equal quantity of red bell peppers for the hot banana peppers.

Grilled Eggplant: Cut eggplant into slices about $1/2$ inch (1 cm) thick. Brush with extra virgin olive oil and place on hot grill, turning once, until lightly browned, about 5 minutes per side. Season with sea salt and freshly ground black pepper to taste.

Zucchini Noodles

I learned how to make zucchini noodles from raw chef Doug McNish and there is no question they are terrific with the wide range of raw sauces he created for his book *Eat Raw, Eat Well*. But I also enjoy them lightly cooked, with a robust sauce, as a substitute for wheat pasta. You can sauté them briefly in extra virgin olive oil with a bit of garlic, or blanche them in a pot of boiling salted water for 1 minute, then drain and rinse under cold running water before topping with any traditional pasta sauce.

I usually use a spiral vegetable slicer to make zucchini "spaghetti" (follow the manufacturer's instructions) but you can also use a julienne vegetable slicer to make julienned zucchini, or a vegetable peeler to make thin strips of the vegetable. You can also use a mandoline, in which case, after slicing the zucchini thinly, stack the slices on top of each other and cut them lengthwise into strips about $1/2$-inch (1 cm) wide. Whatever your technique, you will need about one good-size zucchini per person. For other tasty pasta substitutes, see Kelp Noodles, page 220 or Roasted Spaghetti Squash, page 243.

Meatball Goulash

◆ **Can Be Halved**
(see Tips, below)

Tip

If you are halving this recipe, be sure to use a small (2 to 3½ quart) slow cooker.

Make Ahead

Complete Step 3. Cover and refrigerate for up to 2 days. When you're ready to cook, complete the recipe.

I love the flavors in this sauce — paprika, sweet peppers and tomatoes, with just a hint of caraway seed.

- **Medium to large (3½ to 5 quart) slow cooker**
- **Food processor**

Meatballs

1	onion, quartered	1
2	cloves garlic, chopped	2
½ cup	flat-leaf parsley leaves	125 mL
½ tsp	sea salt	2 mL
	Freshly ground black pepper	
1 lb	lean ground beef	500 g
1 lb	lean ground pork	500 g
¼ cup	almond flour	60 mL
1	egg, beaten	1
2 tbsp	clarified butter or beef tallow, divided	30 mL
2	onions, finely chopped	2
4	cloves garlic, minced	4
1 tsp	caraway seeds	5 mL
½ tsp	each sea salt and cracked black peppercorns	2 mL
1	can (28 oz/796 mL) tomatoes with juice, coarsely chopped (see page 13)	1
1 cup	beef stock	250 mL
2	red bell peppers, seeded and diced	2
1 tbsp	paprika (sweet or hot), dissolved in 2 tbsp (30 mL) lemon juice	15 mL
½ cup	finely chopped fresh dill fronds	125 mL
	Sour cream, optional (see page 14)	

1. *Meatballs:* In a food processor fitted with the metal blade, process onion, garlic, parsley, sea salt and pepper to taste. Process until onion is finely chopped. Add beef, pork, almond flour and egg, in batches, and pulse to combine. Shape mixture into 12 equal balls.

2. In a skillet, heat 1 tbsp (15 mL) of the clarified butter over medium-high heat. Add meatballs, in batches, and brown well, about 5 minutes per batch. Transfer to slow cooker stoneware.

3. Reduce heat to medium. Add remaining tbsp (15 mL) butter to pan. Add onions and cook, stirring, until softened, about 3 minutes. Add garlic, caraway, sea salt and peppercorns and cook, stirring, for 1 minute. Add tomatoes with juice and stock and bring to a boil.

4. Pour over meatballs. Cover and cook on Low for 6 to 8 hours or on High for 3 to 4 hours. Stir in bell peppers and paprika solution. Cover and cook on High for 30 minutes, until peppers are tender and flavors meld. Garnish with dill and a dollop of sour cream, if using.

Catalonian Meatballs

Tips

If you are halving this recipe, be sure to use a small (approx. 1$\frac{1}{2}$ to 3 quart) slow cooker.

If you have access to pure lard, feel free to substitute it for clarified butter in this recipe.

Make Ahead

Complete Step 4, heating 1 tbsp (15 mL) extra virgin olive oil before adding onions to pan. Cover and refrigerate mixture for up to 2 days. When you're ready to cook, complete the recipe.

This is an adaptation of a dish that appears in Anne Willan's book The Country Cooking of France. *These meatballs are traditionally cooked in an earthenware dish known as a cassola, but the slow cooker makes a wonderful substitute.*

• **Medium to large (3$\frac{1}{2}$ to 5 quart) slow cooker**

Meatballs

1 lb	lean ground beef	500 g
8 oz	ground pork	250 g
$\frac{1}{4}$ cup	almond flour + 2 tbsp (30 mL) for dredging	60 mL
4	cloves garlic, minced	4
1	egg, beaten	1
$\frac{1}{2}$ tsp	sea salt	2 mL
	Freshly ground black pepper	
1 tbsp	clarified butter, beef tallow or pure lard	15 mL
2 oz	chunk bacon, diced	60 g

Sauce Rousse

2	onions, finely chopped	2
$\frac{1}{2}$ tsp	cracked black peppercorns	2 mL
1	piece (2 inches/5 cm) cinnamon stick	1
2 cups	beef, chicken or vegetable stock	500 mL
1 tbsp	tomato paste (see page 13)	15 mL
$\frac{1}{2}$ cup	sliced pimento-stuffed olives	125 mL
$\frac{1}{8}$ tsp	cayenne pepper	0.5 mL
$\frac{1}{4}$ cup	finely chopped flat-leaf parsley leaves	60 mL

1. In a large bowl, combine beef, pork, $\frac{1}{4}$ cup (60 mL) almond flour, garlic, egg, sea salt and pepper to taste. Mix well. Shape into 12 equal balls. Spread remaining almond flour on a plate and dredge meatballs in it until lightly coated. Discard any excess almond flour.

2. In a skillet, heat clarified butter over medium-high heat. Add bacon and cook, stirring, until lightly browned, about 5 minutes. Using a slotted spoon, transfer to slow cooker stoneware.

3. Working in batches, add meatballs to pan and cook until lightly browned on all sides, about 6 minutes per batch. Transfer to slow cooker stoneware as completed.

4. *Sauce Rousse:* Add onions to pan and cook, stirring, until softened, about 3 minutes. Add peppercorns and cinnamon stick and cook, stirring, for 1 minute. Stir in stock and tomato paste and bring to a boil.

5. Pour over meatballs. Cover and cook on Low for 6 to 8 hours or on High for 3 to 4 hours, until hot and bubbly and meatballs are cooked through. Add olives and cayenne and stir well. Cover and cook on High for 20 minutes. Garnish with parsley.

Best-Ever Bolognese Sauce

Tip

Bolognese sauce should be thick. Placing the tea towels over the top of the slow cooker absorbs generated moisture that would dilute the sauce.

Make Ahead

Complete Step 2. Cover mixture, ensuring it cools promptly (see Making Ahead, page 21), and refrigerate for up to 2 days. When you're ready to cook, complete the recipe.

This Italian meat sauce and robust porcini mushrooms traditionally develops flavor from long, slow simmering, making it perfect for the slow cooker. I like to serve this over Roasted Spaghetti Squash (page 243) or steamed Zucchini Noodles (page 153).

• **Medium to large (3$\frac{1}{2}$ to 5 quart) slow cooker**

1	package ($\frac{1}{2}$ oz/14 g) dried porcini mushrooms	1
1 cup	hot water	250 mL
1 tbsp	clarified butter, beef tallow or pure lard (approx.)	15 mL
2 oz	chunk pancetta, diced	60 g
1 lb	lean ground beef	500 g
8 oz	ground pork	250 g
2	onions, diced	2
2	stalks celery, diced	2
2	carrots, peeled and diced	2
4	cloves garlic, minced	4
1 tbsp	dried Italian seasoning	15 mL
2	bay leaves	2
$\frac{1}{2}$ tsp	sea salt	2 mL
$\frac{1}{2}$ tsp	cracked black peppercorns	2 mL
$\frac{1}{2}$ tsp	ground cinnamon	2 mL
1 cup	dry red wine	250 mL
1	can (28 oz/796 mL) tomatoes with juice, coarsely chopped	1
$\frac{1}{4}$ cup	tomato paste or $\frac{1}{2}$ cup (125 mL) crushed tomatoes (see page 13)	60 mL

1. In a bowl, combine dried mushrooms and hot water. Let stand for 30 minutes. Drain through a fine sieve, reserving liquid. Pat mushrooms dry with paper towel and chop finely. Set liquid and mushrooms aside.

2. Meanwhile, in a large skillet, heat clarified butter over medium-high heat. Add pancetta and cook, stirring, until browned, about 3 minutes. Using a slotted spoon, transfer to slow cooker stoneware. Add more clarified butter to pan, if necessary. (You should have about 1 tbsp/15 mL.) Add beef, pork, onions, celery and carrots and cook, stirring, until carrots have softened and meat is no longer pink, about 7 minutes. Add garlic, Italian seasoning, bay leaves, sea salt, peppercorns, cinnamon and reserved dried mushrooms and cook, stirring, for 1 minute. Add wine, bring to a boil and boil, stirring and scraping up brown bits from bottom of pan, for 2 minutes. Add reserved mushroom liquid.

3. Transfer to slow cooker stoneware. Add tomatoes with juice and stir well. Stir in tomato paste. Place 2 clean tea towels, each folded in half (so you will have 4 layers), over top of stoneware to absorb moisture. Cover and cook on Low for 6 to 8 hours or on High for 3 to 4 hours.

Osso Buco with Lemon Gremolata

Serves 6 to 8

◆ **Entertaining Worthy**
◆ **Can Be Halved**
(see Tips, below)

Tips

If you are halving this recipe, be sure to use a small (2 to 3½ quart) slow cooker.

Leeks can be gritty. *To clean leeks:* Split leeks in half lengthwise and submerge in a basin of water, swishing them around to remove all traces of dirt. Transfer to a colander and rinse under cold water.

If you are using the outer stalks of celery, peel them before slicing to remove the fibrous exterior.

This is probably my all-time favorite veal dish. I love the wine-flavored sauce and the succulent meat, enhanced with just a soupçon of gremolata, pungent with fresh garlic and lemon zest. But best of all, I adore eating the marrow from the bones, a rare and delicious treat. Pass coffee spoons to ensure that every mouthwatering morsel is extracted from the bone.

• **Large (minimum 5 quart) slow cooker**

1	package (½ oz/14 g) dried porcini mushrooms	1
1 cup	hot water	250 mL
¼ cup	almond flour	60 mL
½ tsp	sea salt	2 mL
½ tsp	freshly ground black pepper	2 mL
6 to 8	sliced veal shanks	6 to 8
2 tbsp	extra virgin olive oil (approx.)	30 mL
3	leeks, white part only, cleaned and thinly sliced (see Tips, left)	3
2	carrots, peeled and diced	2
2	stalks celery, thinly sliced (see Tips, left)	2
2	cloves garlic, minced	2
1 tsp	dried thyme or 2 sprigs fresh thyme	5 mL
½ cup	dry white wine	125 mL

Lemon Gremolata

1 cup	finely chopped flat-leaf parsley leaves	250 mL
2	cloves garlic, minced	2
	Zest of 1 lemon	

1. In a heatproof bowl, combine porcini mushrooms and hot water. Let stand for 30 minutes. Drain through a fine sieve, reserving liquid. Pat mushrooms dry with paper towel and chop finely. Set aside.

2. In a bowl, mix together almond flour, sea salt and pepper. Lightly coat veal shanks with mixture, shaking off excess. Discard any excess.

3. In a large skillet, heat oil over medium heat. Add veal, in batches, and cook until lightly browned on both sides, about 4 minutes per batch, adding more oil, if necessary. Transfer to slow cooker stoneware.

4. Add leeks, carrots and celery to pan and stir well. Reduce heat to low, cover and cook until vegetables are softened, about 10 minutes. Increase heat to medium. Add garlic, thyme and reserved mushrooms and cook, stirring, for 1 minute. Add wine and reserved mushroom liquid and bring to a boil, scraping up brown bits from the bottom of pan. Simmer for 5 minutes to reduce slightly.

Make Ahead

Complete Steps 1 and 4, adding 1 tbsp (15 mL) extra virgin olive oil to pan before softening vegetables. Cover and refrigerate mixture for up to 2 days. When you're ready to cook, complete the recipe.

5. Pour mixture over veal, cover and cook on Low for 8 hours or on High for 4 hours, until veal is very tender.

6. *Lemon Gremolata:* Combine parsley, garlic and lemon zest in a small serving bowl and pass around the table, allowing guests to individually garnish.

Variations

If you prefer a thicker sauce, transfer the cooked veal shanks to a deep platter and keep warm. Using an immersion blender, purée the sauce. (You can also do this in a food processor, in batches.)

Glazed Osso Buco: Preheat broiler. Transfer cooked shanks into a baking/serving dish large enough to accommodate them in a single layer. Spoon approximately 1 tbsp (15 mL) puréed sauce over each shank and heat under broiler until the top looks glazed and shiny, about 5 minutes. Serve remaining sauce in a sauceboat.

Wine-Braised Veal with Rosemary

◆ **Entertaining Worthy**
◆ **Can Be Halved**
(see Tips, below)

Tips

If you are halving this recipe, be sure to use a small (approx. 1½ to 3 quart) slow cooker.

Be aware that if you are using bacon in this recipe, the flavors will not be as pleasingly subtle.

If you are using fresh rosemary and prefer a more pronounced flavor, bury a whole sprig in the meat before adding the sauce. Remove before serving.

If you prefer, substitute an additional ½ cup (125 mL) chicken stock plus 1 tsp (5 mL) freshly squeezed lemon juice for the wine.

Make Ahead

This dish can be partially prepared before it is cooked. Complete Steps 1 and 3, refrigerating mixture for up to 2 days. When you're ready to cook, place veal in slow cooker (don't bother with browning) and continue with Step 4.

This is a delicious Italian-inspired stew that is both simple and elegant. Accompany with steamed broccoli or rapini.

• **Medium to large (3½ to 5 quart) slow cooker**

1 tbsp	clarified butter, beef tallow or lard (approx.) (see page 12)	15 mL
3 oz	pancetta or bacon, cut into ¼-inch (0.5 cm) dice (see Tips, left)	90 g
2 lbs	stewing veal, cut into 1-inch (2.5 cm) cubes and patted dry	1 kg
3	leeks, white part only, cleaned and coarsely chopped	3
3	large carrots, peeled and diced	3
2	stalks celery, diced	2
2	cloves garlic, minced	2
1½ tbsp	chopped fresh rosemary leaves or dried rosemary, crumbled (see Tips, left)	22 mL
½ tsp	sea salt	2 mL
½ tsp	cracked black peppercorns	2 mL
½ cup	dry red wine (see Tips, left)	125 mL
½ cup	chicken stock	125 mL
	Fresh rosemary sprigs, optional	

1. In a skillet, heat clarified butter over medium heat for 30 seconds. Add pancetta and cook, stirring, until browned. Using a slotted spoon, transfer to a bowl and set aside.

2. Add veal to pan, in batches, and cook, stirring, adding a bit more butter, if necessary, just until it begins to brown, about 4 minutes. Using a slotted spoon, transfer to slow cooker stoneware.

3. Add leeks, carrots and celery to pan and cook, stirring, until softened, about 7 minutes. Add garlic, rosemary, sea salt, peppercorns and reserved pancetta and cook, stirring, for 1 minute. Add wine and stock and cook, stirring, until mixture thickens.

4. Pour mixture over meat and stir to combine. Cover and cook on Low for 8 hours or on High for 4 hours, until meat is tender. Garnish with rosemary sprigs, if using, and serve.

Braised Veal with Pearl Onions

Serves 6

◆ **Entertaining Worthy**
◆ **Can Be Halved**
 (see Tips, below)

Tips

If you are halving this recipe, be sure to use a small (approx. 1½ to 3 quart) slow cooker.

To peel pearl onions, cut an "x" in the root end and drop them into a pot of rapidly boiling water for about 30 seconds. Drain in a colander and run under cold running water. The skins should lift off quite easily with a little prodding from you and a sharp paring knife.

Make Ahead

Complete Steps 1 and 3, adding pancetta to vegetable mixture along with the stock. Cover and refrigerate for up to 2 days. When you're ready to cook, complete the recipe.

Here veal is braised in white wine and chicken stock to produce a richly satisfying yet surprisingly light stew.

• **Medium to large (3½ to 5 quart) slow cooker**

2 tbsp	clarified butter or pure lard (approx.), divided (see page 12)	30 mL
2 oz	pancetta, diced	60 g
2 lbs	trimmed stewing veal, cut into 1-inch (2.5 cm) cubes and patted dry	1 kg
¼ cup	almond flour	60 mL
2	carrots, peeled and diced	2
2	stalks celery, diced (see Tips, page 158)	2
2	cloves garlic, minced	2
1 tsp	dried thyme	5 mL
½ tsp	sea salt	2 mL
½ tsp	cracked black peppercorns	2 mL
2	bay leaves	2
1 cup	dry white wine	250 mL
2 cups	chicken or veal stock	500 mL
24	pearl onions, peeled (see Tips, left)	24
2 cups	sweet green peas, thawed if frozen (see page 15)	500 mL
	Freshly ground black pepper	

1. In a skillet, heat 1 tbsp (15 mL) of the clarified butter over medium-high heat. Add pancetta and cook, stirring, until browned, about 3 minutes. Using a slotted spoon, transfer to stoneware. Set pan aside.

2. On a plate or in a plastic bag, dredge veal in almond flour until lightly coated. Return pan to element over medium heat. Add veal, in batches, and brown on all sides, transferring to stoneware as completed and adding more butter, if necessary.

3. Add remaining tbsp (15 mL) of clarified butter to pan. Add carrots and celery and cook, stirring, until softened, about 7 minutes. Add garlic, thyme, sea salt, peppercorns and bay leaves and cook, stirring, for 1 minute. Add wine, bring to a boil and boil for 2 minutes, stirring and scraping up brown bits from the bottom of the pan. Add stock. Return to a boil.

4. Transfer to stoneware. Stir in onions. Cover and cook on Low for 8 hours or on High for 4 hours, until veal is very tender. Add peas and pancetta and cook on High about 10 minutes, until tender. Season with pepper to taste. Serve immediately.

Veal Shank Ragù

Tips

If you are halving this recipe, be sure to use a small (approx. 1½ to 3 quart) slow cooker.

If you prefer, substitute 1 cup (250 mL) chicken stock mixed with 1 tbsp (15 mL) lemon juice for the wine.

Thyme and rosemary are both good seasonings for this ragù. I prefer to use rosemary when I have fresh sprigs on hand. If using fresh rosemary, remove and discard the stems before serving.

Make Ahead

Complete Step 3. Cover and refrigerate for up to 2 days. When you're ready to cook, complete the recipe.

Served over Roasted Spaghetti Squash (page 243) or Zucchini Noodles (page 153), this thick, luscious ragù is the perfect dish for a winter weekend in the country or après-ski. With a fire in the fireplace, a tossed salad and some robust red wine, what could be better?

- **Medium to large (3½ to 5 quart) slow cooker**
- **Large sheet of parchment paper**

1	package (½ oz/14 g) dried porcini mushrooms	1
1 cup	hot water	250 mL
3 tbsp	clarified butter, divided	45 mL
4	veal shanks, each about 12 oz (375 g), patted dry	4
2	onions, finely chopped	2
2	carrots, peeled and diced	2
2	stalks celery, diced (see Tips, page 158)	2
4	cloves garlic, minced	4
1 tsp	dried thyme or 2 sprigs fresh rosemary (see Tips, left)	5 mL
½ tsp	sea salt	2 mL
½ tsp	cracked black peppercorns	2 mL
1 cup	dry white wine (see Tips, left)	250 mL
1	can (14 oz/398 mL) tomatoes with juice, coarsely chopped (see page 13)	1

1. In a heatproof bowl, combine porcini mushrooms and hot water. Let stand for 30 minutes. Drain through a fine sieve, reserving liquid. Pat mushrooms dry with paper towel and chop finely. Set aside.

2. In a skillet, heat 2 tbsp (30 mL) of the clarified butter over medium-high heat. Add veal and cook until lightly browned on both sides, about 4 minutes. Transfer to slow cooker stoneware.

3. Add remaining tbsp (15 mL) of butter to pan. Add onions, carrots and celery and cook, stirring, until softened, about 7 minutes. Add garlic, thyme, sea salt, peppercorns and reserved porcini mushrooms and cook, stirring, for 1 minute. Add wine, bring to a boil and boil, stirring and scraping up brown bits from bottom of pan, for 2 minutes. Add tomatoes with juice and reserved mushroom liquid and bring to a boil.

4. Transfer to stoneware. Place a large piece of parchment over the mixture, pressing it down to brush the food and extending up the sides of the stoneware so it overlaps the rim. Cover and cook on Low for 10 hours or on High for 5 hours, until veal is tender. Lift out parchment and discard, being careful not to spill the accumulated liquid into the sauce. Transfer veal to a cutting board and chop into bite-size pieces. Return to slow cooker. Using a coffee spoon, scoop marrow from the bones and stir into stew. Taste and adjust seasoning.

Chinese-Style Braised Pork

Pork and Lamb

Chinese-Style Braised Pork

◆ **Entertaining Worthy**
◆ **Can Be Halved**
(see Tips, below)

Tips

If you are halving this recipe, be sure to use a small (approx. 1½ to 3 quart) slow cooker.

To purée garlic, use a fine, sharp-toothed grater, such as those made by Microplane.

If the whole piece of pork won't fit in your slow cooker, cut it in half and lay the two pieces on top of each other.

Pork shoulder can be very fatty. If your pork shoulder isn't trimmed of fat when you purchase it, I recommend removing the string and trimming off as much fat as possible before using. Broiling will render some of the fat.

I prefer to make this with dry sherry rather than traditional Chinese Shaoxing rice wine as, in my experience, the North American offerings of this product are extremely salty and combine with the soy sauce to produce a result that tastes overwhelmingly of salt.

This recipe is so easy to make you can dish it up as a weekday meal, but it's also delicious enough to serve to guests. A platter of stir-fried bok choy makes a perfect accompaniment. If you're offering wine, a cold Gewürztraminer is a perfect fit.

- **Medium (3 to 4 quart) slow cooker**
- **Rimmed baking sheet**

6	cloves garlic, puréed (see Tips, left)	6
1 tbsp	finely minced gingerroot	15 mL
1 tsp	cracked black peppercorns	5 mL
1 tsp	dry mustard	5 mL
½ tsp	sea salt	2 mL
3 lb	pork shoulder or blade (butt) roast (see Tips, left)	1.5 kg
½ cup	gluten-free soy sauce or coconut aminos (see page 15)	125 mL
¼ cup	dry sherry (see Tips, left)	60 mL
2 tbsp	coconut sugar	30 mL
3	star anise	3
¼ cup	chopped green onions	60 mL

1. In a small bowl, combine garlic, ginger, peppercorns, mustard and sea salt. Rub all over meat. Cover and refrigerate overnight or for up to 24 hours, turning several times, if possible.

2. When you're ready to cook, preheat broiler. Transfer pork to rimmed baking sheet and broil, turning, until skin and sides brown evenly, about 15 minutes. Transfer to slow cooker stoneware.

3. In a bowl, combine soy sauce, sherry, coconut sugar and star anise. Pour over pork. Cover and cook on Low for 8 hours or on High for 4 hours, until pork falls apart. To serve, cut pork into chunks, spoon pan juices over and garnish with green onions.

Braised Pork with Winter Vegetables

♦ **Can Be Halved**
(see Tips, below)

Tips

If you are halving this recipe, be sure to use a small (2 to 3½ quart) slow cooker.

If you are using chicken stock rather than wine, add 1 tbsp (15 mL) fresh lemon juice along with the stock. The sauce, which has a lovely sweetness from the parsnips, benefits from the hint of acidity.

Make Ahead

Complete Step 2. Cover and refrigerate mixture for up to 2 days. When you're ready to cook, brown the pork and complete the recipe. Or, if you prefer, add the unbrowned pork to the stoneware along with the vegetable mixture, being aware that the result will not be as flavorful as that produced using browned meat.

Here's a simple combination of ingredients that is surprisingly lush — partly due to the wonderful sweetness of the parsnips.

• **Large (approx. 5 quart) slow cooker**

2 tbsp	clarified butter or pure lard, divided (see page 12)	30 mL
2 lb	trimmed boneless pork shoulder or blade (butt), patted dry	1 kg
3	onions, thinly sliced on the vertical	3
3	carrots, peeled and diced	3
3	parsnips, peeled and diced	3
6	cloves garlic, minced	6
1 tsp	dried thyme	5 mL
1 tsp	cracked black peppercorns	5 mL
½ tsp	sea salt	2 mL
1 cup	dry white wine or chicken stock (see Tips, left)	250 mL
1	can (28 oz/796 mL) tomatoes with juice, coarsely chopped (see page 13)	1

1. In a large skillet, heat 1 tbsp (15 mL) of the clarified butter over medium-high heat. Add pork and brown on all sides, about 10 minutes. Transfer to slow cooker stoneware.

2. Reduce heat to medium. Add remaining tbsp (15 mL) of butter to pan. Add onions, carrots and parsnips and cook, stirring, until softened, about 7 minutes. Add garlic, thyme, peppercorns and sea salt and cook, stirring, for 1 minute. Add wine, bring to a boil and boil for 2 minutes, scraping up brown bits from bottom of pan. Add tomatoes with juice and return to a boil.

3. Transfer to slow cooker stoneware. Cover and cook on Low for 8 hours or on High for 4 hours, until meat is very tender.

Savory Braised Pork

◆ Entertaining Worthy

Tips

You can use a bone-in or boneless roast for this recipe, ranging in weight from about 3 to 4 lbs (1.5 to 2 kg). I do, however, suggest you use one from which the skin has been removed, to reduce the quantity of fat.

Pork shoulder can be very fatty. If your pork shoulder isn't trimmed of fat when you purchase it, I recommend removing the string and trimming off as much fat as possible before using.

Make Ahead

Complete Steps 1 and 3. Cover and refrigerate mixtures overnight. When you're ready to cook, brown the pork and continue with the recipe. Or, if you prefer, add the unbrowned marinated pork to the stoneware, then cover with the vegetable mixture, being aware that the result will not be as flavorful as that produced using browned meat.

This pork is very easy to make but it's disproportionately delicious because marinating it overnight imbues the meat with deep flavor. It makes a terrific Sunday dinner.

• **Medium (3 to 4 quart) slow cooker**

2 tsp	coriander seeds	10 mL
2 tsp	cumin seeds	10 mL
1 tsp	cracked black peppercorns	5 mL
6	cloves garlic, puréed (see Tips, page 166)	6
1 tsp	coarse sea salt	5 mL
1 tbsp	extra virgin olive oil	15 mL
1 tbsp	clarified butter or pure lard	15 mL
3 lb	pork shoulder or blade (butt) roast (see Tips, left)	1.5 kg
2	onions, finely chopped	2
2	stalks celery, diced	2
2	carrots, peeled and diced	2
2	bay leaves	2
½ cup	water or chicken stock	125 mL

1. In a skillet over medium heat, toast coriander and cumin seeds until fragrant, about 3 minutes. Transfer to a mortar or a spice grinder. Add peppercorns and coarsely pound or grind. Transfer to a bowl and combine with garlic, sea salt and oil. Make slits all over meat and fill with spice paste. Rub remainder all over meat. Cover and refrigerate overnight or for up to 24 hours, turning several times, if possible.

2. In a skillet, heat clarified butter over medium-high heat. Add pork and brown on all sides, about 10 minutes. Transfer to slow cooker stoneware.

3. Reduce heat to medium. Add onions, celery and carrots and cook, stirring, until softened, about 7 minutes. Stir in bay leaves and water and bring to a boil, scraping up brown bits from bottom of pan.

4. Pour over pork. Cover and cook on Low for 8 hours or on High for 4 hours, until pork is very tender. Transfer meat to a deep platter and keep warm. Transfer sauce to a saucepan and skim off fat. Bring to a boil over medium-high heat and cook until reduced by one quarter, about 7 minutes. Taste and adjust seasoning. Spoon over pork and serve.

Simply Braised Pork with Jerk Spicing

Serves 6

◆ **Entertaining Worthy**
◆ **Can Be Halved**
(see Tips, below)

Tips

If you are halving this recipe, be sure to use a small (approx. 1½ to 3 quart) slow cooker. Reduce cooking time to about 4 hours on Low.

For the best flavor, toast and grind cumin and coriander seeds and allspice berries yourself. *To toast seeds:* Simply stir seeds in a dry skillet over medium heat until fragrant, about 3 minutes. Using a mortar and pestle or a spice grinder, pound or grind as finely as you can.

Be aware that these cooking times are general estimates. Not only do cooking times vary substantially among slow cookers (see Cooking Times, page 18), but people have different preferences with regard to how well they like their meat done. If you prefer fork-tender results, start checking after the food has cooked for 6 hours on Low.

Many years ago I took a trip to Jamaica with a friend who had grown up there. We traveled around that beautiful island eating, among other delights, succulent jerk pork cooked over oil-drum barbecues and sold on the side of the road. Since then, the flavors of Jamaican jerk spicing are among my favorites.

- **Medium (approx. 4 quart) slow cooker**
- **Rimmed baking sheet**
- **Large sheet of parchment paper**

1 tbsp	extra virgin olive oil	15 mL
1 tbsp	minced gingerroot	15 mL
4	green onions, minced	4
4	cloves garlic, puréed (see Tips, page 166)	4
2 tsp	ground cumin (see Tips, left)	10 mL
1 tsp	ground coriander	5 mL
1 tsp	ground allspice (see Tips, left)	5 mL
1 tsp	cracked black peppercorns	5 mL
1 tsp	coarse sea salt, crushed	5 mL
½ tsp	ground cinnamon	2 mL
3 lb	pork shoulder or blade (butt) roast, patted dry (see Tips, page 168)	1.5 kg
1 tsp	finely grated lime zest	5 mL
¼ cup	freshly squeezed lime juice	60 mL
2 tbsp	gluten-free soy sauce or coconut aminos (see page 15)	30 mL
1 to 2	habanero or Scotch bonnet peppers, minced	1 to 2

1. In a small bowl, combine olive oil, ginger, green onions, garlic, cumin, coriander, allspice, peppercorns, sea salt and cinnamon. Rub all over meat. Cover and refrigerate overnight or for up to 24 hours, turning several times, if possible.

2. When you're ready to cook, preheat broiler. Transfer pork to rimmed baking sheet and broil, turning, until skin and sides brown evenly, about 15 minutes. Transfer to slow cooker stoneware.

3. In a bowl, combine lime zest and juice and soy sauce. Pour over pork. Place a large sheet of parchment paper over the pork, pressing it down to brush the meat and extending up the sides of the stoneware so it overlaps the rim. Cover and cook on Low for 6 to 8 hours or on High for 3 to 4 hours, until pork is very tender. Lift off the parchment and discard, being careful not to spill the accumulated liquid, which will dilute the sauce.

4. To serve, tear the pork into chunks (it will pretty well fall apart). Add hot peppers to the pan juices and spoon over pork.

Ancho-Embraced Pork with Tomatillos

◆ **Entertaining Worthy**
◆ **Can Be Halved**
(see Tips, below)

Tips

If you are halving this recipe, be sure to use a small (2½ to 3½ quart) slow cooker.

Many butchers sell cut-up pork stewing meat, which is fine to use in this recipe.

If you prefer, substitute 4 cups (1 L) fresh husked tomatillos for the canned. Place in a saucepan and add water to cover. Bring to a boil, reduce heat and simmer just until tender, about 10 minutes. Drain, let cool and then chop coarsely.

Although ancho chiles are among the mildest chile peppers, 3 chiles produces a zesty dish. If you're heat averse, reduce the quantity to 2.

If you like the taste of cilantro, chop some stems and substitute them for an equal quantity of the leaves called for.

Make Ahead

Complete Step 2. Cover and refrigerate for up to 2 days. When you're ready to cook, complete the recipe.

I love the flavors in this simple but sumptuous stew. Make more than you think you'll need — requests for seconds are the norm.

- **Medium to large (3½ to 8 quart) slow cooker**
- **Blender**

2 tbsp	clarified butter or pure lard, divided	30 mL
2 lb	trimmed pork shoulder or blade (butt), cut into 1-inch (2.5 cm) cubes, and patted dry	1 kg
2	onions, thinly sliced on the vertical	2
2	stalks celery, diced	2
2	carrots, peeled and diced	2
4	cloves garlic, minced	4
2 tsp	ground cumin (see Tips, page 180)	10 mL
2 tsp	dried oregano, preferably Mexican, crumbled	10 mL
2	bay leaves	2
½ tsp	each sea salt and cracked black peppercorns	2 mL
2 tbsp	cider vinegar (see page 15)	30 mL
1	can (28 oz/796 mL) tomatillos, drained and coarsely chopped (see Tips, left)	1
2 cups	chicken stock	500 mL
2 to 3	dried ancho chiles (see Tips, left)	2 to 3
2 cups	boiling water	500 mL
½ cup	packed cilantro leaves (see Tips, left)	125 mL

1. In a skillet, heat 1 tbsp (15 mL) of the butter over medium-high heat. Add pork, in batches, and brown on all sides, about 4 minutes per batch. Transfer to slow cooker stoneware as completed.

2. Reduce heat to medium. Add remaining tbsp (15 mL) of butter to pan. Add onions, celery and carrots and cook, stirring, until vegetables are softened, about 7 minutes. Add garlic, cumin, oregano, bay leaves, sea salt and peppercorns and cook, stirring, for 1 minute. Add vinegar and cook, stirring, for 1 minute, scraping up brown bits from bottom of pan. Add tomatillos and stir well.

3. Transfer to stoneware. Add chicken stock and stir well. Cover and cook on Low for 8 hours or on High for 4 hours, until pork is very tender.

4. About 1 hour before recipe has finished cooking, in a heatproof bowl, soak dried chiles in boiling water for 30 minutes, weighing down with a cup to ensure they remain submerged. Drain, discarding soaking liquid and stems, and chop coarsely. Transfer to a blender along with cilantro. Scoop out ½ cup (125 mL) of the cooking broth from the pork and add to blender. Purée. Stir puréed mixture into stoneware. Cover and cook on High for 30 minutes, until flavors meld.

Pork Roast with Chile-Orange Sauce

Tips

Pork shoulder can be very fatty. If your pork shoulder isn't trimmed of fat when you purchase it, I recommend removing the string and trimming off as much fat as possible before using.

Check your chili powder to make sure it doesn't contain gluten. Some brands do.

Make Ahead

Complete Steps 1 and 3. Cover and refrigerate mixture for up to 2 days. When you're ready to cook, complete the recipe.

There's a lot more to Mexican cuisine than tacos and burritos — as demonstrated by the delicious sweet and spicy flavors of this pork roast. The combination of fruit and chile peppers derives from a simple country dish, but the results should inspire you to learn more about the cuisine of our neighbors to the south.

- **Large (minimum 5 quart) slow cooker**

4	slices bacon, finely chopped	4
3 lb	trimmed boneless pork shoulder or blade (butt) roast, patted dry (see Tips, left)	1.5 kg
2	large onions, thinly sliced	2
3	cloves garlic, minced	3
1 tsp	cracked black peppercorns	5 mL
$\frac{1}{2}$ tsp	sea salt	2 mL
1 tbsp	grated orange zest	15 mL
$1\frac{1}{2}$ cups	freshly squeezed orange juice	375 mL
2	bananas, thinly sliced	2
$1\frac{1}{2}$ tbsp	chili powder (see Tip, left)	22 mL
2	jalapeño peppers, minced	2

1. In a skillet over medium-high heat, cook bacon until crisp. Remove with a slotted spoon to paper towel and drain thoroughly. Set aside.

2. In same pan, brown roast on all sides, about 10 minutes. Transfer to slow cooker stoneware.

3. Reduce heat to medium. Add onions and cook, stirring, until softened, about 3 minutes. Add garlic, peppercorns and salt and cook, stirring, for 1 minute. Add orange zest and juice and bananas and cook, stirring to scrape up any brown bits and mashing bananas into sauce. Stir in bacon pieces.

4. Pour mixture over pork. Cover and cook on Low for 8 hours or on High for 4 hours, until meat is very tender. Fifteen minutes before you are ready to serve, scoop out $\frac{1}{4}$ cup (60 mL) of the cooking liquid and transfer to a small bowl. Stir in chili powder until dissolved. Add to stoneware along with the jalapeño peppers. Cover and cook on High for 10 minutes to blend flavors.

Caribbean Pork Roast with Rum

◆ Entertaining Worthy

Tips

If you are halving this recipe, be sure to use a small (2 to 3½ quart) slow cooker.

This recipe generates a lot of liquid, which I think works well if you're serving it over something such as Cauliflower Mash (page 242) or Roasted Spaghetti Squash (page 243), which will soak up the sauce. If you prefer a thicker sauce and have no problem with starch, you can thicken it with arrowroot, which has some degree of acceptance in the Paleo community.

Make Ahead

If you're pressed for time on the day you plan to serve this dish, I recommend cooking the roast overnight. The next morning, cover and refrigerate. When you're ready to serve, spoon off the congealed fat, remove roast from liquid and slice meat. Place meat in an ovenproof serving dish, cover with foil and place in a warm oven at 325°F (160°C) for 15 to 20 minutes, until meat is heated through. Meanwhile, complete Step 4. Pour sauce over meat and serve.

I love how complex flavors meld in this sauce. It's sweet, yet spicy, with more than a hint of citrus. If you like heat, use a whole chile, and if citrus appeals to you, double the quantity of lime zest and juice. For dinner with a Caribbean theme, serve with baked squash.

- Large (minimum 5 quart) slow cooker
- Preheat broiler

3 lb	trimmed boneless pork shoulder or blade (butt) roast, patted dry	1.5 kg
6	cloves garlic, cut into thin slivers	6
1	piece (2 inches/5 cm) gingerroot, cut in two lengthwise and then into thin slivers	1
20	whole cloves	20
2 tbsp	coconut sugar	30 mL
1 tsp	dry mustard	5 mL
½ cup	dark rum	125 mL
	Zest and juice of 1 lime	
1 tsp	sea salt	5 mL
1 tsp	cracked black peppercorns	5 mL
½	chile pepper (long red, habanero or Scotch bonnet), minced	½
1 tbsp	arrowroot, dissolved in 2 tbsp (30 mL) cold water, optional (see Tips, left)	15 mL

1. On all sides of the meat, make a series of small slits. Insert garlic and ginger slivers and whole cloves. Pat roast dry with paper towel.

2. In a small bowl, combine coconut sugar and mustard. Rub mixture all over roast and place under broiler. Broil, turning to ensure that roast is browned on all sides, about 15 minutes. Transfer to slow cooker stoneware.

3. In a small bowl, combine rum, lime zest and juice, salt and peppercorns. Pour over roast and cook on Low for 8 hours or on High for 4 hours, until pork is tender.

4. Remove roast from slow cooker and keep warm. Skim off accumulated fat, if desired, and pour cooking juices into a medium saucepan. Bring to a boil over medium heat. Add chile pepper and arrowroot mixture, if using, and stir constantly until thickened. Serve in a sauceboat alongside sliced pork.

Tex-Mex Pork Stew

Serves 6

- ◆ Entertaining Worthy
- ◆ Can Be Halved
  (see Tips, below)

Tips

If you are halving this recipe, be sure to use a small (approx. 1½ to 3 quart) slow cooker.

Many butchers sell cut-up pork stewing meat, which is fine to use in this recipe.

If you prefer, instead of wine, substitute 1 cup (250 mL) chicken stock plus 1 tbsp (15 mL) lemon juice.

One jalapeño pepper produces a mildly spiced stew. If you're a heat seeker, use two. If you like a bit of smoke and more spice, substitute an equal quantity of chipotle peppers in adobo sauce. Check the label to make sure the brand you are using doesn't contain gluten.

I love the combination of flavors in this delicious stew, which is a perfect dish for a casual evening with friends.

- **Medium to large (3½ to 8 quart) slow cooker**
- **Blender**

1 tbsp	cumin seeds	15 mL
1 tbsp	coriander seeds	15 mL
1 tbsp	fennel seeds	15 mL
2 lb	trimmed pork shoulder or blade (butt), cut into 1-inch (2.5 cm) cubes, and patted dry	1 kg
2 tbsp	clarified butter or lard, divided (see page 12)	30 mL
2	onions, finely chopped	2
2	carrots, peeled and diced	2
2	stalks celery, diced	2
4	cloves garlic, minced	4
2 tsp	dried oregano	10 mL
2 tsp	dried thyme	10 mL
1 tsp	finely grated lemon zest	5 mL
½ tsp	sea salt	2 mL
½ tsp	cracked black peppercorns	2 mL
1 cup	dry white wine (see Tips, left)	250 mL
2 cups	chicken stock	500 mL
2	dried mild New Mexico, ancho or guajillo chiles	2
2 cups	boiling water	500 mL
½ cup	packed cilantro leaves	125 mL
¼ cup	freshly squeezed lemon juice	60 mL
1 to 2	jalapeño pepper(s), seeded and coarsely chopped (see Tips, left)	1 to 2

1. In a dry skillet over medium heat, toast cumin, coriander and fennel seeds until fragrant, about 3 minutes. Using a mortar and pestle or a spice grinder, pound or grind as finely as you can. Toss with pork. Cover and refrigerate overnight.

2. In a large skillet, heat 1 tbsp (15 mL) of the clarified butter over medium-high heat. Add pork, in batches, and cook, stirring, until lightly browned, about 4 minutes per batch. Transfer to slow cooker stoneware as completed.

3. Reduce heat to medium. Add remaining tbsp (15 mL) of butter to pan. Add onions, carrots and celery and cook, stirring, until carrots have softened, about 7 minutes. Add garlic, oregano, thyme, lemon zest, sea salt and peppercorns and cook, stirring, for 1 minute. Add wine, bring to a boil and boil for 2 minutes, scraping up brown bits from bottom of pan.

Complete Steps 1, 3 and 5. Cover and refrigerate pork, vegetable and chile mixtures separately for up to 2 days. (The chile mixture will lose some of its vibrancy. For best results, complete Step 4 while the stew is cooking.) When you're ready to cook, brown the pork and complete the recipe. Or, if you prefer, add the unbrowned pork to the stoneware along with the vegetable mixture, being aware that the result will not be as flavorful as that produced using browned meat.

4. Transfer to slow cooker stoneware. Add chicken stock and stir well. Cover and cook on Low for 8 hours or on High for 4 hours, until meat is very tender.

5. About 1 hour before the stew has finished cooking, in a heatproof bowl, soak dried chiles in boiling water for 30 minutes, weighing down with a cup to ensure they remain submerged. Drain, discarding soaking liquid and stems, and chop coarsely. Transfer to a blender. Add cilantro, lemon juice, and jalapeño to taste. Purée, scraping down the sides of the blender if necessary.

6. Add chile mixture to stoneware. Cover and cook on High for 30 minutes, until hot and bubbly and flavors meld.

Lard

Contrary to traditional wisdom, old-fashioned animal fats such as lard are healthy alternatives to refined cooking oils. Most of the fat in lard is unsaturated (although it is low in inflammation-producing omega-6 fatty acids) and it has a high smoking point. If you decide to use lard, do not buy packaged lard. It is made from the fat of poorly raised animals and as a result is too high in inflammation-producing omega-6 fatty acids. It is also likely to be hydrogenated, which means it contains deadly trans fats. I buy lard from my butcher, who renders it from the fat of pasture-raised pigs. It keeps for a long time in the freezer.

Farmhouse Pork Stew

♦ **Entertaining Worthy**

♦ **Can Be Halved**
(see Tips, below)

Tips

If you are halving this recipe, be sure to use a small (2½ to 3½ quart) slow cooker.

Many butchers sell cut-up pork stewing meat, which is fine to use in this recipe.

If you prefer, substitute 1 cup (250 mL) chicken stock plus 1 tbsp (15 mL) lemon juice for the wine.

Look for canned tomatoes that are organically grown, with no salt added, and come in glass jars or BPA (bisphenol-A) free cans. When using canned tomatoes (or any canned product) check to make sure they are gluten-free.

Make Ahead

Complete Step 2. Cover and refrigerate for up to 2 days. When you're ready to cook, complete the recipe.

This Italian-inspired stew is rustic and flavorful. On a cold winter's day there is nothing better than a steaming serving accompanied by a bottle of good Chianti. This is delicious over Roasted Spaghetti Squash (page 243).

- Medium to large (3½ to 8 quart) slow cooker

2 tbsp	clarified butter or pure lard, divided	30 mL
2 oz	pancetta, diced	60 g
2 lb	trimmed pork shoulder or blade (butt), cut into 1-inch (2.5 cm) cubes and patted dry (see Tips, left)	1 kg
2	onions, finely chopped	2
2	carrots, peeled and diced	2
2	stalks celery, diced	2
6	cloves garlic, minced	6
½ tsp	sea salt	2 mL
½ tsp	cracked black peppercorns	2 mL
3 to 4	sprigs rosemary with stems, or 1 tbsp (15 mL) dried rosemary	3 to 4
1 cup	dry white wine (see Tips, left)	250 mL
1	can (28 oz/796 mL) tomatoes with juice, coarsely chopped (see Tips, left)	1
2 tbsp	freshly squeezed lemon juice	30 mL
1 tbsp	sweet paprika	15 mL
¼ tsp	cayenne pepper	1 mL

1. In a skillet, heat 1 tbsp (15 mL) of the butter over medium-high heat. Add pancetta and cook, stirring, until crisp. Using a slotted spoon, transfer to slow cooker stoneware. Add pork, in batches, and cook, stirring, until browned, about 4 minutes per batch. Transfer to slow cooker stoneware.

2. Reduce heat to medium. Add remaining tbsp (15 mL) of butter to pan. Add onions, carrots and celery and cook, stirring, until vegetables are softened, about 7 minutes. Add garlic, sea salt, peppercorns and rosemary and toss until coated. Add wine, bring to a boil and cook, stirring for 2 minutes, scraping up brown bits from bottom of pan. Stir in tomatoes with juice. Transfer to slow cooker stoneware. Cover and cook on Low for 8 hours or on High for 4 hours, until meat is very tender.

3. In a small bowl, combine lemon juice, paprika and cayenne, stirring until spices dissolve. Add to slow cooker and stir well. Cover and cook on High for 10 minutes, until flavors meld.

Pork in Mushroom Tomato Gravy

Serves 6

♦ **Can Be Halved**
(see Tips, below)

Tips

If you are halving this recipe, be sure to use a small (2 to 3½ quart) slow cooker. Reduce cooking time to about 4 hours on Low.

To rehydrate mushrooms, place in a bowl with 1 cup (250 mL) hot water. Let stand for 30 minutes. Drain through a fine sieve, reserving liquid. Pat mushrooms dry with a paper towel and chop finely.

If you prefer, substitute 1 cup (250 mL) chicken stock plus 1 tbsp (15 mL) lemon juice for the wine.

Make Ahead

Complete Step 2. Cover and refrigerate mixture for up to 2 days. When you're ready to cook, complete the recipe.

Here's an absolutely luscious way to serve pork — wallowing in a rich tomato gravy flavored with robust porcini mushrooms. Add the cayenne if you like a bit of heat.

• **Large (approx. 5 quart) slow cooker**

1	package (½ oz/14 g) dried porcini mushrooms, rehydrated and chopped (see Tips, left)	1
2 tbsp	clarified butter or pure lard	30 mL
4 oz	chunk pancetta, diced	125 g
3 lb	trimmed pork shoulder or blade (butt) roast, patted dry	1.5 kg
2	onions, finely chopped	2
2	carrots, peeled and diced	2
4	cloves garlic, minced	4
2 tsp	dried oregano	10 mL
1 tsp	dried thyme	5 mL
1 tsp	sea salt	5 mL
1 tsp	cracked black peppercorns	5 mL
2	bay leaves	2
1 cup	dry white wine (see Tips, left)	250 mL
1	can (28 oz/796 mL) tomatoes with juice, coarsely chopped (see Tips, page 176 and page 13)	1
¼ to ½ tsp	cayenne pepper, dissolved in 1 tbsp (15 mL) lemon juice, optional	1 to 2 mL

1. In a large skillet, heat clarified butter over medium-high heat. Add pancetta and cook, stirring, until browned, about 4 minutes. Using a slotted spoon, transfer to slow cooker stoneware. Add pork and brown on all sides, about 10 minutes. Transfer to slow cooker stoneware.

2. Reduce heat to medium. Add onions and carrots to pan and cook, stirring, until carrots are softened, about 7 minutes. Add reserved mushrooms, garlic, oregano, thyme, sea salt, peppercorns and bay leaves and cook, stirring, for 1 minute. Add wine, bring to a boil and boil for 2 minutes. Add tomatoes with juice and reserved mushroom soaking liquid (see Tips, left) and return to a boil, breaking tomatoes up with the back of a spoon and scraping up brown bits from bottom of pan.

3. Transfer to slow cooker stoneware. Cover and cook on Low for 6 to 8 hours or on High for 3 to 4 hours, until pork is very tender. Stir in cayenne solution, if using. Cover and cook on High for 10 minutes.

Ribs in Tablecloth Stainer Sauce

- ◆ **Entertaining Worthy**
- ◆ **Can Be Halved**
  (see Tips, below)

Tips

If you are halving this recipe, be sure to use a small (2 to 3 quart) slow cooker.

This recipe works best if the ribs are in one big piece when cooked. (In my experience, this cut is usually only available from a butcher.) The single piece is easy to turn while broiling and will basically fall apart into individual servings after the meat is cooked.

You can vary the quantity of chiles to suit your taste. Three produce a pleasantly spicy sauce.

Make Ahead

Complete Steps 2 and 4. Cover and refrigerate for up to 2 days, being aware that the chile mixture will lose some of its vibrancy if held for this long. (For best results, rehydrate chiles while the ribs are cooking or no sooner than the night before you plan to cook.) When you're ready to cook, broil the ribs (Step 1) and continue with the recipe.

The colorful name of this sauce, which comes from the city of Oaxaca, in Mexico, is a literal translation from the Spanish. It is distinguished by the addition of fruit, such as pineapple and bananas.

- **Large (minimum 5 quart) slow cooker**
- **Preheat broiler**
- **Blender**

4 lbs	country-style pork ribs (see Tips, left)	2 kg
1 tbsp	clarified butter or pure lard (see page 12)	15 mL
2	onions, thinly sliced on the vertical	2
4	cloves garlic, minced	4
1 tbsp	dried oregano	15 mL
1	piece (2 inches/5 cm) cinnamon stick	1
1 tsp	salt	5 mL
1/2 tsp	cracked black peppercorns	2 mL
6	whole allspice	6
2	apples, peeled, cored and sliced	2
1	can (14 oz/398 mL) diced tomatoes with juice	1
1 cup	chicken broth, divided	250 mL
3	dried ancho chiles (see Tips, left)	3
2 cups	boiling water	500 mL
1	jalapeño pepper, coarsely chopped	1
2	bananas, peeled and sliced	2
1 tbsp	cider vinegar (see page 15)	15 mL
1 cup	pineapple chunks, drained if canned	250 mL

1. Position broiler rack 6 inches (15 cm) from heat source. Broil ribs on both sides, until lightly browned, about 7 minutes per side. Drain on paper towels and transfer to stoneware.

2. In a skillet, heat clarified butter over medium heat. Add onions and cook, stirring, until softened, about 3 minutes. Add garlic, oregano, cinnamon stick, salt, peppercorns and allspice and cook, stirring, for 1 minute. Add apples, tomatoes with juice and 1/2 cup (125 mL) of the broth and bring to a boil.

3. Pour sauce over ribs. Cover and cook on Low for 6 hours or on High for 3 hours, until ribs are tender and falling off the bone.

4. About an hour before recipe has finished cooking, in a heatproof bowl, soak ancho chiles in boiling water for 30 minutes, weighing down with a cup to ensure they remain submerged. Drain, discarding soaking liquid and stems and chop coarsely. Transfer to a blender. Add jalapeño, bananas, vinegar and remaining 1/2 cup (125 mL) of the broth. Purée.

5. Add puréed chiles to stoneware, along with pineapple and stir well. Cover and cook for 30 minutes, until hot and bubbly and flavors meld. Discard allspice and cinnamon stick.

Pork Colombo

Serves 6 to 8

◆ Entertaining Worthy
◆ Can Be Halved
  (see Tips, below)

Tips

If you are halving this recipe, be sure to use a small (2 to 3 quart) slow cooker.

For the best flavor, toast and grind cumin seeds yourself. *To toast seeds:* Place seeds in a dry skillet over medium heat and cook, stirring, until fragrant, about 3 minutes. Immediately transfer to a spice grinder or mortar and grind.

Use a long red or green chile or a habanero or Scotch Bonnet pepper. Be aware that habanero and Scotch Bonnet peppers are among the hottest, so if you're timid about heat you may want to use only half of one.

Make Ahead

Complete Step 2, heating 1 tbsp (15 mL) oil in pan before softening onions. Cover and refrigerate mixture for up to 2 days. When you're ready to cook, complete the recipe.

This rich, flavorful curry is a Caribbean specialty. It has a uniquely spicy taste and is a great centerpiece for a delicious meal.

• **Medium to large (3½ to 6 quart) slow cooker**

1 tbsp	clarified butter or pure lard	15 mL
2 lb	boneless pork shoulder or blade (butt) roast, trimmed, cut into 1-inch (2.5 cm) cubes and patted dry	1 kg
2	onions, finely chopped	2
6	cloves garlic, minced	6
1 tbsp	minced gingerroot	15 mL
2 tsp	ground cumin (see Tips, left)	10 mL
6	whole allspice	6
1	piece (2 inches/5 cm) cinnamon stick	1
1 tsp	cracked black peppercorns	5 mL
½ tsp	sea salt	2 mL
1 cup	chicken broth	250 mL
4 cups	cubed, peeled yellow-fleshed squash, such as acorn or butternut	1 L
1	fresh chile pepper, minced (see Tips, left)	1
1 tsp	grated lime zest	5 mL
2 tbsp	freshly squeezed lime juice	30 mL
	Finely chopped cilantro leaves, optional	

1. In a skillet, heat clarified butter over medium-high. Add pork, in batches, and brown, about 4 minutes per batch. Transfer to slow cooker stoneware.

2. Reduce heat to medium. Add onions and cook, stirring, until softened, about 3 minutes. Add garlic, ginger, cumin, allspice, cinnamon stick, peppercorns and salt and cook, stirring, for 1 minute. Stir in broth and bring to a boil.

3. Add squash to stoneware. Pour contents of pan into slow cooker and stir to combine. Cover and cook on Low for 8 hours or on High for 4 hours, until pork is tender.

4. Stir in chile pepper and lime zest and juice. Cover and cook on High for 10 minutes to meld flavors. Discard cinnamon stick. Garnish with cilantro, if using.

Pork Vindaloo

◆ **Entertaining Worthy**
◆ **Can Be Halved**
(see Tips, below)

Tips

If you are halving this recipe, be sure to use a small (2 to 3 quart) slow cooker.

Ghee is a type of clarified butter, highly valued in Indian cooking because it can be heated to a very high temperature. It's easy to make your own clarified butter (see page 83) but if you prefer, prepared ghee is available in grocery stores specializing in Indian ingredients and will keep, refrigerated. When buying prepared ghee, check the label to make sure it doesn't contain additives.

Make Ahead

This dish must be assembled the night before it is cooked because it needs to be marinated overnight. Follow preparation directions and refrigerate overnight. The next day, transfer to stoneware and cook as directed.

This flavorful pork, marinated and cooked in vinegar and spices, is excellent as part of a buffet or as one dish in an Indian meal.

• **Medium to large (3½ to 6 quart) slow cooker**

1 tbsp	cumin seeds	15 mL
2 tsp	coriander seeds	10 mL
1 tbsp	clarified butter or ghee (see Tips, left)	15 mL
1	onion, finely chopped	1
8	cloves garlic, minced	8
1 tbsp	minced gingerroot	15 mL
1	piece (2 inches/5 cm) cinnamon stick	1
6	whole cloves	6
2 tsp	mustard seeds	10 mL
½ tsp	sea salt	2 mL
¼ tsp	cayenne pepper	1 mL
2 lb	pork shoulder or blade (butt) roast, trimmed, cut into 1-inch (2.5 cm) cubes and patted dry	1 kg
4	bay leaves	4
½ cup	red wine vinegar (see page 15)	125 mL

1. In a skillet over medium heat, toast cumin and coriander seeds, stirring constantly, until they release their aroma, about 3 minutes. Remove pan from heat and transfer seeds to a mortar or a cutting board. Using a pestle or a rolling pin, crush seeds coarsely. Set aside.

2. In a skillet, heat butter over medium heat. Add onion, garlic and ginger and cook for 1 minute. Add reserved toasted cumin and coriander, cinnamon stick, cloves, mustard seeds, salt and cayenne and cook, stirring, for 1 minute. Remove from heat. Let cool.

3. Place pork in a bowl. Add bay leaves and contents of pan. Add vinegar and stir to combine. Cover and marinate overnight in refrigerator. The next day, transfer to slow cooker stoneware, cover and cook on Low for 8 hours or on High for 4 to hours, until pork is tender. Discard bay leaves, cinnamon stick and cloves.

Braised Sauerkraut

♦ **Entertaining Worthy**
♦ **Can Be Halved**
(see Tips, below)

Tips

If you are halving this recipe, be sure to use a small (2 to 3 quart) slow cooker.

For best results, it's important to rinse sauerkraut thoroughly in several changes of water to reduce the bitter taste. Soak it overnight in cold water, then soak and rinse twice more before adding to the recipe.

If you prefer, instead of wine, substitute 1 cup (250 mL) chicken stock plus 1 tbsp (15 mL) lemon juice.

Make Ahead

This dish can be partially prepared before it is cooked. Complete Step 1. Cover and refrigerate bacon and vegetable mixtures separately for up to 2 days. When you're ready to cook, continue with the recipe.

If, like me, you're a fan of sauerkraut, there are few things you enjoy more than a steaming bowl of choucroute garnie, deliciously tart fermented cabbage, garnished with an assortment of vegetables and meat. Many people think they don't like sauerkraut, but I'm sure it's because they have never tasted a good homemade version. One of the most important steps in using sauerkraut is to soak it well. When properly soaked, it is very smooth, like a well-flavored cabbage. This recipe, which I've adapted from Julia Child, is absolutely delicious. You'd be surprised at how many people request seconds. It is a perfect finish for a pork roast or chops.

• **Medium to large (3$\frac{1}{2}$ to 6 quart) slow cooker**

5 cups	sauerkraut, soaked, drained and rinsed (see Tips, left)	1.25 L
8 oz	piece bacon, diced	250 g
1	onion, thinly sliced	1
2	carrots, peeled and diced	2
$\frac{1}{2}$ tsp	cracked black peppercorns	2 mL
1	bay leaf	1
1 cup	dry white wine (see Tips, left)	250 mL
1 cup	chicken stock	250 mL

1. In a skillet, cook bacon over medium heat, until browned. Using a slotted spoon, remove from pan and drain on paper towels. Set aside. Drain all but 2 tbsp (30 mL) fat from pan. Add onion and carrots to pan and cook, stirring, until carrots are softened, about 7 minutes. Add peppercorns and bay leaf and cook, stirring, for 1 minute.

2. Add drained sauerkraut and reserved bacon and toss well. Transfer to slow cooker stoneware. Add wine and chicken stock and stir well. Cover and cook on Low for 6 hours or on High for 3 hours, until hot and bubbly. Discard bay leaf.

Hot Sausage "Sandwiches"

Serves 4

◆ **Can Be Halved**
(see Tip, below)

Tips

If you are halving this recipe, be sure to use a small (approx. 1½ to 3 quart) slow cooker.

Look for canned tomatoes that are organically grown, with no salt added, and come in glass jars or BPA (bisphenol-A) free cans. When using canned tomatoes (or any canned product) check to make sure they are gluten-free.

Make Ahead

Complete Step 1. Cover mixture, ensuring it cools promptly (see Making Ahead, page 21), and refrigerate for up to 2 days. When you're ready to cook, complete the recipe.

These Italian-inspired open-faced sandwiches, served over roasted portobello mushrooms, make a great weeknight meal that's a big hit with both kids and adults. If you like heat, garnish them with roasted banana peppers. All this needs is a tossed salad to complete the meal.

• **Medium to large (3½ to 5 quart) slow cooker**
• **Rimmed baking sheet**

1 tbsp	clarified butter or pure lard	15 mL
1 lb	Italian sausage, casings removed	500 g
1	onion, finely chopped	1
2	stalks celery, diced	2
1	carrot, peeled and diced	1
2 tsp	dried oregano	10 mL
½ tsp	sea salt	2 mL
½ tsp	cracked black peppercorns	2 mL
1	piece (2 inches/5 cm) cinnamon stick	1
½ cup	dry white wine, optional	125 mL
1	can (28 oz/796 mL) diced tomatoes, drained (see Tips, left)	1
4	roasted large portobello mushrooms (see page 242)	4
	Roasted banana peppers, optional	

1. In a skillet, heat clarified butter over medium-high heat. Add sausage, onion, celery and carrot and cook, stirring, until sausage is no longer pink, about 7 minutes. Add oregano, sea salt, peppercorns and cinnamon stick and cook, stirring, for 1 minute. Add wine, if using, bring to a boil and boil, scraping up brown bits from bottom of pan, for 2 minutes. Stir in tomatoes.

2. Transfer to slow cooker stoneware. Cover and cook on Low for 6 to 8 hours or on High for 3 to 4 hours. Discard cinnamon stick

3. To serve, place 1 roasted mushroom on each plate. Spoon sausage mixture over and garnish with hot peppers, if using.

Chipotle Pork "Tacos"

Serves 6

◆ **Can Be Halved**
(see Tips, below)

Tips

If you are halving this recipe, be sure to use a small (approx. 1½ to 3 quart) slow cooker.

In my opinion, this recipe makes slightly too much sauce for the pork, so I spoon it over the shredded pork in a quantity that suits my taste. I refrigerate the excess. When I'm ready for lunch, I heat it to the boiling point and serve it over Napa cabbage.

Chipotle peppers pack quite a wallop, so only add the second one if you're a real heat seeker. Check the label to make sure the brand you are using is gluten-free. If you prefer, substitute 2 minced jalapeño peppers.

Make Ahead

Complete Step 2. Cover and refrigerate mixture for up to 2 days. When you're ready to cook, brown the pork and continue with the recipe. Or, if you prefer, add the unbrowned pork to the stoneware along with the vegetable mixture, being aware that the result will not be as flavorful as that produced using browned meat.

Liberally garnished, these yummy tacos are a meal in themselves. They make a great weeknight dinner, and they're a perfect solution for those nights when everyone is coming and going at different times. Just shred the pork, keep it warm in the sauce and leave the accompaniments within easy reach.

• **Medium to large (3½ to 5 quart) slow cooker**

2 tbsp	clarified butter or pure lard, divided	30 mL
2 lbs	trimmed boneless pork shoulder or blade (butt), patted dry	1 kg
2	onions, thinly sliced on the vertical	2
2	stalks celery, diced	2
4	cloves garlic, minced	4
1 tbsp	ground cumin (see Tips, page 180)	15 mL
1 tbsp	dried oregano	15 mL
1 tsp	cracked black peppercorns	5 mL
½ tsp	sea salt	2 mL
1	piece (2 inches/5 cm) cinnamon stick	1
2	bay leaves	2
1	can (28 oz/796 mL) tomatoes with juice, coarsely chopped (see page 13)	1
1 to 2	chipotle pepper(s) in adobo sauce, minced (see Tips, left)	1 to 2
	Hearts of Romaine lettuce or Napa cabbage leaves	
	Diced avocado tossed in fresh lime juice	
	Finely chopped green or red onion	

1. In a skillet, heat 1 tbsp (15 mL) of the butter over medium-high heat. Add pork and brown well, about 3 minutes per side. Transfer to slow cooker stoneware.

2. Add remaining tbsp (15 mL) of butter to pan. Add onions and celery and cook, stirring, until softened, about 5 minutes. Add garlic, cumin, oregano, peppercorns, sea salt, cinnamon stick and bay leaves and cook, stirring, for 1 minute. Add tomatoes with juice and bring to a boil, scraping up brown bits from bottom of pan.

3. Transfer to slow cooker stoneware. Cover and cook on Low for 8 hours or on High for 4 hours, until pork is very tender. Add chipotle pepper to taste, stir well, cover and cook on High for 10 minutes. Discard cinnamon stick and bay leaves.

4. Transfer pork to a cutting board and, using 2 forks, shred. To serve, spoon pork onto lettuce and spoon sauce to taste over it (see Tips, left). Garnish with avocado and onion. Serve immediately.

Lamb Korma with Spinach

Serves 6 to 8

♦ **Can Be Halved**
(see Tips, below)

Tips

If you are halving this recipe, be sure to use a small (2 to 3½ quart) slow cooker.

Long red or green chiles are about the size of a baby finger. The green variety has been described as a "skinny jalapeño."

Make Ahead

Complete Step 2, heating 1 tbsp (15 mL) oil in pan before softening onions. Cover and refrigerate mixture for up to 2 days. When you're ready to cook, complete the recipe.

A korma is an Indian dish of meat or vegetables braised in a minimal amount of liquid. This version, although very simple, is delicious and benefits from the addition of spinach and yogurt to enrich the sauce.

• **Large (approx. 5 quart) slow cooker**

2 tbsp	clarified butter or ghee	30 mL
2 lb	boneless lamb shoulder roast, trimmed, cut into 1-inch (2.5 cm) cubes and patted dry	1 kg
2	onions, finely chopped	2
4	cloves garlic, minced	4
2 tbsp	minced gingerroot	30 mL
4	cardamom pods, split	4
1 tbsp	ground turmeric	15 mL
1 tbsp	mustard seeds	15 mL
½ tsp	sea salt	2 mL
½ tsp	cracked black peppercorns	2 mL
¼ cup	water	60 mL
1 to 2	long red or green chiles, minced (see Tips, left)	1 to 2
1 lb	fresh spinach, stems removed, or 1 package (10 oz/300 g) spinach, washed and finely chopped	500 g
½ cup	plain full-fat yogurt (see page 14)	125 mL

1. In a skillet, heat clarified butter over medium-high heat. Add lamb, in batches, and brown, about 4 minutes per batch. Using a slotted spoon, transfer to slow cooker stoneware.

2. Reduce heat to medium. Add onions and cook, stirring, until softened, about 3 minutes. Add garlic, ginger, cardamom pods, turmeric, mustard seeds, salt and peppercorns. Cook, stirring, for 1 minute. Add water and stir.

3. Transfer mixture to stoneware and stir well. Cover and cook on Low for 7 to 8 hours or on High for 3 to 4 hours, until lamb is tender.

4. Stir in chile pepper to taste. Add spinach and stir well, pushing leaves down into the hot stew. Cover and cook on High for 20 minutes or until spinach is soft. Stir in yogurt and serve immediately.

Variation

Beef Korma with Spinach: Substitute 2 lbs (1 kg) stewing beef for the lamb.

Irish Stew

♦ **Can Be Halved**
(see Tips, below)

Tips

If you are halving this recipe, be sure to use a small (2 to 3½ quart) slow cooker.

I have included Worcestershire sauce in this recipe because it is a very easy way to enhance the flavor of this dish. If you object to using a prepared sauce, substitute 2 tsp (10 mL) balsamic vinegar and 1 tsp (5 mL) minced anchovies.

If you prefer a thicker gravy-like sauce and have no problem with starch, use the arrowroot solution as a thickener. Arrowroot has varying degrees of acceptance within the Paleo community.

Make Ahead

Complete Step 3, heating 1 tbsp (15 mL) oil in pan before softening vegetables. Cover and refrigerate for up to 2 days. When you're ready to cook, complete the recipe.

This hearty and delicious stew is an old favorite that really can't be improved upon. All it needs is a green vegetable such as string beans or broccoli and a big glass of robust red wine.

- **Large (approx. 5 quart) slow cooker**

2 tbsp	almond flour	30 mL
½ tsp	sea salt	2 mL
½ tsp	cracked black peppercorns	2 mL
2 lbs	stewing lamb, cut into 1-inch (2.5 cm) cubes	1 kg
2 tbsp	clarified butter	30 mL
3	onions, finely chopped	3
2	large carrots, peeled and diced	2
1 tsp	dried thyme	5 mL
2 tbsp	tomato paste or ¼ cup (60 mL) minced reconstituted sun-dried tomatoes (see page 13)	30 mL
1 cup	beef stock	250 mL
4	medium potatoes, peeled and cut into ½-inch (1 cm) cubes	4
1½ cups	sweet green peas (see page 15)	375 mL
1 tbsp	gluten-free Worcestershire sauce (see Tips, left)	15 mL
1 tbsp	arrowroot, dissolved in 3 tbsp (45 mL) water, optional (see Tips, left)	15 mL

1. On a plate, combine almond flour, salt and peppercorns. Lightly coat lamb with mixture, shaking off the excess. Discard any remaining flour mixture.

2. In a skillet, heat butter over medium-high heat. Add lamb, in batches, and brown, about 4 minutes per batch. Transfer to slow cooker stoneware. Reduce heat to medium.

3. Add onions and carrots to pan and cook, stirring, until softened, about 7 minutes. Add thyme and cook, stirring, for 1 minute. Stir in tomato paste and stock and bring to a boil.

4. Place potatoes in stoneware. Add onion mixture and stir to combine. Cover and cook on Low for 8 hours or on High for 4 hours, until mixture is bubbly and lamb is tender. Stir in peas and Worcestershire sauce. Cover and cook on High for 15 to 20 minutes. Add arrowroot solution to slow cooker, if using. Cover and cook on High for 5 minutes, until thickened.

Lamb Tagine with Dates

◆ Entertaining Worthy
◆ Can Be Halved
(see Tip, below)

Tips

If you are halving this recipe, be sure to use a small (2 to 3½ quart) slow cooker.

Tomato paste is, basically, a highly concentrated tomato purée. I buy mine at a natural foods store. It contains only organic tomatoes and salt. However, commercially prepared versions may contain a panoply of dreadful ingredients, from high fructose corn syrup to hidden gluten and even MSG. Check the label. If you can't buy a suitable product or have concerns about using any prepared foods, substitute sun-dried tomatoes.

Make Ahead

Complete Step 1. Cover and refrigerate for up to 2 days. When you're ready to cook, complete the recipe.

If you're in the mood for something a little different, try this. The dates add sumptuous fruity notes that are slightly unexpected when combined with rosemary and a hint of tomato.

- **Large (approx. 5 quart) slow cooker**
- **Food processor**

2	onions, quartered	2
4	cloves garlic, minced	4
1 tbsp	finely chopped fresh rosemary leaves or 2 tsp (10 mL) dried rosemary	15 mL
½ tsp	sea salt	2 mL
½ tsp	cracked black peppercorns	2 mL
1	piece (2 inches/5 cm) cinnamon stick	1
2 lbs	trimmed stewing lamb, cut into 1-inch (2.5 cm) cubes	1 kg
2 tbsp	tomato paste (see Tips, left) or ¼ cup (60 mL) minced reconstituted sun-dried tomatoes	30 mL
2 cups	chicken stock	500 mL
2	sweet potatoes, peeled and cut into 1-inch (2.5 cm) cubes	2
¾ cup	chopped pitted dates (about 4 oz/125 g)	175 mL
	Finely chopped cilantro leaves	

1. In a food processor, pulse onions until a grated consistency is achieved. (You can also do this on a box grater, if you prefer.) Transfer to a bowl. Add garlic, rosemary, sea salt, peppercorns and cinnamon stick and stir well. Add lamb and toss until well coated with mixture. Cover and refrigerate for at least 6 hours or overnight.

2. In slow cooker stoneware, combine tomato paste and chicken stock. Mix well. Add sweet potatoes and lamb mixture. Stir well. Cover and cook on Low for 8 hours or on High for 4 hours, until lamb is very tender. Stir in dates. Cover and cook on High for 15 minutes, until heated through. Discard cinnamon stick. Garnish with cilantro.

Suneeta's Lamb in Almond Sauce

◆ **Entertaining Worthy**
◆ **Can Be Halved**
(see Tips, below)

Tips

If you are halving this recipe, be sure to use a small (approx. 1½ to 3 quart) slow cooker.

To maximize flavor, toast and grind cumin seeds yourself. *To toast seeds:* Place seeds in a dry skillet over medium heat and cook, stirring, until fragrant, about 3 minutes. Using a mortar and pestle or a clean spice grinder, pound or grind as finely as you can.

This is an adaptation of a recipe that appears in Suneeta Vaswani's Complete Book of Indian Cooking. *Suneeta calls it sensuous, an apt description. A side of puréed spinach makes a nice accompaniment.*

• **Medium to large (4 to 6 quart) slow cooker**
• **Blender**
• **Large piece of parchment paper**

1 tsp	saffron threads	5 mL
1 cup	plain full-fat yogurt (see page 14)	250 mL
1 tbsp	ground cumin (see Tips, left)	15 mL
1 tsp	sea salt or to taste	5 mL
½ tsp	cracked black peppercorns	2 mL
2 lbs	trimmed stewing lamb, cut into 1-inch (2.5 cm) cubes	1 kg
¾ cup	blanched almonds	175 mL
¾ cup	very hot water	175 mL
2 tbsp	clarified butter or extra virgin coconut oil (see page 12)	30 mL
1	piece (2 inches/5 cm) cinnamon stick	1
12	green cardamom pods, crushed	12
6	whole cloves	6
3	onions, finely chopped	3
6	cloves garlic, minced	6
2 tbsp	minced gingerroot	30 mL
1 tsp	cayenne pepper	5 mL
1 cup	coconut milk, divided	250 mL
2 tbsp	sliced or slivered almonds, toasted	30 mL

1. In a small bowl, soak saffron threads in 2 tbsp (30 mL) very hot water for 10 minutes.

2. In a large bowl, combine yogurt, cumin, sea salt and peppercorns. Add saffron with soaking liquid and stir well. Stir in lamb until well coated with mixture. Cover and set aside at room temperature for 30 minutes or refrigerate for up to 24 hours.

3. In a bowl, combine blanched almonds and very hot water. Set aside for 10 minutes. Transfer mixture to a blender and purée. Set aside.

4. In a saucepan, heat butter over medium-high heat. Add cinnamon stick, cardamom pods and cloves and sauté for 30 seconds. Add onions and cook, stirring, until golden, about 8 minutes. Add garlic and ginger and cook, stirring, for 1 minute. Stir in almond purée.

Make Ahead

Complete Steps 1, 2, 3 and 4. Cover and refrigerate lamb and onion mixtures separately overnight. When you're ready to cook, complete the recipe.

5. Transfer to slow cooker stoneware. Add meat with marinade and stir well. Place a large piece of parchment paper over the mixture, pressing it down to brush the food and extending up the sides of the stoneware so it overlaps the rim. Cover and cook on Low for 6 to 8 hours or on High for 3 to 4 hours, until meat is tender. Lift out parchment and discard, being careful not to spill the accumulated liquid into the sauce.

6. In a small bowl, blend cayenne with 2 tbsp (30 mL) of the coconut milk until smooth. Stir into lamb. Add remainder of coconut milk and stir well. Cover and cook on High for 15 minutes to meld flavors. Discard cinnamon stick. Garnish with toasted almonds before serving.

Braised Lamb Shanks with Lemon Gremolata

◆ **Entertaining Worthy**
◆ **Can Be Halved**
(see Tips, below)

Tips

If you are halving this recipe, be sure to use a small (2 to 3½ quart) slow cooker.

Whether you cook the lamb shanks whole, halved or have them cut into pieces is a matter of preference. However, if the shanks are left whole, you will be able to serve only four people — each will receive one large shank.

If you prefer, substitute an extra cup (250 mL) of chicken stock plus 1 tbsp (15 mL) lemon juice for the white wine.

Make Ahead

Complete Step 2. Cover and refrigerate for up to 2 days. When you're ready to cook, complete the recipe.

Braised in a light tomato sauce and finished with lemon gremolata, these lamb shanks have Mediterranean overtones.

• **Large (approx. 5 quart) slow cooker**

2 tbsp	clarified butter, divided	30 mL
4	large lamb shanks (about 4 lbs/2 kg), patted dry (see Tips, left)	4
3	onions, finely chopped	3
2	stalks celery, diced	2
2	carrots, peeled and diced	2
6	cloves garlic, minced	6
1 tsp	dried thyme or several whole sprigs, stems and all	5 mL
1 tsp	sea salt	5 mL
1 tsp	cracked black peppercorns	5 mL
1 cup	dry white wine (see Tips, left)	250 mL
1 cup	chicken stock	250 mL
1	can (28 oz/796 mL) tomatoes with juice, coarsely chopped (see page 13)	1

Lemon Gremolata

2	cloves garlic, minced	2
1 cup	finely chopped flat-leaf parsley leaves	250 mL
	Grated zest of 1 lemon	
1 tbsp	extra virgin olive oil	15 mL

1. In a large skillet, heat 1 tbsp (15 mL) of the clarified butter over medium-high heat. Add lamb, in batches, and brown on all sides, about 8 minutes per batch. Transfer to stoneware as completed. Drain off fat from pan.

2. Reduce heat to medium. Add remaining tbsp (15 mL) of butter to pan. Add onions, celery and carrots and cook, stirring, until vegetables are softened, about 7 minutes. Add garlic, thyme, sea salt and peppercorns and cook, stirring, for 1 minute. Add wine, bring to a boil and boil for 2 minutes, scraping up brown bits from bottom of pan. Stir in chicken stock and tomatoes with juice.

3. Transfer to slow cooker stoneware. Cover and cook on Low for 10 to 12 hours or on High for 5 to 6 hours, until meat is falling off the bone.

4. *Lemon Gremolata:* About half an hour before serving, in a small serving bowl, combine garlic, parsley, lemon zest and olive oil. Pass around the table, allowing guests to individually garnish their meat.

Chile-Spiked Lamb Shanks

Serves 4 to 8

◆ **Entertaining Worthy**
◆ **Can Be Halved**
(see Tips, below)

Tips

If you are halving this recipe, be sure to use a small (2 to 3½ quart) slow cooker.

Whether you cook the lamb shanks whole, halved or have them cut into pieces is a matter of preference. However, if the shanks are left whole, you will be able to serve only four people — each will receive one large shank.

For a more sophisticated version, after the dish has finished cooking, transfer the lamb to a deep platter and keep warm. Transfer the sauce to a saucepan and cook over medium heat until reduced by a third, about 10 minutes. Purée using an immersion blender. Pour over shanks and garnish liberally with parsley, if using.

Make Ahead

Complete Step 2. Cover and refrigerate mixture for up to 2 days. When you're ready to cook, complete the recipe.

I love the flavors in this dish — a sweet-and-sour combination with a bit of heat.

• **Large (approx. 5 quart) slow cooker**

2 tbsp	clarified butter, divided	30 mL
4	large lamb shanks (about 4 lbs/2 kg), patted dry (see Tips, left)	4
2	onions, finely chopped	2
2	carrots, peeled and diced	2
2	stalks celery, diced	2
6	cloves garlic, minced	6
1 tsp	dried thyme	5 mL
1 tsp	cracked black peppercorns	5 mL
½ tsp	sea salt	2 mL
1 cup	dry red wine	250 mL
2 tbsp	coconut sugar	30 mL
2 tbsp	red wine vinegar	30 mL
2 cups	chicken stock	500 mL
2 to 4	jalapeño peppers, seeded and diced	2 to 4
	Finely chopped parsley, optional	

1. In a large skillet, heat 1 tbsp (15 mL) of the butter over medium-high heat. Add lamb, in batches, and brown on all sides, about 8 minutes per batch. Transfer to slow cooker stoneware as completed. Drain off fat from pan.

2. Reduce heat to medium. Add remaining tbsp (15 mL) of butter to pan. Add onions, carrots and celery to pan and cook, stirring, until carrots are soft, about 7 minutes. Add garlic, thyme, peppercorns and sea salt and cook, stirring, for 1 minute. Add wine, bring to a boil and boil for 2 minutes, scraping up brown bits from bottom of pan. Add coconut sugar and vinegar and stir well.

3. Transfer to slow cooker stoneware. Stir in chicken stock. Cover and cook on Low for 8 to 10 hours or on High for 4 to 5 hours, until meat is falling off the bone. Stir in jalapeños to taste and cook on High for 15 minutes, until flavors meld. Garnish with parsley, if using.

Just Veggies

Mixed Vegetable
Coconut Curry

Mixed Vegetable Coconut Curry

◆ **Can Be Halved**
(see Tips, below)

Tips

If you are halving this recipe, be sure to use a small (approx. 2 quart) slow cooker.

For the best flavor, toast the cumin and coriander seeds and grind them yourself. *To toast seeds:* Place in a dry skillet over medium heat and cook, stirring, until fragrant, about 3 minutes. Immediately transfer to a spice grinder or mortar and grind finely.

If you are using the outer stalks of celery, peel them before chopping; the top layer is very fibrous. The inner stalks (hearts) can be used without peeling.

Make Ahead

Complete Step 1. Cover and refrigerate for up to 2 days. When you're ready to cook, complete the recipe.

This dish is very versatile. Use it as a vegetable dish to round out an Indian meal, as a tasty side for grilled meat or fish, or increase the portion size and serve it as a main course if you're serving vegetarians. (It is vegan friendly.)

• **Medium to large (4 to 5 quart) slow cooker**

1 tbsp	clarified butter (ghee) or extra virgin coconut oil	15 mL
3 cups	cubed ($\frac{1}{2}$ inch/1 cm) peeled carrots (about 4 medium)	750 mL
2	onions, finely chopped	2
2	stalks celery, diced (see Tips, left)	2
4	cloves garlic, minced	4
1 tbsp	minced gingerroot	15 mL
2 tsp	ground cumin (see Tips, left)	10 mL
2 tsp	ground coriander	10 mL
1 tsp	cracked black peppercorns	5 mL
$\frac{1}{2}$ tsp	sea salt	2 mL
$\frac{1}{2}$ tsp	ground turmeric	2 mL
1	bay leaf	1
1	can (28 oz/796 mL) diced tomatoes with juice (see page 13)	1
4 cups	cubed (1 inch/2.5 cm) peeled winter squash	1 L
1 cup	coconut milk	250 mL
1	red bell pepper, seeded and diced	1
1	long red or green chile pepper, seeded and minced	1

1. In a skillet, heat clarified butter over medium heat. Add carrots, onions and celery and cook, stirring, until softened, about 7 minutes. Add garlic, ginger, cumin, coriander, peppercorns, sea salt, turmeric and bay leaf and cook, stirring, for 1 minute. Add tomatoes with juice and bring to a boil. Transfer to slow cooker stoneware.

2. Stir in squash. Cover and cook on Low for 6 hours or on High for 3 hours. Add coconut milk, bell pepper and chile pepper and stir well. Cover and cook on High for 15 minutes, until peppers are tender.

Parsnip and Coconut Curry with Crispy Shallots

◆ **Entertaining Worthy**
◆ **Can Be Halved**
 (see Tips, below)

Tips

If you are halving this recipe, be sure to use a small (approx. 1½ to 3½ quart) slow cooker.

For best results, toast and grind the cumin yourself. *To toast seeds:* Place in a dry skillet and cook, stirring, until fragrant, about 3 minutes. Immediately transfer to a mortar or a spice grinder and grind.

Make Ahead

Complete Step 1. Cover and refrigerate for up to 2 days. When you're ready to cook, complete the recipe.

The combination of sweet parsnips, spicy curry, mellow coconut milk and crispy shallots is absolutely delicious. It is a perfect dish to serve as part of an Indian food meal. If you are serving vegans, make it with vegetable stock. It can serve double as a main course, served alongside a small platter of stir-fried bok choy drizzled with cold-pressed toasted sesame oil.

• **Small to medium (2 to 4 quart) slow cooker**

1 tbsp	clarified butter (ghee) or extra virgin coconut oil	15 mL
1	large onion, fined chopped	1
4	stalks celery, thinly sliced (see Tips, page 196)	4
6	parsnips, peeled and diced	6
1 tbsp	minced gingerroot	15 mL
2 tsp	ground cumin (see Tips, left)	10 mL
1 cup	vegetable stock	250 mL
2 tsp	curry powder	10 mL
1 tbsp	freshly squeezed lemon juice	15 mL
1 cup	coconut milk	250 mL
1 cup	sweet green peas, thawed if frozen (see page 15)	250 mL

Crispy Shallot Topping

2 tbsp	clarified butter (ghee) or extra virgin coconut oil	30 mL
½ cup	thinly sliced shallots	125 mL
1	red chile pepper, seeded and minced, optional	1

1. In a skillet, heat butter over medium heat. Add onion, celery and parsnips and cook, stirring, until softened, about 7 minutes. Add ginger and cumin and cook, stirring for 1 minute. Stir in vegetable stock. Transfer to slow cooker stoneware.

2. Cover and cook on Low for 6 hours or High for 3 hours, until vegetables are tender. Dissolve curry powder in lemon juice. Add to stoneware along with coconut milk and green peas. Cover and cook on High for 20 to 30 minutes, until peas are cooked and mixture is bubbly.

3. *Crispy Shallot Topping:* In a skillet, heat butter over medium-high heat. Add shallots and cook, stirring, until browned and crispy, about 5 minutes. Add chile pepper, if using, and cook, stirring, for 1 minute. Ladle curry into a serving bowl and top with shallots.

Eggplant Braised with Tomatoes and Mushrooms

Serves 8

♦ **Can Be Halved**
(see Tips, below)

Tips

If you are halving this recipe, be sure to use a small (approx. 1½ to 3½ quart) slow cooker.

To sweat eggplant: Place cubed eggplant in a colander, sprinkle liberally with sea salt, toss well and set aside for 30 minutes to 1 hour. If time is short, blanch the pieces for a minute or two in heavily salted water. In either case, rinse thoroughly in fresh cold water and, using your hands, squeeze out excess moisture. Pat dry with paper towels and it's ready for cooking.

Make Ahead

Complete Steps 1 and 2. Cover and refrigerate for up to 2 days. When you're ready to cook, complete the recipe.

This hearty combination makes a perfect accompaniment to roasted or grilled meat of fish. It can even double as a vegan main course. All you need to add is a simple tossed green salad.

• **Medium (approx. 4 quart) slow cooker**

1	medium eggplant, peeled, cubed (2 inches/5 cm), sweated and drained of excess moisture (see Tips, left)	1
2 tbsp	extra virgin olive oil	30 mL
2	onions, finely chopped	2
4	cloves garlic, minced	4
1 tsp	dried thyme	5 mL
1 tsp	cracked black peppercorns	5 mL
½ tsp	sea salt	2 mL
1	can (28 oz/796 mL) tomatoes with juice, coarsely chopped (see page 13)	1
2	potatoes, peeled and shredded	2
1 lb	cremini mushrooms, trimmed and sliced	500 g
¼ cup	finely chopped flat-leaf parsley leaves	60 mL

1. In a skillet, heat oil over medium heat. Add eggplant, in batches, and cook, stirring, until lightly browned. Transfer to slow cooker stoneware as completed.

2. Reduce heat to medium. Add onions to pan and cook, stirring, until softened, about 3 minutes. Add garlic, thyme, peppercorns and sea salt and cook, stirring, for 1 minute. Stir in tomatoes with juice and bring to a boil. Transfer to slow cooker stoneware.

3. Add potatoes and mushrooms and stir well. Cover and cook on Low for 6 hours or on High for 3 hours, until hot and bubbly. Garnish with parsley.

Ratatouille

◆ **Entertaining Worthy**
◆ **Can Be Halved**
(see Tips, below)

Tips

If you are halving this recipe, be sure to use a small (approx. 1½ to 3½ quart) slow cooker.

Be sure to rinse the salted eggplant thoroughly after sweating. Otherwise it may retain salt and your ratatouille will be too sea salty.

Make Ahead

Complete Steps 1 through 3. Cover and refrigerate eggplant and zucchini mixtures separately for up to 2 days. When you're ready to cook, continue with Step 4.

Ratatouille makes a great accompaniment to grilled meat or fish or a platter of roast vegetables. It is also delicious on its own.

- **Large (approx. 5 quart) slow cooker**
- **Preheat oven to 400°F (200°C)**
- **Rimmed baking sheet, ungreased**

2	medium eggplant (each about 12 oz/375 g), peeled, cubed (1 inch/2.5 cm), sweated and drained of excess moisture (see Tips, left and page 198)	2
3 tbsp	extra virgin olive oil, divided	45 mL
4	medium zucchini (about 1½ lbs/750 g total), peeled and thinly sliced	4
2	cloves garlic, minced	2
2	onions, thinly sliced	2
1 tsp	herbes de Provence	5 mL
½ tsp	sea salt	2 mL
½ tsp	cracked black peppercorns	2 mL
8 oz	cremini mushrooms, sliced	250 g
1	can (28 oz/796 mL) tomatoes with juice, coarsely chopped (see page 13)	1
2	green bell peppers, cut into ½-inch (1 cm) cubes	2
½ cup	chopped flat-leaf parsley or basil leaves	125 mL

1. On baking sheet, toss eggplant with 1 tbsp (15 mL) of the olive oil. Spread evenly on sheet. Cover with foil and bake in preheated oven until soft and fragrant, about 15 minutes. Remove from oven and transfer to slow cooker stoneware.

2. Meanwhile, heat 1 tbsp (15 mL) of oil over medium heat. Add zucchini and cook, stirring, for 6 minutes. Add garlic and cook, stirring, until zucchini is soft and browned, about 1 minute. Transfer to a bowl. Cover and refrigerate.

3. Reduce heat to medium. Add remaining 1 tbsp (15 mL) of oil. Add onions and cook, stirring, until softened, about 3 minutes. Add herbes de Provence, sea salt and peppercorns and cook, stirring, about 1 minute. Add mushrooms and toss until coated. Stir in tomatoes with juice and bring to a boil. Transfer to stoneware.

4. Cover and cook on Low for 6 hours or on High for 3 hours, until vegetables are tender. Add green peppers, reserved zucchini mixture and parsley and stir well. Cover and cook on High for 25 minutes, until peppers are tender and zucchini is heated through.

Louisiana Ratatouille

◆ **Can Be Halved**
(see Tips, below)

Tips

If you are halving this recipe, be sure to use a small (approx. 1½ to 3½ quart) slow cooker.

To sweat eggplant: Place cubed eggplant in a colander, sprinkle liberally with sea salt, toss well and set aside for 30 minutes to 1 hour. If time is short, blanch the pieces for a minute or two in heavily sea salted water. In either case, rinse thoroughly in fresh cold water and, using your hands, squeeze out excess moisture. Pat dry with paper towels and it's ready for cooking.

Okra becomes unpleasantly sticky when overcooked. Choose young okra pods, 2 to 4 inches (5 to 10 cm) long, that don't feel sticky to the touch (if sticky, they are too ripe). Gently scrub the pods and cut off the top and tail. Okra can also be found in the freezer section of the grocery store. Thaw before adding to slow cooker.

Make Ahead

Complete Steps 1 and 2. Cover and refrigerate for up to 2 days. When you're ready to cook, complete the recipe.

Eggplant, tomato and okra stew is a classic Southern dish that probably owes its origins to the famous Mediterranean mélange ratatouille. One secret to a successful result, even on top of the stove, is not overcooking the okra, which should be added after the flavors in the other ingredients have melded.

• **Medium (approx. 4 quart) slow cooker**

2	medium eggplants (each about 12 oz/375 g), peeled, cubed (2 inches/5 cm), sweated and drained of excess moisture (see Tips, left)	2
2 tbsp	extra virgin olive oil	30 mL
2	onions, finely chopped	2
4	cloves garlic, minced	4
1 tsp	dried oregano	5 mL
½ tsp	sea salt	2 mL
½ tsp	cracked black peppercorns	2 mL
1	can (28 oz/796 mL) tomatoes with juice, coarsely chopped (see page 13)	1
2 tbsp	red wine vinegar (see page 15)	30 mL
1 lb	okra, trimmed and cut into 1-inch (2.5 cm) lengths, about 2 cups (500 mL) (see Tips, left)	500 g
1	green bell pepper, diced (¼ inch/0.5 cm)	1

1. In a skillet, heat oil over medium heat. Add eggplant, in batches, and cook, stirring, until lightly browned. Transfer to slow cooker stoneware.

2. Add onions to pan and cook, stirring, until softened, about 3 minutes. Add garlic, oregano, sea salt and peppercorns and cook, stirring, for 1 minute. Stir in tomatoes with juice and red wine vinegar and bring to a boil. Transfer to slow cooker stoneware.

3. Cover and cook on Low for 6 hours or on High for 3 hours, until hot and bubbly. Add okra and bell pepper. Cover and cook on High for 30 minutes, until okra is tender.

Braised Belgian Endive

- ◆ Entertaining Worthy
- ◆ Can Be Halved
  (see Tips, below)

Tip

If you are halving this recipe, be sure to use a small (approx. 1½ to 2 quart) slow cooker.

Endive's bitter flavor can be an acquired taste, but once you "get it," this intriguing vegetable can be mildly addictive. Usually eaten raw, often in salads like its relative radicchio, endive also sparkles when cooked. It lends itself to long, slow braising. This dish makes a great accompaniment to grilled meat or roast chicken.

- **Small to medium (2 to 3½ quart) slow cooker**
- **Large piece of parchment paper**

6	medium Belgian endives	6
3 tbsp	butter or extra virgin olive oil (approx.)	45 mL
½ cup	chicken or vegetable stock	125 mL
1 tbsp	freshly squeezed lemon juice	15 mL
½ tsp	sea salt	2 mL
½ tsp	cracked black peppercorns	2 mL

1. Trim off the stem ends of endives and, using a sharp paring knife, dig out the hard cores and discard. Then halve lengthwise.

2. In a large skillet over medium heat, melt butter. Add endive, cut side down, in batches, if necessary, and cook, stirring, until nicely browned, about 4 minutes per batch, adding more butter, if necessary.

3. Transfer to slow cooker stoneware as completed. Add stock, lemon juice, sea salt and peppercorns to pan and bring to a boil, scraping up brown bits from bottom of pan. Pour over endive. Place a large piece of parchment over the mixture, pressing it down to brush the food and extending up the sides of the stoneware so it overlaps the rim.

4. Cover and cook on Low for 6 hours or on High for 3 hours, until endive is tender. Lift out parchment and discard, being careful not to spill the accumulated liquid into the sauce.

Braised Red Cabbage

◆ **Entertaining Worthy**
◆ **Can Be Halved**
  (see Tips, below)

Tip

If you are halving this recipe, be sure to use a small (approx. 1½ to 3½ quart) slow cooker.

This is one of my favorite winter vegetables — in my opinion, the best possible accompaniment to a pork roast.

• **Medium to large (3½ to 5 quart) slow cooker**

2 tbsp	butter or extra virgin olive oil	30 mL
2	onions, thinly sliced	2
2	apples, peeled, cored and chopped	2
½ tsp	sea salt	2 mL
½ tsp	cracked black peppercorns	2 mL
4	whole cloves	4
1	piece (2 inches/5 cm) cinnamon stick	1
1	small red cabbage, shredded	1
3 tbsp	balsamic vinegar (see page 15)	45 mL
2 tbsp	coconut sugar	30 mL
2 tbsp	water	30 mL

1. In a large skillet over medium heat, melt butter. Add onions and cook, stirring, until softened, about 3 minutes. Add apples, salt, peppercorns, cloves and cinnamon stick and cook, stirring, for 1 minute. Add cabbage, in batches, stirring until it begins to wilt before adding more. Stir in vinegar, coconut sugar and water.

2. Transfer to slow cooker stoneware. Cover and cook on High, stirring once or twice, for 3 hours, until cabbage is tender. Discard cinnamon stick.

Simple Braised Leeks

◆ **Entertaining Worthy**
◆ **Can Be Halved**
(see Tips, below)

Tips

If you are halving this recipe, be sure to use a small (approx. 1½ to 2 quart) slow cooker.

Leeks can be gritty and need to be thoroughly cleaned before cooking. Peel off the tough outer layer(s) and cut off the root. Slice leeks according to recipe instructions and submerge in a basin of lukewarm water, swishing them around to remove all traces of dirt. Transfer to a colander and rinse under cold water.

Leeks have a mild onion flavor that is both delicate and rich. They are a wonderful accompaniment to grilled fish and meats or roast chicken.

• **Small to medium (2 to 4 quart) slow cooker**

6 to 8	leeks, white part only with just a hint of green, cleaned and sliced into quarters on the vertical (see Tips, left)	6 to 8
3 tbsp	melted butter or extra virgin olive oil	45 mL
1 cup	chicken or vegetable stock	250 mL
	Sea salt and freshly ground black pepper	
¼ cup	finely chopped flat-leaf parsley leaves	60 mL

1. Pat leeks dry and place in slow cooker stoneware. Add butter and toss until well coated. Place a clean tea towel, folded in half (so you will have 2 layers), over top of stoneware to absorb moisture. Cover and cook on High for 1 hour. Stir well. Remove tea towel and add stock.

2. Cover and cook on Low for 5 to 6 hours or on High for 2½ to 3 hours, until leeks are very tender. Season with salt and pepper to taste. Garnish with parsley and serve.

Peppery Red Onions

◆ **Can Be Halved**
(see Tip, below)

Tip

If you are halving this recipe, be sure to use a small (1½ to 2 quart) slow cooker.

Make Ahead

Complete Step 1. Cover and refrigerate overnight. The next day, complete the recipe.

I love making this nippy treat in the autumn when the farmers' markets are brimming over with freshly harvested red onions. They are a tasty alternative to creamed onions. I particularly enjoy them as a topping for Roasted Eggplant or Zucchini Boats (page 243).

• **Small to medium (2 to 4 quart) slow cooker**

4	large red onions, quartered	4
1 tbsp	extra virgin olive oil	15 mL
1 tsp	dried oregano	5 mL
¼ cup	water or chicken or vegetable stock	60 mL
	Sea salt and black pepper	
	Hot Pepper Sauce (page 240)	

1. In slow cooker stoneware, combine red onions, olive oil, oregano, water, and salt and pepper, to taste. Stir thoroughly.

2. Cover and cook on Low for 6 hours or on High for 3 hours, until onions are tender. Add hot sauce, to taste, toss well and serve.

Braised Sweet Onions in Balsamic Butter

◆ **Entertaining Worthy**
◆ **Can Be Halved**
(see Tips, below)

Tips

If you are halving this recipe, be sure to use a small (1½ to 2 quart) slow cooker.

If using olive oil rather than butter, drizzle it over the onions before adding the parchment.

Onions are a source of allyl sulfides, which are thought to be anti-carcinogenic.

Onions are the workhorse of almost every kitchen. They are the base for so many soups, stews and sauces that we take them for granted. But cooked properly, they are a delicious vegetable all on their own. Here, sweet onions, which are available in North America throughout the spring, assume a starring role. They are complemented by sweetly pungent balsamic vinegar to produce a simple, but quite magnificent dish.

- **Small to medium (2 to 4 quart) slow cooker**
- **Large sheet of parchment paper**

4 to 6	sweet onions, such as Vidalia, quartered	4 to 6
2 tbsp	balsamic vinegar (see page 15)	30 mL
1 tbsp	extra virgin olive oil	15 mL
½ tsp	sea salt	2 mL
½ tsp	cracked black peppercorns	2 mL
2 tbsp	butter or extra virgin olive oil (see Tips, left)	30 mL
	Finely chopped flat-leaf parsley leaves, optional	

1. In slow cooker stoneware, combine onions, vinegar, olive oil, sea salt and peppercorns. Toss to combine. Dot butter over top. Place a large piece of parchment over the mixture, pressing it down to brush the food and extending up the sides of the stoneware so it overlaps the rim.

2. Cover and cook on Low for 6 hours or on High for 3 hours, until onions are tender. Lift off parchment and discard, being careful not to spill any accumulated liquid into the onions. Garnish liberally with parsley, if using.

New Orleans Braised Onions

♦ **Entertaining Worthy**
♦ **Can Be Halved**
(see Tips, below)

Tips

If you are halving this recipe, be sure to use a small (1½ to 3½ quart) slow cooker, checking to make sure the whole onions will fit.

Onions are high in natural sugars, which long slow simmering brings out, as does the orange juice in this recipe.

I call these New Orleans onions because I was inspired by an old Creole recipe for Spanish onions. In that version, the onions are braised in beef stock enhanced by the addition of liquor such as bourbon or port. After the onions are cooked, the cooking juices are reduced and herbs, such as capers or fresh thyme, may be added to the concentrated sauce. In my opinion, this simplified version is every bit as tasty. If your guests like spice, pass hot pepper sauce at the table.

• **Large (approx. 5 quart) slow cooker**

2 to 3	large Spanish onions	2 to 3
6 to 9	whole cloves	6 to 9
½ tsp	sea salt	2 mL
½ tsp	cracked black peppercorns	2 mL
Pinch	dried thyme	Pinch
	Grated zest and juice of 1 orange	
½ cup	chicken or vegetable stock	125 mL
	Finely chopped flat-leaf parsley leaves, optional	
	Hot Pepper Sauce (page 240), optional	

1. Stud onions with cloves. Place in slow cooker stoneware and sprinkle with salt, peppercorns, thyme and orange zest. Pour orange juice and stock over onions, cover and cook on Low for 6 hours or on High for 3 hours, until onions are tender.

2. Using a slotted spoon, transfer onions to a serving dish and keep warm in a 250°F (120°C) oven. Transfer liquid to a saucepan over medium heat. Cook until reduced by half.

3. When ready to serve, cut onions into quarters. Place on a deep platter and cover with sauce. Sprinkle with parsley, if desired, and pass the hot pepper sauce, if desired.

Ginger-Spiked Sweet Potatoes with Maple Syrup

◆ **Entertaining Worthy**
◆ **Can Be Halved**
(see Tips, below)

Tips

If you are halving this recipe, be sure to use a small (1½ to 2 quart) slow cooker.

Sweet potatoes are neither potatoes nor yams. They are a tuber (like yams) that is native to the Americas. They are quite perishable and don't like the cold. Don't store them at temperatures that are lower than 50°F (10°C).

Sweet potatoes are quite starchy. If you prefer, substitute 2 lbs (1 kg) cubed acorn squash for the sweet potatoes.

Here's a slightly different way of cooking sweet potatoes that is vegan friendly. Simply braised in orange juice, finished with luscious maple syrup and garnished with toasted pecans, they are quite yummy.

• **Small to medium (approx. 2 quart) slow cooker**

4	sweet potatoes, peeled and cut into ½-inch (1 cm) thick rounds (see Tips, left)	4
1 tbsp	finely grated orange zest	15 mL
½ cup	freshly squeezed orange juice	125 mL
1 tbsp	minced gingerroot	15 mL
½ tsp	sea salt	2 mL
½ tsp	cracked black peppercorns	2 mL
¼ cup	pure maple syrup (see page 15)	60 mL
	Toasted pecans	

1. In slow cooker stoneware, combine sweet potatoes, orange zest and juice, ginger, salt and peppercorns. Cover and cook on Low for 6 hours or on High for 3 hours, until potatoes are tender. Using a potato masher or a large fork, mash potatoes. Stir in maple syrup and garnish with toasted pecans.

Sweet Potato Pudding

◆ **Entertaining Worthy**

Tip

Although acceptable on a Paleo diet, sweet potatoes contain quite a bit of starch. If you prefer, substitute an equal quantity of baked acorn squash.

Make Ahead

Complete Step 1. Cover and refrigerate for up to 2 days. When you're ready to cook, continue with the recipe.

This dish makes a wonderful accompaniment to poultry, which is why it is traditionally served with roast turkey. It's slightly sweet, so if you're feeling the urge, enjoy leftovers with a little Coconut Whipped Cream (page 232) for dessert or an afternoon snack.

- **Large (approx. 5 quart) slow cooker**
- **Greased baking dish**
- **Food processor**

4	medium sweet potatoes, cooked and peeled (2 lbs/1 kg) (see Tip, left)	4
2 tbsp	butter	30 mL
2 tbsp	coconut sugar	30 mL
$\frac{1}{2}$ tsp	sea salt	2 mL
$\frac{1}{2}$ tsp	freshly ground black pepper	2 mL
$\frac{1}{2}$ tsp	freshly grated nutmeg	2 mL
2	eggs	2

Topping

$\frac{1}{2}$ cup	chopped pecans	125 mL
$\frac{1}{4}$ cup	almond flour	60 mL
2 tbsp	coconut sugar	30 mL
1 tsp	ground cinnamon	5 mL
2 tbsp	melted butter	30 mL

1. In food processor fitted with the metal blade, combine sweet potatoes, butter, coconut sugar, salt, pepper and nutmeg. Pulse until blended. Add eggs and process until smooth. Transfer to prepared dish. Cover with foil and secure with a string.

2. Place in slow cooker stoneware and pour in enough hot water to come 1 inch (2.5 cm) up the sides of the bowl. Cover and cook on High for 3 to $3\frac{1}{2}$ hours, until pudding is set.

3. *Topping:* In a bowl, combine pecans, almond flour, coconut sugar and cinnamon. Mix well. Add butter and mix to blend. When pudding has finished cooking, preheat broiler. Remove foil and sprinkle topping evenly over pudding. Place under broiler until browned.

Parsnip and Carrot Purée with Cumin

Serves 8

♦ **Can Be Halved**
(see Tips, below)

Tips

If you are halving this recipe, be sure to use a small (1½ to 2 quart) slow cooker.

If you are using very large parsnips, discard the woody core. The easiest way to do this is to cut the parsnips into thirds horizontally and place the flat surface on a cutting board. Using a sharp knife, cut around the core. Discard the core and cut the slices into cubes.

For the best flavor, toast cumin seeds and grind them yourself. *To toast seeds:* Place in a dry skillet over medium heat and cook, stirring, until fragrant, about 3 minutes. Immediately transfer to a spice grinder or mortar and grind finely.

Make Ahead

Peel and cut parsnips and carrots. Cover and refrigerate overnight.

The cumin adds a slightly exotic note to this traditional dish, which makes a great accompaniment to many foods.

• **Medium (approx. 4 quart) slow cooker**

4 cups	cubed (½ inch/1 cm) peeled parsnips (about 8 medium) (see Tips, left)	1 L
2 cups	thinly sliced peeled carrots	500 mL
1 tsp	ground cumin (see Tips, left)	5 mL
2 tbsp	butter or extra virgin olive oil	30 mL
1 tsp	coconut sugar	5 mL
½ tsp	sea salt	2 mL
¼ tsp	freshly ground black pepper	1 mL
¼ cup	water or chicken or vegetable stock	60 mL

1. In slow cooker stoneware, combine parsnips, carrots, cumin, butter, coconut sugar, salt, pepper and water. Cover and cook on Low for 6 hours or on High for 3 hours, until vegetables are tender.

2. Using a potato masher or a food processor or blender, mash or purée mixture until smooth. Serve immediately.

Braised Carrots with Capers

◆ **Entertaining Worthy**
◆ **Can Be Halved**
(see Tips, below)

Tips

If you are halving this recipe, be sure to use a small ($1\frac{1}{2}$ to $3\frac{1}{2}$ quart) slow cooker.

Carrots are high in beta-carotene, an antioxidant that our bodies turn into vitamin A. Cooking actually increases the vegetable's beta-carotene and increases its sweetness.

Make Ahead

Complete Step 1 and refrigerate overnight. The next day, complete the recipe.

This dish is simplicity itself and yet the results are startlingly fresh.

- **Small to medium (2 to 4 quart) slow cooker**

2 tbsp	extra virgin olive oil	30 mL
12	large carrots, peeled and thinly sliced	12
12	cloves garlic, thinly sliced	12
$\frac{1}{2}$ tsp	sea salt	2 mL
$\frac{1}{2}$ tsp	freshly ground black pepper	2 mL
$\frac{1}{2}$ cup	drained capers	125 mL

1. In slow cooker stoneware, combine oil, carrots, garlic, salt and pepper. Toss to combine.

2. Cover and cook on Low for 6 hours or on High for 3 hours, until carrots are tender. Add capers and toss to combine. Serve immediately.

Variation

Braised Carrots with Black Olives: Substitute $\frac{1}{2}$ cup (125 mL) chopped black olives, preferably kalamata, a particularly pungent Greek variety, for the capers

Orange-Spiked Carrots Braised in Vermouth

Serves 6 to 8

◆ **Entertaining Worthy**
◆ **Can Be Halved**
(see Tips, below)

Tip

If you are halving this recipe, be sure to use a small (approx. 1½ to 2 quart) slow cooker.

I love the combination of flavors in this dish, which makes a great accompaniment to just about anything. Served glazed (see Variation, below), it is perfect for a special occasion meal.

• **Medium (approx. 4 quart) slow cooker**

12	carrots, peeled and sliced	12
2 tbsp	melted butter or extra virgin olive oil	30 mL
2 tsp	finely grated orange zest	10 mL
½ tsp	sea salt	2 mL
½ tsp	cracked black peppercorns	2 mL
½ tsp	coconut sugar	2 mL
½ cup	dry vermouth	125 mL
2 tbsp	freshly squeezed orange juice	30 mL

1. In slow cooker stoneware, combine carrots, butter and orange zest. Stir well. Place a clean tea towel, folded in half (so you have 2 layers), over top of stoneware to absorb moisture. Cover and cook on High for 1 hour. Add salt, peppercorns, coconut sugar, vermouth and orange juice. Cover and cook on Low for 4 hours or on High for 2 hours, until carrots are tender.

Variation

I particularly enjoy these carrots in a slightly bumped-up version. After they are cooked, transfer the contents of the slow cooker, including liquid, to a gratin dish. Sprinkle with coconut sugar and, if desired, a bit a cinnamon, to taste. (I've also used vanilla coconut sugar — save the pod from a used vanilla bean and bury it in the sugar until its flavor disperses — which produced excellent results.) Place under a preheated broiler until the sugar glazes. One advantage to this is convenience — you can keep the carrots on Warm in the slow cooker and finish them off (adding the sugar and placing them under the broiler) when the timing suits you.

Fennel Braised with Tomatoes

◆ Entertaining Worthy
◆ Can Be Halved
(see Tips, below)

Tips

If you are halving this recipe, be sure to use a small (approx. 1½ to 2 quart) slow cooker.

If the outer sections of your fennel bulb seem old and dry, peel them with a vegetable peeler before using. *To prepare fennel:* Chop off the top shoots (which resemble celery) and discard. If desired, save the feathery green fronds to use as a garnish.

I like to use parchment when cooking this dish because it doesn't contain much liquid. Creating a tight seal ensures that none evaporates and that the vegetables are well basted in their own juices.

Here's a perfectly luscious side dish that makes a great companion for grilled or roasted fish and meats.

- **Medium (approx. 3½ quart) slow cooker**
- **Large piece of parchment paper**

2 tbsp	extra virgin olive oil	30 mL
1	onion, thinly sliced on the vertical	1
3	bulbs fennel, cored and thinly sliced on the vertical (see Tips, left)	3
4	cloves garlic, minced	4
½ tsp	sea salt	2 mL
½ tsp	cracked black peppercorns	2 mL
1	can (14 oz/398 mL) diced tomatoes with juice (see page 13)	1
	Fennel fronds, optional	

1. In a large skillet, heat oil over medium heat. Add onion and fennel, in batches, if necessary, and cook, tossing, until fennel begins to brown, about 5 minutes. Add garlic, salt and peppercorns and cook, stirring, for 1 minute. Add tomatoes with juice and bring to a boil.

2. Transfer to slow cooker stoneware. Place a large piece of parchment over the mixture, pressing it down to brush the food and extending up the sides of the stoneware so it overlaps the rim.

3. Cover and cook on Low for 6 hours or on High for 3 hours, until fennel is tender. Lift out parchment and discard, being careful not to spill the accumulated liquid into the sauce. Garnish with fennel fronds, if using.

Orange-Braised Fennel

◆ **Can Be Halved**
(see Tips, below)

Tips

If halving this recipe, be sure to use a small (approx. 2 quart) slow cooker.

For the best flavor, toast coriander seeds and grind them yourself. *To toast seeds:* Place in a dry skillet over medium heat and cook, stirring, until fragrant, about 3 minutes. Immediately transfer to a spice grinder or mortar and grind finely.

If you're looking for something that tastes deliciously different, try this. The flavors of orange and coriander combine intriguingly with the fennel, which is slightly more intensely flavored than usual because it has been browned before braising. Serve this with anything that benefits from a hint of tartness.

- **Small to medium (1½ to 3½ quart) slow cooker**
- **Large sheet of parchment paper**

2 tbsp	extra virgin olive oil	30 mL
3	bulbs fennel, trimmed, cored and thinly sliced on the vertical (see Tips, page 214)	3
2	cloves garlic, minced	2
1 tsp	ground coriander (see Tips, left)	5 mL
½ tsp	sea salt	2 mL
½ tsp	cracked black peppercorns	2 mL
	Grated zest and juice of 1 orange	

1. In a large skillet, heat oil over medium heat. Add fennel, in batches, if necessary, and cook, stirring, just until it begins to brown, about 5 minutes per batch. Transfer to slow cooker stoneware as completed. When last batch of fennel is almost browned, add garlic, coriander, salt, peppercorns and orange zest to pan and cook, stirring, for 1 minute. Transfer to slow cooker stoneware and stir in orange juice.

2. Place a large piece of parchment over the fennel, pressing it down to brush the food and extending up the sides of the stoneware so it overlaps the rim. Cover and cook on Low for 6 hours or on High for 3 hours, until fennel is tender. Lift out the parchment and discard, being careful not to spill the accumulated liquid into the stoneware.

Braised Butternut Squash

◆ **Entertaining Worthy**
◆ **Can Be Halved**
(see Tips, below)

Tips

If you are halving this recipe, be sure to use a small (approx. 1½ to 2 quart) slow cooker.

I like to use parchment when cooking this dish because the recipe doesn't contain much liquid. Creating a tight seal ensures that the ingredients baste in their own juices, intensifying the flavors.

If you prefer, substitute another winter squash, such as acorn, calabaza or pumpkin.

One advantage to making squash in the slow cooker is that you can get it ready and forget about it until it's cooked, which is a big help if you're preparing a multi-course meal. Another is that you can cook in a minimum amount of liquid, conserving precious nutrients and flavor.

- **Medium (3½ quart) slow cooker**
- **Large piece of parchment paper (see Tips, left)**

6 cups	cubed (1 inch/2.5 cm) butternut squash (about 1 large) (see Tips, left)	1.5 L
1 tbsp	extra virgin olive or coconut oil, or butter	15 mL
1	onion, finely chopped	1
1 tsp	coconut sugar	5 mL
½ tsp	sea salt	2 mL
½ tsp	cracked black peppercorns	2 mL
½ cup	water or beef, chicken or vegetable stock	125 mL
3 tbsp	coconut milk	45 mL
1 tbsp	fresh thyme leaves or finely snipped chives	15 mL

1. Place squash in slow cooker stoneware. In a skillet heat oil over medium heat. Add onion and cook, stirring, until it begins to turn golden, about 5 minutes. Add coconut sugar, sea salt and peppercorns and cook, stirring, for 1 minute. Add water and bring to a boil, scraping up brown bits from the bottom of the pan.

2. Transfer to slow cooker stoneware. Stir well. Place a large piece of parchment paper over the squash, pressing it down to brush the food and extending up the sides of the stoneware so it overlaps the rim. Cover and cook on Low for 6 hours or on High for 3 hours, until squash is very tender. Remove and discard parchment, being careful not to spill accumulated liquid onto squash. Using a wooden spoon, mash squash until desired consistency is achieved. Stir in coconut milk and thyme. Serve hot.

Collard Greens in Tomato Sauce

◆ **Can Be Halved**
(see Tips, below)

Tips

If you are halving this recipe, be sure to use a small (approx. 1½ to 2 quart) slow cooker.

You'll need 2 bunches of greens for this recipe.

Collards require a thorough washing before being cooked. Soak the trimmed greens in several changes of tepid water, agitating to remove grit. Then rinse thoroughly, in a colander, under cold running water.

Collard greens, which are popular in the South, are a particularly tasty member of the cabbage family. Unlike most vegetables, they are very tolerant of long, slow cooking.

• **Medium (approx. 3½ quart) slow cooker**

2	slices bacon	2
2	onions, finely chopped	2
2	cloves garlic, minced	2
½ tsp	sea salt	2 mL
½ tsp	cracked black peppercorns	2 mL
2 cups	tomatoes, coarsely chopped, including juice	500 mL
2 lbs	fresh collard greens, tough stems removed and chopped into 2-inch (5 cm) lengths (see Tips, left)	1 kg
	Hot Pepper Sauce (page 240), optional	
	Red wine vinegar, optional	

1. In a skillet, cook bacon over medium heat, until crisp. Drain on paper towel and crumble. Set aside. Drain all but 1 tbsp (15 mL) fat from pan, if desired, and reduce heat to medium.

2. Add onions to pan and cook, stirring, until softened. Add garlic, salt and peppercorns and cook, stirring, for 1 minute. Add tomatoes and bring to a boil.

3. Place greens in slow cooker stoneware. Add tomato mixture and stir to combine. Cover and cook on Low for 6 hours or on High for 3 hours, until greens are tender. Add reserved bacon and cook until heated through, about 10 minutes. Serve with hot pepper sauce or a splash of vinegar, if desired.

Cumin Beets

Tips

For the best flavor, toast cumin seeds and grind them yourself. *To toast seeds:* Place in a dry skillet over medium heat and cook, stirring, until fragrant, about 3 minutes. Immediately transfer to a spice grinder or mortar and grind finely.

Peeling the beets before they are cooked ensures that all the delicious cooking juices end up on your plate.

Make Ahead

Complete Step 1. Cover and refrigerate for up to 2 days. When you're ready to cook, complete the recipe.

I love the simple, but unusual and effective combination of flavors in this dish, which is inspired by Indian cuisine. It's my favorite way of cooking small summer beets fresh from the garden because I don't have to heat up my kitchen with a pot of simmering water on the stove top. If you prefer a spicy dish, add hot pepper sauce, to taste, after the beets have finished cooking.

- Small (approx. 2 quart) slow cooker

1 tbsp	extra virgin olive oil	15 mL
1	onion, finely chopped	1
3	cloves garlic, minced	3
1 tsp	ground cumin (see Tips, left)	5 mL
1/2 tsp	sea salt	2 mL
1/2 tsp	freshly ground black pepper	2 mL
2	medium tomatoes, peeled and coarsely chopped	2
1 cup	water	250 mL
1 lb	beets, peeled and used whole, if small, or sliced thinly (see Tips, left)	500 g
	Hot Pepper Sauce (page 240), optional	

1. In a skillet, heat oil over medium heat. Add onion and cook, stirring, until softened, about 3 minutes. Stir in garlic, cumin, sea salt and pepper and cook, stirring, for 1 minute. Add tomatoes and water and bring to a boil.

2. Place beets in slow cooker stoneware and pour tomato mixture over them. Cover and cook on Low for 6 hours or on High for 2 hours, until beets are tender. Pass hot pepper sauce at the table, if using.

Basic Tomato Sauce

Makes about 8 cups (2 L)

◆ **Can Be Halved**
(see Tips, below)

Tips

If you are halving this recipe, be sure to use a small (1$\frac{1}{2}$ to 3$\frac{1}{2}$ quart) slow cooker.

If you are in a hurry, you can soften the vegetables on the stove top. Heat oil in a skillet for 30 seconds. Add onions and carrots and cook, stirring, until carrots are softened, about 7 minutes. Add garlic, thyme and peppercorns and cook, stirring, for 1 minute. Transfer to slow cooker stoneware. Add tomatoes with juice and continue with Step 2.

Not only is this sauce tasty and easy to make, it is also much lower in sodium than prepared sauces. It keeps covered for up to 1 week in the refrigerator and can be frozen for up to 6 months.

• **Medium to large (3$\frac{1}{2}$ to 5 quart) slow cooker**

1 tbsp	extra virgin olive oil	15 mL
2	onions, finely chopped	2
2	carrots, peeled and diced	2
4	cloves garlic, minced	4
1 tsp	dried thyme, crumbled	5 mL
$\frac{1}{2}$ tsp	cracked black peppercorns	2 mL
2	cans (each 28 oz/796 mL) tomatoes with juice, coarsely chopped (see page 13)	2
	Sea salt, optional	

1. In slow cooker stoneware, combine olive oil, onions and carrots. Stir well to ensure vegetables are coated with oil. Cover and cook on High for 1 hour, until vegetables are softened. Add garlic, thyme and peppercorns. Stir well. Stir in tomatoes with juice.

2. Place a clean tea towel, folded in half (so you will have two layers), over top of stoneware to absorb moisture. Cover and cook on Low for 6 hours or on High for 3 hours, until sauce is thickened and flavors are melded. Season to taste with sea salt, if using.

Kelp Noodles

Kelp noodles, which are made from kelp (a sea vegetable), water and a natural salt, are both low cal and low carb. They are also neutral in taste, which makes them a great partner for virtually any hot pasta sauce. Just rinse them well under cold running water, add to your sauce and stir well. Cook gently until the noodles are heated through, about 5 minutes. They will be a bit crunchy, but if you haven't tried them before, you will be surprised at how well they work in pasta sauces, from traditional Bolognese to the most robust ragù. (See also Zucchini Noodles, page 153).

Mushroom Tomato Sauce

◆ **Can Be Halved**
(see Tip, below)

Tips

If you are halving this recipe, be sure to use a small (1½ to 3½ quart) slow cooker.

Look for canned tomatoes that are organically grown, with no salt added, and come in glass jars or BPA (bisphenol-A) free cans. When using canned tomatoes (or any canned product) check to make sure they are gluten-free.

Make Ahead

Complete Step 1. Cover and refrigerate for up to 2 days. When you're ready to cook, complete the recipe.

Serve this classic sauce over Roasted Spaghetti Squash (page 243) or Roasted Eggplant or Zucchini Boats (page 243). Accompanied by a tossed green salad, it makes a great weeknight meal — perfect if you are serving vegans.

• **Medium to large (3½ to 5 quart) slow cooker**

1 tbsp	extra virgin olive oil	15 mL
1	onion, finely chopped	1
2	stalks celery, diced	2
4	cloves garlic, minced	4
1 tbsp	finely chopped fresh rosemary or 2 tsp (10 mL) dried rosemary, crumbled	15 mL
½ tsp	sea salt	2 mL
½ tsp	cracked black peppercorns	2 mL
8 oz	cremini mushrooms, sliced	250 g
½ cup	dry white wine or chicken or vegetable stock	125 mL
1 tbsp	tomato paste or 2 tbsp (30 mL) minced reconstituted sun-dried tomatoes	15 mL
1	can (28 oz/796 mL) tomatoes with juice, coarsely chopped (see Tips, left)	1
	Hot pepper flakes, optional	

1. In a skillet, heat oil over medium heat. Add onion and celery and cook, stirring, until softened, about 5 minutes. Add garlic, rosemary, salt and peppercorns and cook, stirring, for 1 minute. Add mushrooms and toss to coat. Add wine and cook for 1 minute. Stir in tomato paste and tomatoes with juice and bring to a boil. Transfer to slow cooker stoneware.

2. Place a clean tea towel, folded in half (so you will have two layers), over top of stoneware to absorb moisture. Cover and cook on Low for 6 hours or on High for 3 hours, until hot and bubbly. Stir in hot pepper flakes, if using.

Variation

Double Mushroom Tomato Sauce: Soak 1 package (½ oz/14 g) dried porcini mushrooms in 1 cup (250 mL) hot water for 20 minutes. Drain, pat dry and chop finely. Save soaking liquid for another use. Add mushrooms to pan along with peppercorns.

Syracuse Sauce

Serve this rich and delicious sauce over Zucchini Noodles (page 153), Roasted Spaghettis Squash (page 243) or Kelp Noodles (page 220) for a great Italian-themed meal. Add a simple green salad to complete the meal.

• **Medium to large (3½ to 5 quart) slow cooker**

1	large eggplant, peeled, cubed (2 inches/5 cm), sweated and drained of excess moisture (see Tips, left)	1
2 tbsp	extra virgin olive oil, divided (approx.)	30 mL
2	onions, finely chopped	2
4	cloves garlic, minced	4
1	can (28 oz/796 mL) tomatoes with juice, coarsely chopped (see Tips, page 221)	1
1 tbsp	tomato paste or 2 tbsp (30 mL) minced reconstituted sun-dried tomatoes	15 mL
2	roasted red bell peppers, diced	2
½ cup	black olives, pitted and chopped (about 20 olives)	125 mL
½ cup	finely chopped flat-leaf parsley leaves	125 mL
2 tbsp	capers, drained and minced	30 mL
1 tbsp	brown rice miso, optional (see Tips, left)	15 mL

1. In a skillet, heat 1 tbsp (15 mL) of the oil over medium-high heat. Add sweated eggplant, in batches, and cook until lightly browned, adding more oil as necessary. Transfer to slow cooker stoneware.

2. Add onions to pan, adding oil, if necessary, and cook, stirring, until softened, about 3 minutes. Add garlic and cook, stirring, for 1 minute. Add tomatoes with juice and tomato paste and bring to a boil. Transfer to slow cooker stoneware.

3. Place a clean tea towel, folded in half (so you will have two layers), over top of stoneware to absorb moisture. Cover and cook on Low for 6 hours or on High for 3 hours, until hot and bubbly. Add roasted red peppers, olives, parsley, capers and miso, if using. Stir well. Cover and cook on High for 20 minutes, until heated through.

Arugula-Laced Caramelized Onion Sauce

◆ **Entertaining Worthy**
◆ **Can Be Halved**
(see Tips, below)

Tips

If you are halving this recipe, be sure to use a small (1½ to 3½ quart) slow cooker.

If you're pressed for time soften the onions on the stove top. Heat the oil over medium heat in a large skillet. Add the onions and cook, stirring, until softened, about 5 minutes. Transfer to stoneware and continue with Step 2.

If you prefer a smoother sauce, combine the arugula with 1 cup (250 mL) of tomato sauce in a food processor and pulse until arugula is finely chopped. Add to onion mixture along with the remaining sauce.

Make Ahead

Complete Steps 1 and 2. Cover and refrigerate onions for up to 2 days. When you're ready to complete the recipe, in a saucepan, bring tomato sauce, miso and caramelized onions to a simmer over medium heat. Add arugula, return to a simmer and cook until nicely wilted.

I love the bittersweet flavor of caramelized onions but on the stove top caramelizing onions is a laborious process of slow, constant stirring. Made in the slow cooker, caramelized onions require almost no attention. In this recipe, I have added a bit of coconut sugar to the onions to ensure deeper flavor. Serve this luscious sauce over Roasted Spaghetti Squash (page 243), Roasted Eggplant or Zucchini Boats (page 243), Kelp Noodles (page 220) or Zucchini Noodles (page 153). Complete the meal with a tossed green salad topped with shredded carrots for a splash of healthy color.

● **Medium to large (3½ to 5 quart) slow cooker**

2 tbsp	extra virgin olive oil	30 mL
6	onions, thinly sliced on the vertical (about 3 lbs/1.5 kg)	6
1 tsp	coconut sugar	5 mL
1 tsp	cracked black peppercorns	5 mL
1 tbsp	brown rice miso, optional (see Tips, page 222)	15 mL
3 cups	tomato sauce (see recipe, page 220 and page 14)	750 mL
2	bunches arugula, stems removed and chopped (see Tips, left)	2

1. In slow cooker stoneware, combine olive oil and onions. Stir well to coat onions thoroughly. Cover and cook on High for 1 hour, until onions are softened (see Tips, left).

2. Add coconut sugar and peppercorns and stir well. Place a clean tea towel, folded in half (so you will have two layers), over top of stoneware to absorb moisture. Cover and cook on High for 4 hours, stirring two or three times to ensure that the onions are browning evenly and replacing towel each time.

3. Remove towels, add miso, if using, and stir well to ensure it is well integrated into the onions. Add tomato sauce and arugula and stir well to blend. Cover and cook on High for 30 minutes, until mixture is hot and flavors have blended.

Down-Home Tomatoes with Okra

◆ **Entertaining Worthy**
◆ **Can Be Halved**
(see Tips, below)

Tips

If you are halving this recipe, be sure to use a small (approx. 1½ to 2 quart) slow cooker.

Okra, a tropical vegetable, has a great flavor but becomes unpleasantly sticky when overcooked. Choose young okra pods 2 to 4 inches (5 to 10 cm) long that don't feel sticky to the touch (if sticky, they are too ripe). Gently scrub the pods and cut off the top and tail. Okra can also be found in the freezer section of the grocery store. Thaw before adding to the slow cooker.

This is a great side dish. A particularly mouthwatering combination of flavors, it makes a perfect accompaniment to grilled meat, fish or seafood. Leftovers make a delicious filling for an omelet.

• **Medium (approx. 3½ quart) slow cooker**

1 tbsp	clarified butter or pure lard	15 mL
4 oz	chunk bacon, diced, optional	125 g
1	onion, finely chopped	1
2	cloves garlic, minced	2
1 tsp	cracked black peppercorns	5 mL
½ tsp	sea salt	2 mL
1	can (28 oz/796 mL) tomatoes with juice (see page 13)	1
1	green bell pepper, seeded and diced	1
2 cups	sliced (½ inch/1 cm) okra, about 12 oz (375 g) (see Tips, left)	500 mL

1. In a skillet, heat butter over medium-high heat. Add bacon, if using, and cook, stirring, until nicely browned, about 4 minutes. Using a slotted spoon, transfer to slow cooker stoneware. Add onion and cook, stirring, until softened, about 3 minutes. Add garlic, peppercorns and salt and cook, stirring, for 1 minute. Add tomatoes with juice and bring to a boil. Transfer to slow cooker stoneware.

2. Cover and cook on Low for 6 hours or on High for 3 hours, until hot and bubbly. Add bell pepper and okra. Cover and cook on High for about 30 minutes, until okra is tender.

Desserts

Gingery Pears Poached
in Green Tea

Gingery Pears Poached in Green Tea

Serves 8

◆ **Entertaining Worthy**
◆ **Can Be Halved**
(see Tips, below)

Tips

If you are halving this recipe, be sure to use a small (1½ to 2 quart) slow cooker.

When poaching, use firmer pears, such as Bosc, for best results.

I prefer a strong ginger taste in these pears, but some might feel it overpowers the taste of the pears. Vary the amount of ginger to suit your preference.

Make Ahead

This dessert should be made early in the day or the night before so it can be well chilled before serving.

I love the combination of ginger and pears in this light but delicious dessert. Sprinkle with toasted almonds and top with a dollop of Coconut Whipped Cream for a perfect finish to a substantial meal.

• **Small (maximum 3½ quart) slow cooker**

4 cups	boiling water	1 L
2 tbsp	green tea leaves	30 mL
1 to 2 tbsp	grated gingerroot (see Tips, left)	15 to 30 mL
½ cup	liquid honey	125 mL
1 tsp	pure almond extract	5 mL
1 tsp	grated lemon zest	5 mL
8	firm pears, such as Bosc, peeled, cored and cut into quarters lengthwise	8
	Toasted sliced almonds, optional	
	Coconut Whipped Cream, optional (see page 232)	

1. In a pot, combine boiling water and green tea leaves. Cover and let steep for 5 minutes. Strain through a fine sieve into slow cooker stoneware.

2. Add ginger, honey, almond extract and lemon zest and stir well. Add pears. Cover and cook on Low for 6 hours or on High for 3 hours, until pears are tender. Transfer to a serving bowl, cover and chill thoroughly. Serve garnished with toasted almonds and a dollop of Coconut Whipped Cream, if using.

The Ultimate Baked Apples

Serves 8

◆ **Entertaining Worthy**
◆ **Can Be Halved**
  (see Tips, below)

Tips

If you are halving this recipe, you will need a smaller oval slow cooker (approx. 3 quart) that will comfortably accommodate 4 apples.

When buying nuts, be sure to source them from a purveyor with high turnover. Because nuts are high in fat (but healthy fat), they tend to become rancid very quickly. This is especially true of walnuts. In my experience, the vast majority of walnuts sold in supermarkets have already passed their peak. Taste before you buy. If they are not sweet, substitute an equal quantity of pecans.

These luscious apples, simple to make yet delicious, are the definitive autumn dessert. If you feel like gilding the lily, serve them with a dollop of Coconut Whipped Cream (page 232) or cultured coconut.

• **Large (minimum 5 quart) oval slow cooker**

½ cup	chopped toasted walnuts (see Tips, left)	125 mL
½ cup	dried cranberries	125 mL
2 tbsp	coconut sugar	30 mL
1 tsp	grated orange zest	5 mL
8	apples, cored	8
1 cup	pure pomegranate juice	250 mL

1. In a bowl, combine walnuts, cranberries, sugar and orange zest. To stuff the apples, hold your hand over the bottom of the apple and, using your fingers, tightly pack core space with filling. One at a time, place filled apples in slow cooker stoneware. Drizzle pomegranate juice evenly over tops.

2. Cover and cook on Low for 6 hours or on High for 3 hours, until apples are tender.

3. Transfer apples to a serving dish and spoon cooking juices over them. Serve hot.

Chocolate Flan with Toasted Almonds

◆ **Entertaining Worthy**

Tips

If you prefer, make this dessert in 6 individual tall ramekins or 4- to 6-ounce (125 to 175 mL) mason-type jars. Just make sure your slow cooker is large enough to accommodate the vessels. Mason jars are particularly functional if you are transporting this dessert. Instead of covering the jars with foil, use the lids and screw tops. Add enough hot water to come half way up the sides of the jars and reduce the cooking time to about 1½ hours.

Heatproof silicone bands, available in kitchen supply stores, are useful for securing the foil tops on both a baking dish and ramekins.

Here's a deliciously decadent chocolate dessert. Save it for special occasions or treat yourself and enjoy. For a real treat, finish with a dollop of Coconut Whipped Cream.

- **6-cup (1.5 L) lightly greased mold or soufflé dish (see Tips, left)**
- **Large (minimum 5 quart) oval slow cooker**

Caramel

¾ cup	coconut sugar	175 mL
⅓ cup	water	75 mL
¼ cup	toasted slivered almonds	60 mL

Flan

3½ oz	bittersweet chocolate, broken into chunks	105 g
1	can (10 oz/400 mL) coconut milk (about 1½ cups/375 mL)	1
⅓ cup	coconut sugar	75 mL
2	eggs	2
2	egg yolks	2
	Coconut Whipped Cream (page 232), optional	

1. *Caramel:* In a heavy-bottomed saucepan over medium heat, bring coconut sugar and water to a boil, stirring until sugar dissolves. Cook without stirring until mixture is very syrupy, about 6 minutes. Pour into prepared dish and, working quickly, tip mixture around the dish until sides are well coated. Sprinkle almonds over bottom of dish and set aside.

2. *Flan:* In a heatproof bowl, place chocolate. In a clean saucepan, bring coconut milk and sugar just to a boil, stirring until sugar dissolves. Pour over chocolate and stir until mixture is smooth and chocolate is melted.

3. In a bowl, beat eggs and egg yolks. Gradually add chocolate mixture, beating constantly until incorporated. Pour into caramel-coated dish. Cover with foil and secure tightly. Place dish in slow cooker stoneware and add enough hot water to come 1 inch (2.5 cm) up the sides. Cover and cook on High for 2 hours, or until a knife inserted in custard comes out clean. Remove and refrigerate for 4 hours or overnight.

4. When ready to serve, remove foil. Run a sharp knife around the edge of the flan and invert onto a serving plate. Serve with Coconut Whipped Cream, if desired.

Ginger-Spiked Apple Cider Compote

Tip

Apple cider differs from apple juice in that it is pressed juice that is unfiltered and has much more flavor. In this recipe, use naturally sweet cider, not the hard cider, which is fermented.

If you've gone apple picking and are wondering what to do with all that luscious fruit you have on hand, try this deliciously different compote. It's very refreshing and, topped with Coconut Whipped Cream is, good enough to serve to guests.

Small to medium (2 to 3½ quart) slow cooker

3 cups	apple cider (see Tip, left)	750 mL
½ cup	coconut sugar	125 mL
2	slices (¼ inch/0.5 cm) peeled gingerroot	2
6	firm apples, peeled, cored and quartered	6
	Coconut Whipped Cream (see below)	

1. In slow cooker stoneware, combine apple cider, coconut sugar and gingerroot. Add apples and stir well.

2. Cover and cook on High about 2 hours, until apples are al dente. Transfer into a serving dish and chill thoroughly. To serve, ladle into bowls and top with Coconut Whipped Cream.

Coconut Whipped Cream

Coconut whipped cream is a great finish for many desserts. The secret to a successful result is ensuring that your coconut milk and the bowl and beaters used for whipping are all thoroughly chilled.

1	can (10 oz/400 mL) coconut milk, refrigerated for at least 4 hours	1
2 tsp	coconut sugar (see Variations, below)	10 mL
½ tsp	vanilla extract (see Variations, below)	2 mL

1. Skim off the thick layer of cream on top of the milk and transfer to a chilled mixing bowl. (Save the remaining liquid for another use.) Add sugar and vanilla and using an electric mixer beat on low speed to incorporate ingredients. Increase to high and beat until peaks form, about 2 minutes. Serve immediately.

Variations

You can vary the flavor of the cream to complement the dish you are serving it with. Substitute pure maple syrup and maple extract for the coconut sugar and vanilla or, for a more intense coconut flavor, coconut extract for the vanilla.

Maple Surprise

Serves 6 to 8

◆ **Entertaining Worthy**
◆ **Can Be Halved**
  (see Tips, below)

Tips

If you are halving this recipe, be sure to use a small (1½ to 2 quart) slow cooker.

Recent research is showing that pure maple syrup, which Native North American hunter-gatherers taught the early settlers to make, may actually be a superfood. It is loaded with beneficial compounds, which may be anti-inflammatory and of benefit to people managing type-2 diabetes.

I buy organic ginger, which has been coated in raw cane sugar, at my local natural foods store.

This delicious purée makes a great way to finish a meal. If you don't identify the key ingredient for your guests, they'll enjoy guessing. Some will think it's a particularly good applesauce, but won't be able to pinpoint the unusual flavoring. Serve this on its own with a good dollop of Coconut Whipped Cream (page 232), or over a complementary frozen non-dairy dessert, such as apple-ginger or pear sorbet, non-dairy coconut ice cream or cultured coconut, which is a tasty yogurt substitute.

• **Small (maximum 3 quart) slow cooker**

4 cups	squash or pumpkin, peeled and cut into 1-inch (2.5 cm) cubes	1 L
½ cup	pure maple syrup (see Tips, left)	125 mL
2 tbsp	melted butter	30 mL
1	vanilla bean, seeds scraped, pod reserved	1
Pinch	salt	Pinch
¼ cup	walnuts pieces, finely chopped	60 mL
3 tbsp	candied ginger, finely chopped (see Tips, left)	45 mL

1. In slow cooker stoneware, combine squash, maple syrup, butter, vanilla seeds and pod and salt. Stir well. Cover and cook on Low for 6 hours or on High for 4 hours, until squash is very tender. Remove and discard vanilla pod.

2. Using a wooden spoon or potato masher, crush mixture to a smooth purée. Stir in walnuts and ginger. Serve warm or let cool.

Poached Pears in Chocolate Sauce

◆ Entertaining Worthy

◆ Can Be Halved
(see Tip, below)

Tips

If you are halving this recipe, be sure to use a small (approx. 1½ to 3½ quart) slow cooker.

Coconut cream is a thicker, richer version of coconut milk. You can purchase it in stores with a well-stocked Asian foods section. If you can't find it, spoon off the thick layer that rises to the top of a can of coconut milk.

Nothing could be simpler than these pears poached in a simple syrup enhanced with vanilla and a hint of cinnamon. The fruit is delicious on its own, but if, like me, you enjoy gilding the lily, add the luscious chocolate sauce, which is very easy to make.

- **Medium to large (3½ to 5 quart) slow cooker**

	Finely grated zest of 1 lemon	
2 tbsp	freshly squeezed lemon juice	30 mL
6	firm pears, such as Bosc or Bartlett, peeled, cored and cut into quarters on the vertical	6
½ cup	liquid honey	125 mL
1	piece (2 inches/5 cm) cinnamon stick	1
1	vanilla bean, seeds scraped, pod reserved	1

Chocolate Sauce

½ cup	coconut cream (see Tips, left)	125 mL
1 tbsp	coconut sugar	15 mL
4 oz	bittersweet chocolate, chopped	125 g

1. In a large bowl, combine 4 cups (1 L) water and lemon juice. After preparing the pears immediately drop them into the lemon juice solution. (This will prevent the fruit from turning brown.)

2. In slow cooker stoneware, combine 2 cups (500 mL) water, honey, cinnamon stick, vanilla seeds and pod and lemon zest. Stir well. Drain pears and add to stoneware. Cover and cook on Low for 6 hours or on High for 3 hours, until pears are tender. Remove and discard vanilla pod. Transfer pears and liquid to a large bowl. Cover and chill thoroughly.

3. *Chocolate Sauce:* When you're ready to serve, combine coconut cream and coconut sugar in a saucepan over medium heat. Heat until bubbles form around the edges. Remove from heat. (If you have a true simmer feature on your stove you can leave it on the element; it will speed things up a bit.) Add chocolate and stir until melted. Set aside at room temperature until ready to use, for up to 1 hour. To serve, transfer pears to a plate, using a slotted spoon, and top with chocolate sauce.

Poached Quince

◆ **Entertaining Worthy**
◆ **Can Be Halved**
  (see Tips, below)

Tips

If you are halving this recipe, be sure to use a small (1½ to 2 quart) slow cooker.

Quinces are a fabulous winter fruit that are made for the slow cooker because they demand cooking. Raw, the quince is a tough, fibrous ball. Softened by slow cooking, it turns a beautiful shade of pink and melts in your mouth, releasing a panoply of complex flavors.

• **Small to medium (2 to 4 quart) slow cooker**

½ cup	water	125 mL
½ cup	liquid honey	125 mL
	Zest of 1 orange	
4	quinces (about 2 lbs/1 kg), peeled, cored and sliced	4
	Coconut Whipped Cream (see page 232)	
	Toasted chopped walnuts or toasted coconut, optional	

1. In slow cooker stoneware, combine water, honey and orange zest. Add quinces and stir well. Cover and cook on Low for about 8 hours, until quinces are tender and turn pink. Serve warm or chilled. To serve, top with Coconut Whipped Cream. Sprinkle with walnuts, if using.

Oven-Baked Kale Chips
with Caper-Studded
Caponata (page 28)

Condiments and Accompaniments

Paleo Mayo

Tips

This recipe contains raw eggs. If you have any food safety concerns, cook the egg yolk with the lemon juice over very low heat in a small saucepan, whisking constantly until it begins to thicken. If the egg starts to curdle, whisk in 1 tbsp (15 mL) boiling water. Transfer to food processor and continue with Step 1.

It is important to process the egg mixture until it is very creamy and thick before adding the oil. This helps to ensure that the oil will be properly emulsified.

Dijon mustard is a robust blend of mustard seeds, white wine, herbs and seasoning and it should not contain gluten. However, gluten has made its way into many condiments, so check the label.

This mayonnaise is a delicious and healthy alternative to commercially prepared varieties. The combination of extra virgin olive and cold-pressed flax oil is a feast of healthy fats, including those hard-to-obtain omega-3's. If you prefer, substitute organic cold-pressed canola oil for the flax. The results taste virtually identical, but the flax oil contains more omega-3 fatty acids. Double or triple the recipe to suit your needs.

• Food processor

1	egg yolk, from organically fed naturally raised chickens (see Tips, left)	1
2 tbsp	freshly squeezed lemon juice	30 mL
1 tsp	Dijon mustard, optional (see Tips, left)	5 mL
1/4 tsp	fine sea salt	1 mL
1/8 tsp	cayenne pepper	0.5 mL
1/3 cup	extra virgin olive oil	75 mL
3 tbsp	cold-pressed flax oil	45 mL

1. In food processor fitted with the metal blade, process egg yolk, lemon juice, mustard, if using, salt and cayenne until pale and creamy.
2. In a measuring cup, combine olive and flax oils. With motor running, very slowly pour oil down the feed tube, watching to ensure the oil is becoming emulsified with the egg mixture. (It will thicken visibly.) If it is not thickening, stop adding oil until you can see the mixture coming together. Serve immediately, or cover and refrigerate for up to 1 week.

Variations

Dill Paleo Mayo: Add 2 tbsp (30 mL) chopped dill fronds to the finished mayo and pulse 2 or 3 times to blend.

Chive Paleo Mayo: Add 2 tbsp (30 mL) chopped fresh chives to the finished mayo and pulse 2 or 3 times to blend.

Tarragon Paleo Mayo: Add 2 tbsp (30 mL) chopped fresh tarragon leaves to the finished mayo and pulse 2 or 3 times to blend.

Anchovy Paleo Mayo: Add 4 to 6 (or to taste) chopped anchovy fillets to the finished mayo and pulse 2 or 3 times to blend.

Roasted Garlic Aïoli: Add 1 tbsp (15 mL) roasted garlic (or to taste) to the finished mayo and pulse to blend.

Harissa

**Makes about
½ cup (125 mL)**

Tips

Use sun-dried tomatoes packed in extra virgin olive oil, or dry-packed sun-dried tomatoes, which should be soaked in 1 cup (250 mL) boiling water for 15 minutes before being used. In case you have any concerns about sun-dried tomatoes being "Paleo" according to James Trager (in his book *Food Chronology*) humans were drying and smoking food as early as 12,000 B.C.

If you have a mini bowl attachment for your food processor, this is the perfect time to use it.

Harissa is a hot pepper paste that is used extensively in North African cuisine. It is available in specialty shops, but it is very easy to make your own.

• **Food processor or blender**

12	dried red chile peppers, stems removed	12
2 tsp	caraway seeds	10 mL
2 tsp	coriander seeds	10 mL
1 tsp	cumin seeds	5 mL
2	reconstituted sun-dried tomatoes (see Tips, left)	2
2	cloves garlic	2
2 tbsp	freshly squeezed lemon juice	30 mL
½ tsp	sea salt	2 mL
¼ cup	extra virgin olive oil	60 mL

1. Place peppers in a bowl. Add boiling water to generously cover. Ensure peppers are submerged and set aside for 30 minutes until soft. Drain. Transfer to food processor fitted with the metal blade (see Tips, left; you can also do this in a blender.)

2. Meanwhile, in a skillet over medium heat, toast caraway, coriander and cumin seeds, stirring until fragrant, about 3 minutes. Transfer to a mortar or a spice grinder and grind. Add to peppers in food processor.

3. Add sun-dried tomatoes, garlic, lemon juice and salt and process until chopped. Add olive oil and process, stopping the motor 3 or 4 times, as necessary, and scraping down the sides of the bowl, until mixture forms a smooth paste. (You will still have some seeds and bits of chile pepper.) Transfer to a clean jar and store covered in the refrigerator for up to 1 month. Add a bit of olive oil to cover the paste every time you use it.

Homemade Horseradish

**Makes about
2 cups (500 mL)**

Tip

Once shredded, horseradish releases allyl sulfide, a very pungent gas. The addition of vinegar stops this action. However, be sure to process fresh horseradish in a well-ventilated area.

Making your own horseradish is a good idea because it is fresher tasting than prepared versions and you know every ingredient that it contains.

• Food processor

1	small horseradish (about 12 oz/375 g), peeled	1
1/4 cup	white wine vinegar	60 mL
1 tsp	coconut sugar	5 mL
1/4 cup	water	60 mL
1/2 tsp	salt	2 mL

1. In food processor fitted with the shredding blade, shred horseradish. (You will need about 2 cups/500 mL). Replace shredding blade with metal blade.

2. In a small bowl, combine vinegar and coconut sugar. Stir until sugar dissolves. Add to food processor along with water and salt and pulse until very fine but not puréed, stopping and scraping down the sides of the bowl once. Transfer to a bowl or glass preserving jar and refrigerate until ready to use or for up to 2 weeks.

Hot Pepper Sauce

**Makes about
1/4 cup (60 mL)**

Tip

If you are concerned about intestinal permeability (also known as leaky gut), limit your consumption of chile peppers, which are thought to exacerbate the condition.

If you don't want to use a prepared hot pepper sauce, this makes a fine substitute.

Food processor or blender

15	dried red chile peppers, stems removed	15
1/4 cup	distilled white vinegar	60 mL
1/2 tsp	fine sea salt	2 mL

1. Place peppers in a bowl. Add boiling water to cover generously. Ensure peppers are submerged and set aside for 30 minutes until soft. Drain. Transfer to food processor fitted with the metal blade or blender. Add vinegar and salt and process until puréed. Strain into a clear jar, pressing out solids. Cover tightly and store in the refrigerator for up to 1 month.

Oven-Baked Kale Chips

Makes about 5 chips per stem

Tips

When trimming the kale, remove the tough stem right to the end of the leaf (it has an unpleasantly chewy texture) and discard. Then cut the pieces crosswise into "chips."

I like to use lacinto (also known as black or dinosaur kale) when making chips because its long, relatively solid leaves allow for the creation of a "chip" that has enough heft to support a spread or to be used as a dipper. However, other types of kale also make delicious chips.

In the past few years, kale chips have become very popular, with good reason. They are tasty and nutritious, perfect as a gluten-free dipper or on their own as a satisfying snack. And, if you make your own, you can be sure they don't contain any nasty additives. Increase the quantity to suit your needs.

- **Preheat oven to 350°F (180°C)**

Per stem of kale:

1	leaf lacinto (or other type) kale, trimmed and chopped (see Tips, left)	1
1 tsp	extra virgin olive oil	5 mL
	Fine sea salt	
	Sweet or hot paprika, regular or smoked, optional	

1. In a salad spinner, thoroughly dry kale. Place olive oil in a bowl and add kale, in batches, if necessary. Using your hand, toss kale until evenly coated with oil.

2. Place on a baking sheet in a single layer. Bake in preheated oven until leaves crisp up, about 10 minutes. Remove from oven and sprinkle lightly with sea salt, and paprika, if using.

Cauliflower Mash

Tip

If you are serving Cauliflower Mash with a dish with a complementary flavor profile, substitute rendered bacon fat for the butter. It is very tasty.

If you can't eat potatoes, here is a perfect alternative. This makes a great accompaniment to stews and pot roasts, among other dishes.

4 cups	cauliflower florets (about 1 small)	1 L
2 tbsp	butter or extra virgin olive oil	30 mL
	Sea salt and freshly ground black pepper	
2 tbsp	finely chopped parsley, chives or green onions, optional	30 mL

1. In a large pot of boiling water, cook cauliflower just until tender, about 5 minutes. Drain well and transfer to a food processor fitted with the metal blade. Add butter, salt and pepper and purée.
2. Season with salt and freshly ground pepper to taste. Transfer to a warm serving bowl and garnish with parsley, if using.

Roasted Portobello Mushrooms

Tip

You can use any good fat that complements your recipe, from melted coconut oil to leftover bacon fat.

These make a great base for sauces and work well as "bread" for dishes such as sausage sandwiches.

- **Preheat oven to 425°F (220°C)**
- **Rimmed baking sheet**

4	large portobello mushrooms, stems and gills removed	4
¼ cup	extra virgin olive oil or melted butter (see Tip, left)	60 mL

1. Brush mushrooms liberally on both sides with oil. Place on baking sheet, cap side up. Roast on center rack of preheated oven for 8 minutes. Turn gill side up and roast until sizzling, about 8 minutes more.

Roasted Eggplant Boats

Tip

Double or triple this recipe to suit your needs.

Eggplant (or zucchini) boats make a great accompaniment to dishes such as Sloppy Joes (page 151).

- Preheat oven to 425°F (220°C)
- Rimmed baking sheet

1	medium eggplant (about 12 ounces/375 g), halved lengthwise	1
¼ cup	extra virgin olive oil or melted butter	60 mL
	Salt and freshly ground black pepper	

1. Using a grapefruit spoon, make a small trough down the center of each eggplant half. Brush both sides liberally with oil and place on baking sheet, cut side down.
2. Bake in preheated oven until cut surface is nicely browned, about 15 minutes. Turn and roast until tender, about 15 minutes. Season with salt and freshly ground pepper to taste.

Variation

Roasted Zucchini Boats: Substitute 2 medium zucchini for the eggplant.

Roasted Spaghetti Squash

Tip

Unlike traditional pasta, spaghetti squash is low in calories and carbs and is low on the glycemic index. It also provides a wide range of vitamins and minerals.

Here is a perfect gluten-free alternative to pasta.

- Preheat oven to 400°F (200°C)
- Rimmed baking sheet

1	large spaghetti squash (about 3 lb/1.5 kg) halved lengthwise	1
2 tbsp	melted butter or extra virgin olive oil (approx.)	30 mL

1. Scrape out seeds and stringy fibrous parts of the squash and discard. Brush cut surfaces with melted butter and place on baking sheet, cut side down.
2. Bake in preheated oven until squash feels soft and begins to lose its firmness, about 30 minutes. Remove from oven and set aside until cool enough to handle.
3. Using a fork, scrape out spaghetti strands and transfer to a warm serving bowl or platter. Drizzle with additional melted butter, if desired.

Resources

Bitterman, Mark. *Salted, A Manifesto on the World's Most Essential Mineral, with Recipes* (Ten Speed Press, New York, 2010)

Cordain, Loren. *The Paleo Diet: Lose Weight and Get Healthy by Eating the Foods You Were Designed to Eat* (Revised Edition) (John Wiley & Sons, Inc. Hoboken, New Jersey, 2011)

Katz, Sandor Ellix. *The Art of Fermentation: An In-Depth Exploration of Essential Concepts and Processes from Around the World* (Chelsea Green Publishing, White River Junction, Vermont, 2012)

McLagan, Jennifer. *Fat: An Appreciation of a Misunderstood Ingredient, with Recipes* (McClelland & Stewart, Toronto, 2008)

Outram, Alan K. "Hunter-Gatherers and the First Farmers" in *Food: The History of Taste* Paul Freedman ed. (University of California Press, Berkeley, Los Angeles, 2007)

Quinn, Neely and Glaspey, Jason. *The Complete Idiot's Guide to Eating Paleo* (Alpha Books, New York, 2012)

Sanfilippo, Diane. *Practical Paleo: A Customized Approach to Health and a Whole-Foods Lifestyle* (Victory Belt Publishing, Las Vegas, 2012)

Taubes, Gary. *Good Calories, Bad Calories* (Alfred A. Knopf, New York, 2007)

Trager, James. *The Food Chronology: A Food Lover's Compendium of Events and Anecdotes, from Prehistory to the Present* (Owl Books, New York, 1995)

Wolf, Robb. *The Paleo Solution: The Original Human Diet* (Victory Belt Publishing, Las Vegas, 2010)

Library and Archives Canada Cataloguing in Publication

Finlayson, Judith, author
  The 163 best paleo slow cooker recipes : 100% gluten-free / Judith Finlayson.

Includes index.
ISBN 978-0-7788-0464-2 (pbk.)

  1. Electric cooking, Slow. 2. High-protein diet--Recipes. 3. Gluten-free diet—Recipes.
4. Cookbooks. I. Title. II. Title: One hundred sixty-three best paleo slow cooker recipes.

TX827.F55195 2013   641.5'884   C2013-903352-1

Index

(v) = Variation

More great books by Judith Finlayson

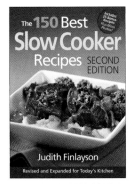

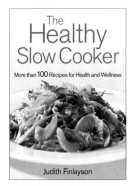

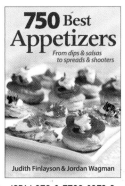
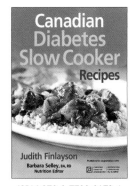
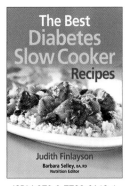
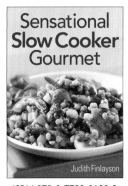
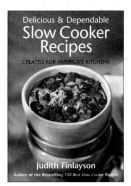
Available wherever books are sold
Visit us at www.robertrose.ca

Robert
ROSE